Deliberat
Pedagog.

TRANSFORMATIONS IN HIGHER EDUCATION: THE SCHOLARSHIP OF ENGAGEMENT

Deliberative Pedagogy

Teaching and Learning for Democratic Engagement

Edited by TIMOTHY J. SHAFFER, NICHOLAS V. LONGO,
IDIT MANOSEVITCH, and MAXINE S. THOMAS

Michigan State University Press | East Lansing

⊗ The paper used in this publication meets the minimum requirements
of ANSI/NISO Z39.48-1992 (R 1997) (Permanence of Paper).

Michigan State University Press
East Lansing, Michigan 48823-5245

Printed and bound in the United States of America.

26 25 24 23 22 21 20 19 18 17   1 2 3 4 5 6 7 8 9 10

LIBRARY OF CONGRESS CATALOGING-IN-PUBLICATION DATA IS AVAILABLE
Names: Shaffer, Timothy J., editor.
Title: Deliberative pedagogy : teaching and learning for democratic engagement / edited by
Timothy J. Shaffer, Nicholas V. Longo, Idit Manosevitch, and Maxine S. Thomas.
Description: East Lansing : Michigan State University Press, [2017] | Series:
Transformations in higher education: the scholarship of engagement
| Includes bibliographical references and index.
Identifiers: LCCN 2016041049| ISBN 9781611862492 (pbk. : alk. paper)
| ISBN 9781609175313 (pdf) | ISBN 9781628953015 (epub) | ISBN 9781628963014 (kindle)
Subjects: LCSH: Citizenship—Study and teaching. | Democracy and education.
Classification: LCC LC1091 .D38 2017 | DDC 370.115—dc23 LC record available at
https://lccn.loc.gov/2016041049

Book design by Charlie Sharp, Sharp Designs, East Lansing, MI
Cover design by Shaun Allshouse, www.shaunallshouse.com
Cover photograph by Hugh Cox is used courtesy of the photographer and the San Diego
Deliberation Network (www.sddn.org) with permission. All rights reserved.

Michigan State University Press is a member of the Green Press Initiative and
is committed to developing and encouraging ecologically responsible publishing
practices. For more information about the Green Press Initiative and the use
of recycled paper in book publishing, please visit *www.greenpressinitiative.org.*

Visit Michigan State University Press at *www.msupress.org*

Transformations in Higher Education: Scholarship of Engagement

T he Transformations in Higher Education: Scholarship of Engagement book series is designed to provide a forum where scholars can address the diverse issues provoked by community-campus partnerships that are directed toward creating innovative solutions to societal problems. Numerous social critics and key national commissions have drawn attention to the pervasive and burgeoning problems of individuals, families, communities, economies, health services, and education in American society. Such issues as child and youth development, economic competitiveness, environmental quality, and health and health care require creative research and the design, deployment, and evaluation of innovative public policies and intervention programs. Similar problems and initiatives have been articulated in many other countries, apart from the devastating consequences of poverty that burdens economic and social change. As a consequence, there has been increasing societal pressure on universities to partner with communities to design and deliver knowledge applications that address these issues, and to co-create novel approaches to effect system changes that can lead to sustainable and evidence-based solutions. Knowledge generation and knowledge application are critical parts of the engagement process, but so too are knowledge dissemination and preservation. The Transformations in Higher Education: Scholarship of Engagement series was designed to meet one aspect of the dissemination/preservation dyad.

This series is sponsored by the National Collaborative for the Study of University Engagement (NCSUE) and is published in partnership with the Michigan State University Press. An external board of editors supports the NCSUE editorial staff in order to insure that all volumes in the series are peer reviewed throughout the publication process. Manuscripts embracing campus-community partnerships are invited from authors regardless of discipline, geographic place, or type of transformational change accomplished. Similarly, the series embraces all methodological approaches from rigorous randomized trials to narrative and ethnographic studies. Analyses may span the qualitative to quantitative continuum, with particular emphasis on mixed-model approaches. However, all manuscripts must attend to detailing critical aspects of partnership development, community involvement, and evidence of program changes or impacts. Monographs and books provide ample space for authors to address all facets of engaged scholarship thereby building a compendium of praxis that will facilitate replication and generalization, two of the cornerstones of evidence-based programs, practices, and policies. We invite you to submit your work for publication review and to fully participate in our effort to assist higher education to renew its covenant with society through engaged scholarship.

HIRAM E. FITZGERALD
BURTON BARGERSTOCK
LAURIE VAN EGEREN

Contents

FOREWORD, *David Mathews* ·ix

PREFACE, *Maxine S. Thomas* ·xiii

INTRODUCTION, *Nicholas V. Longo, Idit Manosevitch, and Timothy J. Shaffer* · · · · · · · · · · · · · · ·xix

Part 1. Theory and History of Deliberative Pedagogy

Deliberative Pedagogy as Critical Connective: Building Democratic Mind-Sets
and Skill Sets for Addressing Wicked Problems, *Martín Carcasson* · 3

Democracy and Education: Historical Roots of Deliberative Pedagogy, *Timothy J. Shaffer* · · · · 21

Talking Out of School: Using Deliberative Pedagogy to Connect Campus
and Community, *Nicholas V. Longo and Cynthia M. Gibson* · 37

Part 2. Classroom Practices: New Ways of Teaching and Learning

Deliberative Pedagogy as a Central Tenet: First-Year Students Develop a Course
and a Community, *Leila R. Brammer* · 51

Deliberative Pedagogy in Israeli Higher Education: A Course Curriculum for Preparing
a Deliberative Student Conference, *Idit Manosevitch* · 61

Deliberative Pedagogy in the Communication Studies Curriculum,
Sara A. Mehltretter Drury and Martín Carcasson · 71

Deliberative Pedagogy in Undergraduate Science Courses, *Sara A. Mehltretter Drury* · · · · · · · · 79

Part 3. Comparative, Gender, and Cross-Cultural Deliberative Pedagogy Practice

Deliberative Pedagogy's Feminist Potential: Teaching Our Students to Cultivate
a More Inclusive Public Sphere, *J. Cherie Strachan* · 89

Russian and American Students Deliberating Online: Complementing Core Courses with Intercultural Communication Skills, *Ekaterina Lukianova and Jack Musselman* ········· 99

Tackling the "Savior" Complex: Teaching Introduction to Women's and Gender Studies through Deliberation, *Ibtesam Al-Atiyat* ··· 107

Deliberative Pedagogy for the Entire Student Body, *Ferenc Hammer* ····················· 115

Part 4. Deliberative Pedagogy and Institutional Change

Educating for Democracy, *Scott London* ·· 127

Kansas State University's Institute for Civic Discourse and Democracy: Developing Civic Agency, *Timothy Steffensmeier and David Procter* ································· 135

Practical Application: A National Issues Forum at a Historically Black College, *Marshalita Sims Peterson* ·· 143

Part 5. Bridging Campus and the Community

Deliberative Pedagogy and Journalism Education: Lessons from Classroom–Community Projects in Four Countries, *Angela Romano* ··· 153

I Understand that Infrastructure Affects People's Lives: Deliberative Pedagogy and Community-Engaged Learning in a South African Engineering Curriculum, *Janice McMillan* ··· 159

Transporting Communication: Community College Students Facilitate Deliberation in Their Own Communities, *Rebecca M. Townsend* ································· 169

Part 6. Assessing Deliberative Pedagogy

The Value of Longitudinal Assessment: The Impact of the Democracy Fellows Program over Time, *Katy J. Harriger, Jill J. McMillan, Christy M. Buchanan, and Stephanie Gusler* ····· 179

Assessment through a Deliberative Pedagogy Learning Outcomes Rubric, *Sara A. Mehltretter Drury, Leila R. Brammer, and Joni Doherty* ····················· 191

Assessing Language and Power in Deliberative Conversations in Educational Settings, *Telma Gimenez and Andressa Molinari* ··· 203

CONCLUSION, *Nancy L. Thomas* ·· 215

ABOUT THE CONTRIBUTORS ··· 223

INDEX ·· 231

Foreword

David Mathews

People aren't born knowing how to be citizens in a democracy. It is something they have to learn. Colleges can have a significant effect on what students see as their role in a democracy and how they make a difference in their communities and their countries.

What role people play depends on how they understand democracy. Conventionally, democracy is defined as a system of contested elections that produce representative governments. Citizens are voters. They play by the rules, pay their taxes, and obey the laws. They should be well informed. If there is anything more, it is that citizens should be good people who help others and support beneficial institutions like the schools.

Being a good citizen in this sense is commendable. But it isn't enough. It isn't enough because there are difficult problems that can't be solved without collective action by citizens. It isn't enough because people can't act together when they disagree about how to act. It isn't enough because, without joining forces, citizens don't have the power to make a difference in their communities and beyond.

Democracy is more than contested elections and representative governments. And citizens have to be more than voters. They have to be producers; that is, they have to be able to work with others (who may neither be like them nor even like them) to make things that combat common problems and create a life that is better for everyone. What only citizens can produce is also needed to make their institutions effective. These things may be local, like a sports program for youngsters, or nationwide, like the MADD campaign against drunk driving.

In a word, democracy is work, and citizens need to know how to do the work that gives them power. The only way they can learn how the work is done is by actually doing it. So academic institutions have to combine classroom experiences with experiences working in communities.

The work citizens do requires making good decisions about what that work should be. And this inevitably provokes disagreements, which are difficult because they turn on normative questions about what is the right thing to do. Since there aren't any infallible experts on questions of what should be, people have to exercise their best judgments. Happily, human beings have a faculty for judgment, although it isn't always used because it involves making difficult trade-offs among the many things people hold dear—their security, their freedom, their desire to be treated fairly. To reach shared and reflective judgments, people must recognize the tensions among the things they consider valuable and carefully consider the implications for various alternatives for action. For instance, what will make us secure can restrict our freedom. Without this careful weighing, conversations easily degenerate into personal pleadings, sound bites, and partisan rancor. Or to avoid facing up to the tensions, people opt for polite discussion, which doesn't lead to collective efforts. Tensions, never worked through, are pushed into the background only to resurface later.

Ancient languages have left us a clue as to how we can make use of our faculty for judgment. The clue is the word *deliberation*, which is found in different written forms from Egyptian hieroglyphics to old Chinese characters. In Latin, the word is drawn from the act of weighing, as done on a scale, to determine something's value. To deliberate is to carefully weigh possible civic actions, laws, or policies against the various things that people hold dear in order to settle on a direction to follow or purpose to pursue.

This weighing requires the exercise of our faculty for judgment. Judgment informs our decisions, making them sound. Personally, I like Pericles's concept of deliberation as the talk used before people act in order to first teach themselves how to act.[1] Also Isocrates, in the *Antidosis*, usefully distinguishes deliberation from purely logical reasoning and scientific analysis. And Aristotle equates deliberation with moral reasoning and the creation of practical wisdom (*phronesis*).[2] As you can see, deliberation isn't unique to the United States, and it certainly isn't a Kettering Foundation methodology.

Today, deliberation isn't defined in exactly the same way by everyone. What I am reporting is how the foundation has come to understand it. We have seen it become a gateway into a concept of democratic politics that puts citizens and their work at the center. Public deliberation can open the door to all of the other practices essential to doing the work of citizens. These practices aren't just tools or techniques; they have an intrinsic worth; they promote democratic values like fairness and freedom. They are ways of both learning and doing simultaneously. Here are six of the practices that are used in the work of citizens:

1. Naming problems to reflect the things people consider valuable and hold dear.
2. Framing issues for decision-making that not only takes into account what people feel is valuable but also lays out fairly all the major options for acting—with full recognition of the tensions growing out of the advantages and disadvantages of each option.
3. Making decisions deliberatively to move opinions from first impressions to more shared and reflective judgment.
4. Identifying and committing all the resources people have, including their talents and experiences, which become more powerful when combined. These are assets that often go unrecognized and unused.
5. Organizing civic actions so they complement one another, which makes the whole of people's efforts more than the sum of the parts.
6. Learning as a community all along the way to keep up civic momentum.

This understanding of democratic politics doesn't require people to do something out of the ordinary (we all have a faculty for judgment) but rather to do what is done routinely a bit differently. For instance, problems that are named in expert terms (for good reason) can additionally be named in terms of what people hold dear. The point is that there are opportunities to turn ordinary routines into democratic practices. And learning where these opportunities are is crucial to the experiences in citizenship that college students must have.

Fortunately, the Kettering Foundation has gotten to know faculty members from a wide range of institutions and disciplines who are developing courses that prepare students to do the work of citizens. Their disciplines range from biology to law and drama. They come from the Middle East, Latin America, Europe, and elsewhere. Many faculty members call what they do *deliberative pedagogy*. And in this book, some of them explain what they are doing and why.

They are also beginning to report on the results. A student who was introduced to deliberative decision-making in a college course wrote that what he had learned wasn't just about the practice of deliberating but about himself. He learned his voice had more power than he realized. He could express opinions, weigh options with others, and make better decisions for himself and his community. He felt that his fellow students could create a community that would be more than "various individuals squawking over hard pressed issues," a community that would be reasonably coherent and reasonably cohesive. And he knew how to make that community stronger: he could begin by joining his voice with others.[3] He understood what to do to be a producer as a citizen—what to do to make a difference.

The most extensive research on results has been done at Wake Forest University and is reported on in this volume. So I won't discuss it here, except to say that I was impressed by the richer understanding of politics that Wake Forest students developed, which had implications for their daily lives. Politics was no longer seen as something only politicians do.[4]

Deliberative pedagogy also has implications for the institutions where it is being used. Some institutions have used deliberation to deal with highly sensitive campus issues like racial discrimination. Others have used it to engage the public they serve more effectively by joining citizens in deliberating on town–gown issues. Having faculty and students familiar with deliberative forums on campus has been quite helpful when the forums moved off campus.

Some of these off-campus forums have been on the role and mission of colleges and universities. These forums have the potential to bring institutions into a different relationship with the public. Public deliberations aren't just about what should be done; they are about who should act. Citizens have to consider their own responsibilities. That is crucial for many issues academic institutions face. Take the case of improving the community or neighborhood where a campus is located. No institution can make those improvements without the participation of the local residents. Academic institutions also give the work they do *for* citizens greater legitimacy when it is done *with* citizens. What is more, a habit of deliberating with citizens can fundamentally change the way institutions see them—not just as consumers of services but as producers working with others to combat common problems.

Deliberative pedagogy is focused first, as it should be, on the classroom and on the challenge of giving students an understanding of citizenship they can use every day. But it also has the potential to spread from the classroom to the institution as a whole—and the potential to bring the institution into a more productive relationship with the public. Those are all good reasons to learn more about this pedagogy from those who are pioneering it.

NOTES

1. See Thucydides, *History of the Peloponnesian War*, 2.40.2.

2. Isocrates, "Antidosis," in *Isocrates*, trans. George Norlin, vol. 2 (New York: G. P. Putnam's Sons, 2000), 179–365, and Aristotle, *The Ethics of Aristotle: The Nicomachean Ethics*, trans. J. A. K. Thomson (London: Penguin Books, 1956), 84–87, 176–84.

3. Nick McNamara, "Social and Public Deliberation Reflection" (class assignment in Dr. Wanda Minor's course titled Social and Public Deliberation, Monmouth University, West Long Branch, NJ, April 2011).

4. Other studies show that college students welcome opportunities to engage in deliberations. See Abby Kiesa et al., *Millennials Talk Politics: A Study of College Student Political Engagement* (College Park, MD: Center for Information and Research on Civic Learning and Engagement, 2007).

Preface

Maxine S. Thomas

This volume is rooted in innovative approaches to teaching in higher education that developed over the course of more than a decade, with the encouragement of the Charles F. Kettering Foundation.[1] The foundation brought together faculty members from across the country several times a year to share experiences and collaborate on the ideas that would form the basis of this volume. These efforts involved serendipity, lessons learned, and, occasionally, struggles with change. The result was a new way of thinking about the role of the college classroom in educating students that put deliberation at the center of how people were teaching.

Before I describe this journey and its gratifying end, it may be helpful to provide some background on the Kettering Foundation's citizen-centered view of what makes democracy work. The Kettering Foundation is deeply rooted in democratic ideas, which put citizens at the forefront of what must be done in communities if democracy is to work as it should.[2] It focuses its research on the role of government, institutions, and citizens in shaping democratic life. This approach is not new. It's as familiar as the tradition of gathering together for barn raisings and quilting bees.[3] It involves people offering their skills and ideas to consider solutions to the problem at hand and organizing to get work done.

This type of collective work is concerned not only with solving problems but also with how skills are transmitted to the next generation. In communities, people teach each other how to do what is needed. Often traditions of work are handed down through families. Sometimes the process is so embedded in the fabric of a community that people don't even remember where they learned how to come together to produce what the community needs.

The same is true in politics. Traditionally, town meetings were the places where people came together to talk about community challenges or to take advantage of new community opportunities. These political traditions were handed down through geographically close-knit groups, whether they were hunter-gatherers or rural farmers. But over time as communities grew in size and diversity, they deferred much of the teaching of community roles and decision-making to a professional class of politicians, who changed not only what people did in community but ultimately what the community itself did.

People began to back out of barn raisings or sewing circles, instead hiring contractors and quilters. With the rise of other entertainment outlets, people didn't come together as much. Gatherings to talk, exchange ideas, and help with decisions were replaced with solitary work, and as people pulled further and further back from the commons, they became more and more critical of the professionals who had replaced them. This criticism led to increasing distrust of politics by the early 1990s. Richard Harwood summarized the implications of this shift for succeeding generations when he wrote, "The challenge, then, facing the country is how to educate young Americans so that they see the relevance of politics in their lives."[4] Harwood's research found that while students' parents were cynical about politics and politicians, young people were downright disgusted. They wanted nothing to do with it.

Kettering research suggested that for the pubic to reprise its role in politics, we would need to bring not only adults but also young people back into the political arena. Key to this process was discovering how young people were learning about politics—and what they needed to learn to do the work of citizens in a democracy. It took a while, but eventually we found a focused group of like-minded professors to study these questions.

This small cadre of professors questioned what their students were learning in college, including how classroom work prepared young people for the challenges they would face in the future. Believing that students could best learn democratic skills and ideals by practicing them, these professors began to hold student-led forums to deliberate on the thorny choices involved in seeking solutions to our most difficult public problems. Deliberation is a way of discussing such issues that emphasizes understanding the trade-offs inherent to every solution. It encourages empathy and respect for the views of others, even in the face of disagreement.

In 2002 Kettering brought together these professionals to begin research on what the next generation needed to learn if they were to be prepared for the tasks necessary to help democracy survive. From the start, this was a motley crew. Many noted that they were the only person on their campus involved in this work, as democracy education had little relevance for tenure, promotion, and other faculty rewards. In fact, deans, department heads, and peers often discouraged these professors from continuing this line of research.[5]

When this small but tenacious group arrived at Kettering, many were just glad to know they had coconspirators. They had found their tribe. Early meetings often involved commiserating about how faculty priorities made it hard to continue this work. But over time they began to take responsibility for what was happening. As many matured through the faculty ranks, they persevered at studying these ideas and using them in their classrooms. They also began to organize to find out how this experimental work might come together to develop a new field.

Kettering called this work *using deliberation in the classroom*, because the locus was the classroom and the experience was deliberation. But as the small (yet steadily growing) group of faculty members continued to define what they thought was necessary if this work was to survive on each of their campuses, they referred to their work as *deliberative pedagogy*.[6] They focused on training and research on how to use deliberation in classroom teaching and in communities, how to assess that work, and how to expand the field. They traded syllabi, exchanged stories, and collaborated on the development of an assessment rubric.

Other scholars were doing parallel research. Wake Forest University professors Jill J. McMillan and Katy J. Harriger embarked on a major longitudinal study of a group of students who would practice and study the work of citizenship throughout their college career. This group of thirty Democracy Fellows spent the entire four years of their experience at Wake Forest learning about, framing, and convening deliberative forums. Their work included learning to structure deliberative conversations, researching and holding deliberations in the classroom, and organizing community forums.

The longitudinal study of this work constituted a major step forward. The results—published by the Kettering Foundation in 2007[7]—suggest that this work might reintroduce young people to democratic ideas and give them a new and lasting understanding of politics. Although this program involved only one group of students from one university, the study offered suggestions for how deliberative practices might be adopted at other institutions.

In 2008 the Kettering Foundation published *Deliberation and the Work of Higher Education*, edited by John R. Dedrick, Laura Grattan, and Harris Dienstfrey. This volume explored experiments from a wide variety of people who used forums in their classrooms and in the community. It shared findings from professors across institutions and disciplines who recognized the importance of deliberative teaching approaches in higher education.

Armed with these preliminary findings from McMillan, Harriger, and Dedrick et al., the newly named Deliberative Pedagogy group concluded that if these ideas were to thrive and if new faculty were to adopt them, the field needed a compilation of theory, practice, and relevant research that would make it possible for others to experiment. The group began to identify what faculty would need if they were to consider using deliberation and related ideas in their classrooms. Clearly, they would need more than the exchange of syllabi and stories. Group members began to plan a book. Kettering could publish work that came out of this effort, but many of these faculty were young professors, and publications needed to count for promotion and tenure and be recognized by their peers. The group decided to develop a research dissemination strategy that would include journal articles, presentations at relevant conferences and meetings, and exploration of a publishing contract.

During that time, I learned of a new experiment that one of Kettering's former researchers, living in Israel, was doing in her college classroom and community. Intrigued, we invited her to join one of our Deliberative Pedagogy meetings. Recognizing that she was probably not the only one outside of the United States using these ideas, we began to ask what faculty members in other countries were doing in their classrooms. We invited some of them to be a part of our research. In the spring of 2014 this international group met at the Kettering Foundation with our Deliberative Pedagogy group. With interest from a book publisher, we moved to the editing, refining, and ultimate publication of this research, including models and views from the United States and around the world.

We learned that we could come together as a group to make an important contribution to the ideas around deliberative pedagogy, encouraging members to publish in different journals and books the ideas that are central to our research.[8] We encouraged young professors to work on deliberation in the classroom and community in a wide array of disciplines. Cross-cultural linkages and research in comparative and comparable efforts enriched our work, as did examples of what these ideas look like in the context of other countries and cultures.

Fundamentally, deliberative pedagogy looks at democracy and citizenship in a variety of ways. It looks at the role of students and graduates of colleges and universities and the way they see their role in a democratic society. It seeks to make it more likely that students see themselves as agents capable of playing a role in the development of their communities. It also looks at the role educators play in helping students realize their efficacy to participate as citizens in communities. This civic awakening is central to the broader civic engagement movement on campuses, and it depends on a different kind of faculty and different kinds of classrooms. This volume focuses on these first two. But this is just the beginning of the work. We are already looking forward. The questions that remain are many: What do faculty need to do to prepare themselves to be guides to students who engage in their communities? How do you get beyond the college campus to those who do not, cannot, and will not go to college? How does the work of students become more integral to communities and less of just a good deed? What should public life look like? What role should colleges and universities play in the development of students for participation in the public life of communities? The ultimate question is what are the next steps of this work.

What is clear is the need to engage not only with other students and faculty but with the broader communities. There must be robust interactions between students and communities. In fact, campuses and communities share many common concerns: the effects of student use of alcohol on campus, the sheer overcrowding of streets and local stores on game days, as well as basic concerns about safety and crime. These beg for campuses and communities to talk. But not just any talk—deliberative discussion. This requires not only students, but faculty, staff, and administration of the institution as well, to join with community institutions and citizens. Students and colleges need to be more than just resources to communities. They need to be active partners in addressing concerns about local development, to be among the first responders to natural disasters in communities, and to join in the naming of the problems the broader community (of which they are a part) faces. It is not enough to simply prepare students to do these things in the future. They need to do them now by developing relationships with community members.

The series of meetings that started in 2002 with interested faculty members simply sharing experiences, syllabi, and challenges turned into something that was much larger than our modest plan. Ultimately, colleagues from different states and from around the world reminded us that these deliberative practices and ideas are not owned by any one region or country. They strengthen all of our communities, and in so doing, enrich all of our lives. We view this book as a critical contribution to what we see as a pedagogical approach and field of practice only beginning to be realized.

NOTES

1. Early meetings of this group began in 2002.

2. See David Mathews, *Politics for People: Finding a Responsible Public Voice*, 2nd ed. (Urbana: University of Illinois Press, 1999).

3. See David Mathews, "Why We Need to Change Our Concept of Community Leadership," *Community Education Journal* 23, nos. 1–2 (Fall 1995/Winter 1996): 9–18.

4. Richard Harwood, *College Students Talk Politics* (Dayton, OH: Kettering Foundation, 1993), 4.

5. See Claire Snyder-Hall, *Civic Aspirations: Why Some Higher Education Faculty Are Reconnecting Their Professional and Public Lives* (Dayton, OH: Kettering Foundation, 2015).

6. The name itself was the subject of an extended deliberation, in which faculty, joined by foundation staff, shared what they meant by *deliberative pedagogy*.

7. Katy J. Harriger and Jill J. McMillan, *Speaking of Politics: Preparing College Students for Democratic Citizenship through Deliberative Dialogue* (Dayton, OH: Kettering Foundation Press, 2007).

8. See, for example, Sara A. Mehltretter Drury, "Deliberation as Communication Instruction: A Study of a Climate Change Deliberation in an Introductory Biology Course," *Journal on Excellence in College Teaching* 26, no. 4 (2015): 51–72; N. V. Longo, "Deliberative Pedagogy in the Community: Connecting Deliberative Dialogue, Community Engagement, and Democratic Education," *Journal of Public Deliberation* 9, no. 2 (2013), Article 16. T. J. Shaffer, "Teaching deliberative democracy deliberatively," *eJournal of Public Affairs* 5, no. 2 (2016): 92–114.

Introduction

Nicholas V. Longo, Idit Manosevitch, and Timothy J. Shaffer

All social change begins with a conversation.
—Margaret J. Wheatley (2002)

In contested spaces across the globe, a new model of teaching and learning is emerging in higher education. This approach goes well beyond the old, passive instructional paradigm that asks students to be consumers of their education, instead creating space for participants to be cocreators of their own learning through deliberative conversations. It also goes beyond the "active learning" strategies that have become more robust in recent years. While it includes a diversity of methods, the model we term *deliberative pedagogy* encompasses a common commitment that sets it apart from other approaches: a connection between education and democracy.

This connection has relevance in countries across the globe. Deliberative pedagogy is engaging students as productive citizens on a variety of issues at a diverse range of institutions. In South Africa, for example, the lasting effects of apartheid still abound, as do calls for transformation and actions to bring about decolonization. At the University of Cape Town, students of color have organized highly touted efforts leading to victories such as the removal of symbols of white oppression on campus and an end to proposed tuition increases. On a smaller yet possibly more profound scale, transformation means students from different backgrounds and races coming together as part of their education to have deliberative conversations about the possibilities for a more just and equitable society—and their roles in creating this society as citizens and future professionals.

Providence College, a Catholic liberal arts institution in Rhode Island, makes space for deliberative conversations across diverse communities in a neighborhood setting. Like many urban campuses in the United States, Providence College has a long history of distrust between the campus and the local community. To overcome this distrust, the campus and community have developed a storefront space in the heart of the Smith Hill neighborhood. The Providence College/Smith Hill Annex provides a free space to foster ongoing conversations and trusting relationships between neighbors. Like other "third places," the Annex hosts courses for students and community members, youth programming, and dialogues on pressing issues (Oldenburg, 1999, p. xvii).

These kinds of deliberative conversations are taking place in an assortment of disciplines in higher education, especially communication studies. At Kansas State University, communication studies faculty became increasingly concerned about the tremendous influence of political elites in setting the political agenda and driving public policy. Realizing that citizens needed a real voice, department faculty, in collaboration with other colleagues and with robust institutional support, began to implement deliberative approaches. The university has now embedded deliberative pedagogy in undergraduate curricula, graduate curricula, and research. In addition, it offers community-based educational opportunities to train citizens in facilitation techniques and deliberative methods for greater civic engagement.

The Future of Teaching and Learning in Higher Education

These stories from campuses illustrate, perhaps more than anything else, that new models for teaching and learning in the future will need to include public deliberation—a process through which a range of stakeholders come together to share ideas and perspectives and then make collective decisions that form the basis for public action (Longo, 2013). This process for coming to public judgment about difficult issues has been "part of the ongoing development of democracy" (Leighninger, 2012, p. 19); more than that, it has for many centuries been at the core of what makes communities work (London, 2010; Mathews, 1999; Nabatchi, Gastil, Leighninger & Weiksner, 2012).

Public deliberation has been used since ancient times as a basis for public governance in societies around the world. Foundational examples include the ancient Greek assemblies, the centuries-spanning Buddhist councils in India, the Jewish law debates in Late Antiquity, and the seventh-century Japanese constitution, among many others (Blum-Kulka, Blondheim & Hacohen, 2002; Marin, 2006; Sen, 2003). In recent centuries, deliberation was central to the labor, women's, and civil rights movements, along with settlement houses, social centers, citizenship schools, popular education practices, participatory budgeting processes, folk schools, indigenous people's efforts, truth and reconciliation commissions, the kibbutz model, and countless other civic engagement projects globally (Barker, McAfee & McIvor, 2012b; Leighninger, 2012; McIlrath, Lyons & Munck, 2012; Röcke, 2014; Rosner, 1973).

As the field of public deliberation has grown over the past two decades, much research has been done to study the historical and philosophical foundations of deliberative democracy, including what works in practice and how public deliberation supports the civic mission of higher education (Dedrick, Grattan & Dienstfrey, 2008; Gastil & Levine, 2005; Harriger & McMillan, 2007; Nabatchi, Gastil, Leighninger & Weiksner, 2012; Thomas & Carcasson, 2010). The efficacy of this approach in grappling with complex issues has prompted its incorporation into domains beyond public policy or the political sphere.

One of the most prominent of these areas is education, where deliberation is emerging as a distinct pedagogy. Scholars have written about the democratic classroom creating a learning environment that models democratic habits and practices, but few have included deliberation. In contrast to deliberative politics, which couples deliberative decision-making with public action, deliberative pedagogy integrates deliberative processes of working through issues with teaching, learning, and engagement—inside the classroom as well as in community settings.

This book is among the first instances in which deliberative pedagogy has been used explicitly in the way we have conceptualized it: as a way of teaching and learning for democracy (see also Dedrick, Grattan & Dienstfrey, 2008; Doherty, 2012; Longo, 2013; Shaffer 2016). Scholars have written about deliberative pedagogy in connection with school settings in Sweden (Roth, 2010); others more loosely connect deliberative forums with pedagogy as it connects to democratic education (Laker, Naval & Mrnjaus, 2014; McGregor, 2004; Waghid, 2014). This book goes one step further, describing deliberative pedagogy as an essential component of the future of teaching and learning in higher education, especially arguing for this kind of civic purpose in how colleges and universities understand their mission.

Writing about the establishment of a teaching and learning seminar for faculty members at Elon University, Stephen Bloch-Schulman quotes a colleague engaged in democratic education: "democratic pedagogy ought to foster and embody both respect and resistance, and the tensions and difficulties of doing so are the richness and challenge of truly democratic teaching and thinking" (2010, p. 409). While this quote seemingly aligns with the practices described in this volume, the article from which this quote is taken speaks to the need for educating for democracy without ever mentioning the word *deliberation*.

If we expand our language from deliberation to discussion and/or dialogue, we find more scholarly interest in the roles of discourse and engagement in higher education settings (Brookfield & Preskill, 2005; Colby, Beaumont, Ehrlich & Corngold, 2007; Isgro & Deal, 2013; Palmer, Zajonc & Scribner, 2010). Further, like engaged scholarship—teaching, research, and service—deliberative pedagogy attempts to break the detached, expert-driven model by utilizing engaged pedagogical approaches to address complex, adaptive public problems (Fitzgerald, Burack & Seifer, 2010; Hoy & Johnson, 2013; Swaner, 2012; Thomas & Levine, 2011; Wolf & Loker, 2012). Despite these similarities (indeed, many contributors to this volume view themselves as engaged scholars), the concept of deliberative pedagogy should not be conflated with the wider civic engagement movement. In our view, deliberative pedagogy is concerned primarily with the role of education in democracy, making pedagogical issues related to civic education and experiential learning central, while also firmly grounding this work in deliberative democracy theory and practice. This focus on pedagogy has been too often minimized in wider calls for civic renewal.

This book focuses specifically on deliberative pedagogy in higher education. Deliberative pedagogy is a democratic educational process and a way of thinking that encourages students to encounter and consider multiple perspectives, weigh trade-offs and tensions, and move toward action through informed judgment. It is simultaneously a way of teaching that is itself deliberative and a process for developing the skills, behaviors, and values that support deliberative practice. Perhaps most important, the work of deliberative pedagogy is about space-making: creating and holding space for authentic and productive dialogue, conversations that can ultimately be not only educational but also transformative.

New Terrain in Pedagogical Practice

The scholars and practitioners who have contributed to this volume—and to the broader conversation about deliberative pedagogy—offer frameworks and examples that help us begin to imagine what the future of teaching and learning might look like. In addressing questions such as "What makes pedagogy deliberative?" we attempt to elucidate what is otherwise a foreign or confusing concept for those in teaching environments.

Such questions also help illuminate practices with a long history, albeit one that has been largely subterranean. Deliberative pedagogy is an approach to education that has "freeing powers" for learners, as Jane Addams (1902, p. 84) described. It has also been central to social movements in the past, as seen with the learning circle tradition at places like the Highlander Folk School during the labor and civil rights movements (Longo, 2007). Understanding this history helps chart new possibilities for education, including how a different kind of learning can lead to action.

Deliberative pedagogy connects deliberative dialogue, democratic education, and, often, community engagement. It also attempts to create spaces for reciprocal conversations, grounded in real-world experiences, which lead to collective action. Ultimately, deliberative pedagogy challenges our ideas about politics, engagement, and education, as illustrated in the chapters in this book. The more we can work to develop a deeper understanding of this concept, based on actual experiences across the globe, the more we can make progress in addressing the polarization in our politics, the inefficacy of our engagement, and the inequities in our education.

We focus on higher education for a few reasons. First, higher education has long allowed greater freedom and flexibility than other institutions when it comes to pedagogical approaches. More important, higher education has a unique dual role of educating the next generation while also being able to unleash significant resources to contribute to addressing today's pressing problems. Colleges and universities, as Harry Boyte writes in *Democracy's Education*, are essential mediating and educational institutions for civic education and democratic renewal. The university, in short, serves as "a crucial *anchoring institution of citizenship*" (Boyte, 2015, p. 3).

Many are involved in what we call deliberative pedagogy, even if they give it another name. On college campuses, deliberation has grown as a form of civic education in recent years. To illustrate, 80 percent of U.S. institutions hosted and/or funded public dialogues on current issues in 2014, according to a survey by Campus Compact (2014). Further, there is a growing infrastructure on college campuses for dialogue and deliberation—mirroring the capacity for other engaged pedagogies, such as service-learning and multicultural education. As Scott London points out in his chapter in this volume, centers for public life are now operating in almost every U.S. state and in about a dozen other countries, including places as diverse as Russia, Brazil, Israel (Manosevitch, 2016), and Colombia.

Support structures for this work are varied and growing. Multiple consortiums promote dialogue and deliberation, including the Deliberative Democracy Consortium and the National Coalition for Dialogue and Deliberation; endowed institutions such as the Kettering Foundation and Everyday Democracy support research and practice; an academic journal, the *Journal of Public Deliberation*, offers a venue to share research, projects, experiments, and experiences of academics and practitioners in the multidisciplinary field of deliberative democracy; and a multitude of practices in higher education are emerging from the National Issues Forums Institute, Study Circles, the Sustained Dialogue Institute, Difficult Dialogue Initiative, the Public Conversations Project, and the Program on Intergroup Relations, among many others.

Although this approach is not yet widely used in higher education, the contributors to this book highlight the breadth of its early adopters across institutional types—community colleges, regional universities, research-intensive universities, private liberal arts institutions, and historically black colleges and universities—in varying regions in the world, including Latin America, Africa, Europe, North America, and the Middle East. Significantly, this book is comprised of chapters that speak to nuanced approaches to integrating deliberation in teaching in the classroom and the community in a wide range of settings.

Our own work, along with conversations with scholars and practitioners from across the globe, helped us begin to ask: What does a twenty-first-century teaching and learning model look like? What is the relationship between education and democracy in a rapidly changing, globalized world? How would we prepare young people to practice this new form of education? Given the role of higher education in preparing young people for leadership in all sectors—public, private, and nonprofit—how can colleges and universities transform their approach to educate in ways that better reflect the challenges and trends in our world?

Those were the questions with which we found ourselves grappling as we began discussing this project in 2011. From the beginning of the conversation about deliberative pedagogy at regular meetings convened by the Kettering Foundation in Dayton, Ohio, the participants have been intentional about keeping this effort from spilling over into the expansive literature focusing on civic engagement in higher education. While informed by the emergence of both the theory and practice of higher education's greater response to public problems through engaged teaching and research, our conversations have focused on deliberation as a pedagogical approach. Pedagogical concerns are not limited to the confines of the classroom, however. As Nicholas V. Longo and Cynthia M. Gibson demonstrate in their chapter, deliberative pedagogy can play a critical role in bridging the divide between campuses and surrounding communities.

What might be most helpful at the onset of this volume is a clarification about what we mean by terms such as *deliberation* and *pedagogy*. We borrow heavily from the increasingly robust field of democratic theory since the deliberative turn more than two decades ago (Dryzek, 2000). The following section offers a brief explanation of deliberative democracy that goes well beyond higher education but that lays out tenets that must be integrated into a democratic classroom if it is to be deliberative.

The diversity of settings we explore in this book also offers insights into the contested nature of deliberation and dialogue, even when connected to the academic curriculum. While in the U.S. context we often think of higher education as a site for academic freedom and free space, where no topic is off limits, our work illustrates this is not true, even in Western-style democracies. Deliberative conversations about abortion or gay marriage are contentious and often silenced on faith-based campuses, for instance. Academic freedom is being stripped away at places such as the University of Wisconsin system that has historically been a pioneer in engagement dating back to the "Wisconsin Idea." And conversations about race, racism, and Black Lives Matter on campuses across the United States illustrate the discrimination facing historically marginalized communities in American higher education. These challenges can be even more pronounced in some places in Eastern Europe, the Middle East, and Africa, where free speech may not be enshrined in constitutions, and discussions about political topics can lead to severe repercussions and punishments. Even where academic freedom is taken for granted, differences in sociopolitical situations or speech cultures may have important implications for the practice of deliberative pedagogy. In addition, institutional issues such as budget constraints, tenure and promotion expectations, and lack of support can limit possibilities for engaging in this work.

Thus, we have come to realize that engaging in deliberative pedagogy often takes courage and leadership as well as flexibility and attentiveness to the nuances of context. Most important, deliberative pedagogy requires a shift in the role of the faculty member from primarily teaching content to primarily facilitating learning. This shift requires faculty to rethink their professional roles and identities as reflective practitioners, moving toward what John Saltmarsh, director of the New England Resource Center for Higher Education, describes as a "process of collaboration with students and community to build democracy" (personal interview with Longo & Gibson).

(Briefly) Defining Deliberative Democracy

Deliberative pedagogy is rooted in the tradition of deliberative theory and put into practice in educational spaces. In its classic version, deliberative democracy is based on two principles: reasoning between people rather than bargaining or aggregating private preferences and having the giving, weighing, acceptance, or rejection of reasons be a public act. Ideally, no force except that of the better argument is exercised (Habermas, 1975). Thus, the ability to use reasoned judgment is central to deliberative democracy and individuals should put forth justifications for making arguments and for supporting or criticizing them.

Recent approaches have broadened the notion of deliberative democracy by emphasizing not only the informed public process for addressing issues but also the social values that govern it. Accordingly, John Gastil (2008) conceptualizes public deliberation as entailing two processes that must occur in tandem. The analytic process constitutes the substantive dimensions of the issue that are necessary for reaching an informed decision: specifically, reason giving and careful consideration of all options and their trade-offs. At the same time, the social process of deliberation constitutes the norms and values underlying the discussion: mutual respect and equal opportunity to speak and to be heard and understood. Others have similarly identified requirements for deliberation as including reason giving, universalism, inclusivity, rationality, agreement, and political efficacy (Jacobs, Cook & Delli Carpini, 2009; Gutmann & Thompson, 2004).

Through the sharing of information and knowledge, and careful listening to people's personal narratives and perspectives, public deliberation can transform individuals' understanding and grasp of complex problems and allow them to see elements of an issue they had not considered previously. This reliance on inclusive public reasoning has led some to believe that "deliberative democracy is the best conception of democratic procedure because it can generate 'best' decisions; that is, produce outcomes that are the most thoroughly examined, justified and, hence, legitimate" (Held, 2006, pp. 237–38). Adherence to deliberative values and norms of conversation is a necessary condition for such a process to unfold. Participants in deliberative democracy must understand the importance of listening to a broad range of voices. Further, they must have the skills and opportunity to exercise such listening, along with a willingness to consider reasoning offered on its merits.

Deliberative theory, however, is not without critique. The ideals of deliberation raise numerous challenges, mainly around issues of power and inclusion for women and diverse populations (Fung, 2005; Karpowitz & Raphael, 2014; Sanders, 1997; Young, 2000, 2001). Others have challenged the sometimes-vague connections between talk and action (Barker, McAfee & McIvor, 2012a; Boyte, 2012; Levine, 2013). But deliberative theory and practice have worked to overcome these critiques, drawing on a framing of politics that shifts away from expert-centric institutions to those that identify the environments and practices in which diverse citizens can engage in public problem-solving and deliberative public work (Boyte, 2004, 2012; Kim & Kim, 2008; Mansbridge, 1999; Mathews, 1999, 2014).

(Briefly) Defining Engaged Pedagogy

Deliberative pedagogy is likewise rooted in a particular conception of pedagogy. Fundamentally, pedagogy is the method and practice of teaching an academic subject or theoretical concept. The deliberative—and engaged—aspect of pedagogy builds on the foundational work of education philosopher John Dewey (1910, [1916] 1997), whose seminal writings focus on experience being central to learning, along with the work of educator Paulo Freire (1974, 2000), whose theory of praxis drew a distinction between the "banking" and "dialogic" models of education. An assortment of other educational writers, from bell hooks (1994) to Myles Horton (1998), invites us to make the central pedagogical shift to viewing students as sources, rather than simply receptacles, of knowledge.

Along these lines, Malcolm S. Knowles (1980), a scholar of adult education, noted an approach to learning grounded in one's experience—including problem-solving, deliberation, and engagement in and with communities. Matthew Johnson and colleagues use this lens when they write that public deliberation "aligns with the learning paradigm as the teacher acts as a guide through the public deliberation process as opposed to delivering content about the process to students. Students undertake a process of discovery . . . and work alongside teachers to engage in reflective, often transformational, dialogue in which they gain self-awareness and discover multiple possibilities for collective action" (Johnson et al., 2014, p. 97). All involved in this type of education take on roles and responsibilities to both teach and learn from and with one another.

Thus, deliberative pedagogy builds on an important conceptual shift in higher education that Robert Barr and John Tagg (1995) flagged just over twenty years ago—in which colleges began to see their primary function as providing learning rather than instruction. By doing so, colleges were recognizing their responsibility to "create environments and experiences that allow students to discover and construct knowledge for themselves and to become members of communities of learning that make discoveries and solve problems" (Barr & Tagg, 1995, p. 15).

More recently, scholars concerned with engaged pedagogies have articulated nuanced dynamics of what it means to approach academic content, students, and communities through more collaborative, participatory, and democratic approaches (Eyler & Giles, 1999; Longo & Gibson,

2016; Saltmarsh, 2010; Stoecker, Tryon & Hilgendorf, 2009; Zlotkowski, 2000). An essential part of engaged pedagogy is participatory educational practices—what George Kuh (2008) refers to as a set of "high-impact practices" for student learning. These engaged learning practices include curricular interventions (e.g., first-year seminars, capstone courses, global learning), student life experiences (common intellectual experiences and learning communities), off-campus engagement (internships, service-learning courses), and classroom practices (intensive writing, undergraduate research, collaborative assignments).

Deliberative pedagogy is another such practice that enables us to look for opportunities to acknowledge the complexity of our positions and views alongside those we teach and work with every day. To help students learn about democracy, we can't just talk about it as being "out there"; we also need to acknowledge it as something that happens in classrooms and through community partnerships—through an engaged pedagogy. Deliberative pedagogy thus addresses what Benson, Harkavy, and Puckett term the "Dewey Problem" (2007, p. 33) by helping us construct a participatory democratic society through education. The chapters in this volume embody this articulation of pedagogy in a multitude of settings.

Overview of Contents

The book is divided into six parts, each including three to four chapters that speak to distinct elements of deliberative pedagogy. Building on the need to reconceptualize the role of higher education in connecting education with democracy, the first section of this book sets the groundwork for understanding deliberative pedagogy with an overview of the theoretical concepts and historical underpinnings of this approach to teaching and learning. Parts 2 through 5 are best described as stories of deliberative pedagogy in practice. Part 6 focuses on the issue of assessment, and the book concludes with Nancy L. Thomas offering insight and suggestions for deliberative pedagogy's place in the higher education civic movement.

Part 1: Theory and History of Deliberative Pedagogy

Part 1 of the book describes what makes deliberative pedagogy unique and how it connects with other civic practices in higher education, both historically and today. In the first chapter, Martín Carcasson offers an important framework for thinking about deliberative pedagogy: as a pedagogy rooted in the classroom but also transcending that setting. Deliberative pedagogy, according to Carcasson, is a "teaching philosophy focused on equipping students with the mind-sets and skill sets necessary for high-quality participatory decision-making in the face of 'wicked' problems." Carcasson focuses on the need to make sense of—and address—complex problems, partially by preparing students to participate effectively in and lead critical conversations.

Next, Timothy J. Shaffer offers a perspective on the history of deliberation as an important element of education in the United States. Tracing its roots back through the New England town meeting, lyceums, and Chautauqua movement, Shaffer focuses on the role of deliberation in American society and through higher education. His chapter explores the role of discussion and deliberation in the disciplines, especially communication and its willingness to embrace group discussion, as well as the ways in which higher education institutions helped facilitate community discussion and deliberation in the 1930s and early 1940s. Understanding these historical roots can help to ground our current discussion.

In their chapter, Nicholas V. Longo and Cynthia M. Gibson point out that deliberative pedagogy often takes place outside the boundaries of the classroom. Drawing on interviews with leading scholars, Longo and Gibson offer a context for deliberative pedagogy as a citizen-centered approach that connects classroom learning with community engagement. "As the approach gains recognition," they argue, "it has the potential to transform teaching and learning in a way that has powerful implications for civic education, community problem-solving, and democracy." These chapters offer a broader theoretical and conceptual framing that ground the following sections.

Part 2: Classroom Practices: New Ways of Teaching and Learning

The calls from authors in part 1 for a more democratic and collaborative public sphere are echoed in classrooms and communities across the globe. Parts 2 through 5 illuminate these practices with a series of chapters devoted to the implementation of deliberative pedagogy in higher education by scholars from around the world. These scholars come from a wide range of academic institutions—from small, private liberal arts colleges to large universities to minority-serving institutions—in the Middle East, Europe, Russia, and the United States. These authors manifest the relevance and applicability of deliberative pedagogy to a variety of subject fields as well as the challenges faced by educators coming from different social and political contexts. The natural setting for teaching in higher education is the classroom. Accordingly, part 2 begins with deliberative pedagogy practices designed primarily around classroom experiences. Leila R. Brammer describes her implementation of a first-year seminar at Gustavus Adolphus College in Minnesota, in which deliberation served as the course's key organizing principle. Guided by the perspective of the class as a community, Brammer discusses the risks and challenges that arise from utilizing deliberative pedagogy as a core tenet in course construction, as well as the outcomes for student learning and empowerment.

Idit Manosevitch of Netanya Academic College discusses the particular challenges of implementing deliberative pedagogy in a deeply divided society such as Israel's. She offers a detailed syllabus of a course in which students learned the principles and values of deliberation through designing and implementing a deliberative issue conference. Manosevitch explains the transformational power of such an experience, particularly with regard to students' deliberative faith, which is particularly significant given the deeply conflicted political context and the highly aggressive nature of Israeli public debate.

Sara A. Mehltretter Drury and Martín Carcasson provide a compelling case for the inherent connection between deliberative pedagogy and communication courses, advocating for the promotion of these connections across their field's curricula. The authors provide specific recommendations for ways of integrating deliberative pedagogy in core elements of communication courses, including public speaking, group communication, argumentation, and research.

Turning to the natural sciences, Sara A. Mehltretter Drury uses the concept of wicked problems to demonstrate the relevance and importance of deliberative pedagogy in teaching science subjects.

She details her multiyear experience of engaging non–science majors in introductory biology and chemistry courses using the public issues of climate change and energy. She also points to useful resources for implementing deliberative pedagogy in the sciences and elsewhere.

Part 3: Comparative, Gender, and Cross-Cultural Deliberative Pedagogy Practice

Deliberative pedagogy spans many divides, including national borders. Part 3 offers chapters that explore the growing global network of scholars engaging in this work through technology-aided conversations, collaborations in fields such as feminist studies and journalism education, and even cross-cultural deliberative experiences. J. Cherie Strachan offers a critical perspective of deliberative pedagogy's potential to create inclusive public spaces. Drawing on feminist and political theory, Strachan emphasizes the need to address inequity when it comes to women participating in democracy—whether in the classroom or, more broadly, in public life. Noting the history of women's "deliberative disempowerment," Strachan writes that "failing to make any effort to address women's historic exclusion from deliberative decision-making is not only irresponsible, but a lost opportunity to help our students become the type of citizens who will help build a more inclusive and egalitarian public sphere for everyone."

Ekaterina Lukianova previously of Saint Petersburg State University and now at the Kettering Foundation and Jack Musselman of St. Edward's University lay out their experience conducting a deliberative pedagogy experiment with students in Russia and the United States. The authors illustrate how instructors from different parts of the world may collaborate and overcome geographic constraints by using readily accessible digital networks. They discuss the challenges involved in cross-border deliberative pedagogy, as well as the unique opportunities that such collaboration brings for internationalizing deliberation, enhancing opportunities for cultural exchange, and reconciling differences.

Ibtesam Al-Atiyat of St. Olaf College in Minnesota builds on Strachan's earlier discussion of the relevance of deliberative pedagogy to gender studies. She describes global debates surrounding the feminist movement, noting that despite growing criticism from third world feminists, Western feminism often assumes that women from developing and Muslim countries are in need of "saving" from oppressive situations. The importance of this debate, she explains, transcends academic and professional spheres, as it affects political decisions regarding invasion, war, and aid. Al-Atiyat details several deliberative pedagogy exercises in which she engaged her students in globally focused deliberation about these issues.

The final chapter of this part offers a dramatic example of student movement building at Eötvös Loránd University in Hungary. Ferenc Hammer uses personal interviews and participatory observations to detail and analyze the grassroots, participatory forums that students led around a variety of public issues, including educational funding and political accountability. Hammer concludes with recommendations for student-led and other deliberative efforts, based on the creative and open-ended forums in Hungary.

Part 4: Deliberative Pedagogy and Institutional Change

Using deliberative pedagogy as a means of democratic engagement ultimately requires changing the very structures that underpin institutions of higher education. The chapters in part 4 offer different ways institutional change can be achieved through and in support of deliberative practices. Scott London chronicles the growing number of centers for public life located on college campuses. These centers—operating often in almost every U.S. state and in about a dozen other countries—provide what Sara Evans and Harry Boyte (1992) term "free spaces" for civic action and public problem-solving.

Timothy Steffensmeier and David Procter provide an example of how deliberative pedagogy can be embedded into university practice through their cutting-edge efforts at Kansas State University. The authors describe how the Institute for Civic Discourse and Democracy has been advancing its mission of building civic capacity through deliberative pedagogy in the university curriculum and in public issues workshops for citizens and professionals since its founding in 2004.

Finally, Marshalita Sims Peterson demonstrates the possibilities for engaging a wide range of stakeholders in deliberative pedagogy at historically black colleges and universities. Peterson examines a year-long process at Spelman College in which students organized and facilitated public dialogues and led deliberative forums on campus. She uses this case study to develop an integrated model for connecting forums with the civic mission of higher education, concluding that "A commitment to civic engagement and public deliberation provides the foundation for creating meaningful curricular and civic experiences that can stay with students through college and beyond."

Part 5: Bridging Campus and the Community

It can be argued that the most meaningful examples of deliberative pedagogy occur when students and faculty get outside of the campus "bubble." The chapters in part 5 provide models that bridge campus and community. These examples also continue to illustrate what deliberative pedagogy in the community can look like in very different contexts, with examples from urban research universities in Australia and South Africa, as well as a community college in the United States.

Angela Romano of Queensland University of Technology takes us into the realm of deliberative pedagogy in journalism education. Building on interviews with educators from Australia, South Africa, the United States, and New Zealand, Romano explains that deliberative pedagogy extends the purview of vocational journalism education by teaching students deliberative engagement as a means of bringing community members into the news media conversation. Focusing on the notion of public listening as a core component of deliberative journalism, she also outlines methods students can use to gain a deep understanding of community dynamics.

Next, Janice McMillan of the University of Cape Town provides a compelling example of how deliberative pedagogy can connect with community-engaged learning. The course described, Social Infrastructures: Engaging with Community for Change, illustrates how deliberative pedagogy can take place in a setting that at first glance may not seem ideal for participatory, engaged learning: a large classroom with preprofessional students studying engineering. It also illustrates how universities in the Global South are leading efforts to engage in real-world problem-solving. In discussing core aspects of her pedagogical practice, McMillan connects deliberative pedagogy with university and societal transformation in postapartheid South Africa.

Rebecca M. Townsend describes the use of deliberative pedagogy in transportation planning courses at Manchester Community College. The courses, in which students use deliberative discussion as a method of researching community transportation needs, offer an innovative model for the more than one thousand community colleges in the United States. This highly regarded work illustrates how deliberative processes can engage citizens with policymakers on key community issues while improving student learning and skill development.

Part 6: Assessing Deliberative Pedagogy

While they are buzzwords in virtually all sectors of public life, evaluation and assessment are not only a necessary dimension of contemporary higher education but also tools we should embrace for making sense of the diverse range of efforts and claims made by the authors of this volume. One challenge is determining how to evaluate and assess engagement and participation in deliberative settings (Rayner, 2003). The chapters in part 6 offer insight into how scholars have approached this question, including developing tools like longitudinal studies and student learning rubrics, taking a critical view of how educators use language in deliberative forums, and thinking about ways to attend to the larger political realities and dynamics shaping our lives. These chapters make clear that assessment can be critical in garnering support for deliberative pedagogies by demonstrating the impact of these methods.

Katy J. Harriger, Jill J. McMillan, Christy M. Buchanan, and Stephanie Gusler offer a longitudinal assessment of the Democracy Fellows program, an intensive dialogue and deliberation experiment at Wake Forest University. In analyzing this program, they make a case for the importance of assessment more generally. As they note, "it is clear that we live in a larger political and economic environment that is . . . skeptical and that requires systematic assessment to make the case for supporting deliberative work." It is exactly because of that skeptical world—of university administrators, legislators, funders, parents, and students—that we must often justify what we are doing and why it matters.

Given this need, Sara A. Mehltretter Drury, Leila R. Brammer, and Joni Doherty offer a sophisticated rubric-based methodology for assessing deliberative learning in the classroom. This rubric is intended to advance learning of deliberative democratic practices in a progressive way through the integration of a variety of deliberation activities. While similar measures have been developed to assess pedagogy and learning outcomes in the broader area of civic engagement, this rubric is among the first to look specifically at deliberative pedagogy.

Finally, Telma Gimenez and Andressa Molinari use linguistic analysis to assess deliberative pedagogy, particularly issues of language and power. They use critical discourse analysis to judge the exercise of power in the use of language in deliberative forums introduced into a language-teacher education program at Universidade Estadual de Londrina in Brazil.

Conclusion

In the conclusion, Nancy L. Thomas offers a critical assessment of the role of deliberative pedagogy as an important element of the movement to integrate deliberation into the work of educating for democracy. As she notes, "Deliberation advocates need to renew the case for educating for democracy while simultaneously helping educators overcome [the] barriers [to it]. The authors in this book offer strategies for tackling the most immediate barrier: unease with the method." In her view, those of us considering or using democratic approaches in our classrooms must concern ourselves equally with the political world beyond our campuses. Democratic habits can and should be learned in educational settings, which will help them flourish in our everyday lives.

Moving Forward

While this book offers what we hope is an important and broad introduction to the theory and practice of deliberative pedagogy, it is in no way meant to be the final word. It is meant to start a conversation. This book is best understood as a collection of useful demonstrations and explanations of how scholars from diverse contexts have understood, employed, and assessed deliberative pedagogy as an approach to student learning and public problem-solving. While we encourage readers to draw on these chapters in their own thinking, we do not suggest these are the only examples of what deliberative pedagogy looks like or how it should be approached. In fact, faculty members on campuses not included in this book are also engaging in this work and making significant contributions to this developing literature.

Nevertheless, we hope this volume makes an important contribution to the conversations about the future of civic engagement, teaching and learning, and higher education. As David Mathews observes, "Deliberative democracy challenges academic institutions at every level: from the nature of teaching and the character of the extracurricular program to the very meaning of scholarship" (2009, p. 13). This book offers important insights into these challenges. Importantly, we view this book as a conversation for those within higher education as well as those closely connected with the civic engagement movement transforming colleges and universities. Thus, our intended audience focuses on faculty members interested in deliberative pedagogy, academic professionals who help to support teaching and learning in classrooms and communities, and administrators who want to see students, faculty, and community partners flourish through such efforts. As such, the book is limited in the exposure of community voices. The chapters in this book are written from the perspective of faculty members and those with experience in higher education settings. While we have made efforts to include a range of voices, perspectives, and experiences from diverse institutional types and geographical settings, we acknowledge the inherent limitations set forth in such a collected volume and see promising future research that elevates the voices of students and community partners who experience deliberative pedagogy from places other than as an instructor or someone within higher education institutions.

At its core, deliberative pedagogy offers a glimpse into what the next paradigm of teaching and learning is likely to look like. By giving students agency in the classroom, making learning collaborative and engaging, and recognizing the connections between learning and social action, deliberative pedagogy represents a new model of learning for a globalized, networked society. Deliberative pedagogy also connects education with democracy by providing an example of the type of civic innovation needed for colleges and universities to respond to the complex challenges facing society. This idea also echoes those of education luminaries like John Dewey (1910), who believed that knowledge and learning are most effective when people work collaboratively to solve real-world problems. *Deliberative Pedagogy* builds on this thinking with an in-depth examination of the theory, processes, and practice of deliberative pedagogy—offering a way of teaching, learning, and engaging that cultivates spaces for diverse voices and perspectives to listen, speak, and act.

REFERENCES

Addams, J. (1902). *Democracy and social ethics.* New York: Macmillan.

Barker, D. W. M., McAfee, N., & McIvor, D. W. (2012a). Introduction: Democratizing deliberation. In D. W. M. Barker, N. McAfee & D. W. McIvor (Eds.), *Democratizing deliberation: A political theory anthology* (pp. 1–17). Dayton, OH: Kettering Foundation Press.

Barker, D. W. M., McAfee, N., & McIvor, D. W. (Eds.). (2012b). *Democratizing deliberation: A political theory anthology.* Dayton, OH: Kettering Foundation Press.

Barr, R. B., & Tagg, J. (1995). From teaching to learning: A new paradigm for undergraduate education. *Change,* 27(6), 12–25.

Benson, L., Harkavy, I. R., & Puckett, J. L. (2007). *Dewey's dream: Universities and democracies in an age of education reform.* Philadelphia: Temple University Press.

Bloch-Schulman, S. (2010). When the "best hope" is not so hopeful, what then? Democratic thinking, democratic pedagogies, and higher education. *Journal of Speculative Philosophy,* 24(4), 399–415.

Blum-Kulka, S., Blondheim, M., & Hacohen, G. (2002). Traditions of dispute: From negotiations of talmudic texts to the arena of political discourse in the media. *Journal of Pragmatics,* 34(10), 1569–94.

Boyte, H. C. (2004). *Everyday politics: Reconnecting citizens and public life.* Philadelphia: University of Pennsylvania Press.

Boyte, H. C. (2012). Constructivist politics as public work: Organizing the literature. In D. W. M. Barker, N. McAfee & D. W. McIvor (Eds.), *Democratizing deliberation: A political theory anthology* (pp. 153–82). Dayton, OH: Kettering Foundation Press.

Boyte, H. C. (2015). Reinventing citizenship as public work. In H. C. Boyte (Ed.), *Democracy's education: Public work, citizenship, and the future of colleges and universities* (pp. 1–33). Nashville: Vanderbilt University Press.

Brookfield, S., & Preskill, S. (2005). *Discussion as a way of teaching: Tools and techniques for democratic classrooms.* San Francisco: Jossey-Bass.

Campus Compact. (2014). *2014 annual member survey: Three decades of institutionalizing change.* Boston: Campus Compact.

Colby, A., Beaumont, E., Ehrlich, T., & Corngold, J. (2007). *Educating for democracy: Preparing undergraduates for responsible political engagement.* San Francisco: Jossey-Bass.

Dedrick, J. R., Grattan, L., & Dienstfrey, H. (Eds.). (2008). *Deliberation and the work of higher education: Innovations for the classroom, the campus, and the community.* Dayton, OH: Kettering Foundation Press.

Dewey, J. (1910). *How we think*. Boston: D. C. Heath.

Dewey, J. ([1916] 1997). *Democracy and education: An introduction to the philosophy of education*. New York: Free Press.

Doherty, J. (2012). Deliberative pedagogy: An education that matters. *Connections*, 24–27.

Dryzek, J. S. (2000). *Deliberative democracy and beyond: Liberals, critics, contestations*. New York: Oxford University Press.

Evans, S. M., & Boyte, H. C. (1992). *Free spaces: The sources of democratic change in America*. Chicago: University of Chicago Press.

Eyler, J., & Giles, D. (1999). *Where's the learning in service-learning?* San Francisco: Jossey-Bass.

Fitzgerald, H. E., Burack, C., & Seifer, S. D. (Eds.). (2010). *Handbook of engaged scholarship: Contemporary landscapes, future directions* (Vols. 1 & 2). East Lansing: Michigan State University.

Freire, P. (1974). *Education for critical consciousness*. New York: Continuum.

Freire, P. (2000). *Pedagogy of the oppressed* (M. B. Ramos, Trans.; 30th anniversary ed.). New York: Continuum.

Fung, A. (2005). Deliberation before the revolution: Toward an ethics of deliberative democracy in an unjust world. *Political Theory*, 33(3), 397–419.

Gastil, J. (2008). *Political communication and deliberation*. Thousand Oaks, CA: SAGE Publications.

Gastil, J., & Levine, P. (Eds.). (2005). *The deliberative democracy handbook: Strategies for effective civic engagement in the twenty-first century*. San Francisco: Jossey-Bass.

Gutmann, A., & Thompson, D. F. (2004). *Why deliberative democracy?* Princeton, NJ: Princeton University Press.

Habermas, J. (1975). *Legitimation crisis* (T. McCarthy, Trans.). Boston: Beacon Press.

Harriger, K. J., & McMillan, J. J. (2007). *Speaking of politics: Preparing college students for democratic citizenship through deliberative dialogue*. Dayton, OH: Kettering Foundation Press.

Held, D. (2006). *Models of democracy* (3rd ed.). Stanford, CA: Stanford University Press.

hooks, b. (1994). *Teaching to transgress: Education as the practice of freedom*. New York: Routledge.

Horton, M. (1998). *The long haul: An autobiography*. New York: Teachers College Press.

Hoy, A., & Johnson, M. (Eds.). (2013). *Deepening community engagement in higher education: Forging new pathways*. New York: Palgrave Macmillan.

Isgro, K., & Deal, M. (2013). The colloquium as a pedagogy of dialogue. *College Teaching*, 61(3), 90–94.

Jacobs, L. R., Cook, F. L., & Delli Carpini, M. X. (2009). *Talking together: Public deliberation and political participation in America*. Chicago: University of Chicago Press.

Johnson, M., Partlo, M., Hullender, T., Akanwa, E., Burke, H., Todd, J., & Alwood, C. (2014). Public deliberation as a teaching andragogy: Implications for adult student learning from a doctoral higher education policy course. *Journal of the Scholarship of Teaching and Learning*, 14(1), 95–108.

Karpowitz, C. F., & Raphael, C. (2014). *Deliberation, democracy, and civic forums: Improving equality and publicity*. New York: Cambridge University Press.

Kim, J., & Kim, E. J. (2008). Theorizing dialogic deliberation: Everyday political talk as communicative action and dialogue. *Communication Theory*, 18(1), 51–70.

Knowles, M. S. (1980). *The modern practice of adult education: From pedagogy to andragogy* (rev. ed.). Englewood Cliffs, NJ: Cambridge Adult Education Company.

Kuh, G. D. (2008). *High-impact educational practices: What they are, who has access to them, and why they matter*. Washington, DC: Association of American Colleges & Universities.

Laker, J., Naval, C., & Mrnjaus, K. (Eds.). (2014). *Civic pedagogies in higher education: Teaching for democracy in Europe, Canada and the USA*. New York: Palgrave Macmillan.

Leighninger, M. (2012). Mapping deliberative civic engagement: Pictures from a (r)evolution. In T. Nabatchi, J. Gastil, M. Leighninger & G. M. Weiksner (Eds.), *Democracy in motion: Evaluating the practice and impact of deliberative civic engagement* (pp. 19-39). New York: Oxford University Press.

Levine, P. (2013). *We are the ones we have been waiting for: The promise of civic renewal in America*. New York: Oxford University Press.

London, S. (2010). *Doing democracy: How a network of grassroots organizations is strengthening community, building capacity, and shaping a new kind of civic education*. Dayton, OH: Kettering Foundation.

Longo, N. V. (2007). *Why community matters: Connecting education with civic life*. Albany: SUNY Press.

Longo, N. V. (2013). Deliberative pedagogy in the community: Connecting deliberative dialogue, community engagement, and democratic education. *Journal of Public Deliberation*, 9(2), Article 16.

Longo, N. V., & Gibson, C. (2016). Collaborative engagment: The future of teaching and learning in higher education. In M. A. Post, E. Ward, N. V. Longo & J. Saltmarsh (Eds.), *Publicly engaged scholars: Next generation engagement and the future of higher education*. Sterling, VA: Stylus.

Manosevitch, I. (2016). *Politics for People* in the Israeli context: An introduction to the Hebrew translation of *Politics for People*. In D. Mathews, *Politics for people: Finding a responsible public voice*. (Hebrew edition). Charles F. Kettering Foundation Working Paper [2016:3]. Dayton, OH: Kettering Foundation.

Mansbridge, J. (1999). Everyday talk in the deliberative system. In S. Mancedo (Ed.), *Deliberative politics: Essays on democracy and disagreement* (pp. 211-39). New York: Oxford Universisty Press.

Marin, I. (Ed.). (2006). *Collective decision making around the world: Essays on historical deliberative practices*. Dayton, OH: Kettering Foundation Press.

Mathews, D. (1999). *Politics for people: Finding a responsible public voice* (2nd ed.). Urbana: University of Illinois Press.

Mathews, D. (2009). Ships passing in the night? *Journal of Higher Education Outreach and Engagement*, 13(3), 5-16.

Mathews, D. (2014). *The ecology of democracy: Finding ways to have a stronger hand in shaping our future*. Dayton, OH: Kettering Foundation Press.

McGregor, C. (2004). Care(full) deliberation: A pedagogy for citizenship. *Journal of Transformative Education*, 2(2), 90-106.

McIlrath, L., Lyons, A., & Munck, R. (Eds.). (2012). *Higher education and civic engagement: Comparative perspectives*. New York: Palgrave Macmillan.

Nabatchi, T., Gastil, J., Leighninger, M., & Weiksner, G. M. (Eds.). (2012). *Democracy in motion: Evaluating the practice and impact of deliberative civic engagement*. New York: Oxford University Press.

Oldenburg, R. (1999). *The great good place: Cafés, coffee shops, bookstores, bars, hair salons, and other hangouts at the heart of a community*. Cambridge, MA: Da Capo Press.

Palmer, P. J., Zajonc, A., & Scribner, M. (2010). *The heart of higher education: A call to renewal*. San Francisco: Jossey-Bass.

Rayner, S. (2003). Democracy in the age of assessment: Reflections on the roles of expertise and democracy in public-sector decision making. *Science and Public Policy*, 30(3), 163-70.

Röcke, A. (2014). *Framing citizen participation: Participatory budgeting in France, Germany and the United*

Kingdom. New York: Palgrave Macmillan.

Rosner, M. (1973). Direct democracy in the kibbutz. In R. M. Kanter (Ed.), *Communes: Creating and Managing the Collective Life* (pp. 178–91). New York: Harper and Row.

Roth, K. (2010). Deliberative pedagogy and the rationalization of learning. In J. Zajda & M. A. Geo-Jaja (Eds.), *The politics of education reforms* (pp. 209–18). New York: Springer Netherlands.

Saltmarsh, J. (2010). Changing pedagogies. In H. E. Fitzgerald, C. Burack & S. D. Seifer (Eds.), *Handbook of engaged scholarship: Contemporary landscapes, future directions* (Vol. 1: *Institutional Change*, pp. 331–52). East Lansing: Michigan State University Press.

Sanders, L. M. (1997). Against deliberation. *Political Theory, 25*(3), 347–76.

Sen, A. (2003). Democracy and its global roots. *New Republic*, October 6, 28–35.

Shaffer, T. J. (2016). Teaching deliberative democracy deliberatively. *eJournal of Public Affairs, 5*(2), 92–114.

Stoecker, R., Tryon, E. A., & Hilgendorf, A. (Eds.). (2009). *The unheard voices: Community organizations and service learning.* Philadelphia: Temple University Press.

Swaner, L. E. (2012). The theories, contexts, and multiple pedagogies of engaged learning: What succeeds and why? In D. W. Harward (Ed.), *Transforming undergraduate education: Theory that compels and practices that succeed* (pp. 73–89). Lanham, MD: Rowan & Littlefield.

Thomas, N. L., & Carcasson, M. (2010). Editors' introduction: Special issue on higher education. *Journal of Public Deliberation, 6*(1), Article 11.

Thomas, N. L., & Levine, P. (2011). Deliberative democracy and higher education: Higher education's democratic mission. In J. Saltmarsh & M. Hartley (Eds.), *"To serve a larger purpose": Engagement for democracy and the transformation of higher education* (pp. 154–76). Philadelphia: Temple University Press.

Waghid, Y. (2014). *Pedagogy out of bounds: Untamed variations of democratic education.* Rotterdam: Sense Publishers.

Wheatley, M. J. (2002). Some friends and I started talking. . . . *UTNE Reader*, July/August, 55–60.

Wolf, T., & Loker, W. M. (2012). Public sphere pedagogy: Connecting student work to public arenas—California State University, Chico. In D. W. Harward (Ed.), *Transforming undergraduate education: Theory that compels and practices that succeed* (pp. 309–12). Lanham, MD: Rowan & Littlefield.

Young, I. M. (2000). *Inclusion and democracy.* New York: Oxford University Press.

Young, I. M. (2001). Activist challenges to deliberative democracy. *Political Theory, 29*(5), 670–90.

Zlotkowski, E. (2000). Civic engagement and the academic disciplines. In T. Ehrlich (Ed.), *Civic responsibility and higher education* (pp. 309–22). Phoenix, AZ: Oryx Press.

PART 1

Theory and History of Deliberative Pedagogy

Deliberative Pedagogy as Critical Connective: Building Democratic Mind-Sets and Skill Sets for Addressing Wicked Problems

Martín Carcasson

Deliberative pedagogy is best understood as a teaching philosophy focused on equipping students with the mind-sets and skill sets necessary for high-quality participatory decision-making in the face of "wicked" problems. Most complex social and public policy issues are wicked problems (Rittel & Webber, 1973)—that is, problems that have no technical solution, but that call for ongoing communicative processes of broad engagement to address underlying competing values and tensions. Such engagement helps communities and organizations develop mutual understanding across perspectives, negotiate the underlying competing values, and invent, support, and constantly adapt collaborative actions (Carcasson & Sprain, 2016).

Deliberative pedagogy is designed to prepare students to participate effectively in these critical conversations. It focuses on decision-making at the community level, but the skills it develops are often transferable to many other organizational and business contexts. Due to a wide variety of factors, however, our colleges and universities often do not sufficiently equip students with these deliberative skills. Some may argue that such civic skills are secondary to the workforce focus of modern students, but in reality deliberative skills have very broad application. Indeed, the ability to address complex problems in the face of uncertain information and competing underlying values is highly prized by employers (Hart Research Associates, 2013), so there is no need to pit democratic education against education for the workforce.

Unfortunately, although our campuses certainly have all the necessary resources for deliberative pedagogy, their use is too often episodic, disconnected, underfunded, less prestigious, and/or voluntary. This chapter provides a model for deliberative pedagogy at the college level that attempts to respond to the needs of our diverse communities and the limitations of higher education, as well as to students' needs and the needs of employers. The model adapts Sam Kaner's (2014) diamond model of participatory decision-making as a basis for outlining the arguments for and key aspects of deliberative pedagogy. The model involves three distinct yet connected stages: divergent thinking, working through, and convergent thinking leading to a decision point. As such, it provides a useful mechanism for conceptualizing how the broad skill sets critical to addressing wicked problems are interconnected and helps highlight ways to overcome current limitations and weaknesses of both human nature and dominant pedagogical perspectives on campus.

The Need for a Deliberative Mind-Set

Our communities are awash with wicked problems. Almost all issues facing our communities can be understood through a wicked-problem lens that focuses on the competing underlying values that make simple solutions impossible. These competing values create tensions, paradoxes, and tough choices that cannot be resolved, although they can certainly be managed better (or worse). Whether *community* is interpreted as applying to the global, national, regional, local, or campus level, it is clear that we are struggling with how to respond effectively to myriad issues.

In several of my past writings (Carcasson, 2013a, 2013b; Carcasson & Sprain, 2016), I have argued for the need to increase deliberative engagement in our communities in order to improve how we manage wicked problems. The basis of the argument is that wicked problems are inherent to diverse democracies and complex organizations and require ongoing, high-quality communication and collaboration in order to address them. For example, the inherent tensions between and within dominant American values such as freedom, security, equality, and justice will always be with us, as will the critical tension between individual rights and the common good. Management scholars similarly argue that organizations are constantly addressing a variety of tensions—for example, short term versus long term, cooperation versus competition, flexibility versus efficiency, and tradition/stability versus innovation/change (Quinn, 1988; Cameron & Quinn, 1988; Senge, 2006; Smith & Lewis, 2011; Johnson, 1996). The two currently dominant problem-solving models—adversarial and expert—are ill equipped to address such wicked problems and are often subject to perverse incentives that actually make it harder to tackle them productively. Adversarial processes incentivize simplistic and manipulative strategic frames that create polarization and cynicism, whereas expert processes are often too narrow and technical. Both are overly focused on certainty, and both clearly avoid the necessary engagement with values and value dilemmas.

The deliberative mind-set, on the other hand, focuses precisely on the hard work of addressing wicked problems, particularly the need to engage the natural tensions, trade-offs, tough choices, dilemmas, and paradoxes embedded within issues. Taking a wicked-problem perspective essentially shifts the focus away from the adversarial emphasis on wicked people (i.e., people with bad values who are often seen as the primary cause of problems) and the expert "quest for certainty" (Dewey, 1929; Kadlec, 2007), and toward the ongoing collaborative management of the wicked problem. The deliberative mind-set starts with the question, "What should we do about X?" Particular emphasis is placed on the "we," and since it is assumed that no technical or final solution exists, the answer should spark an ongoing conversation predominantly focused on negotiating tensions while periodically moving toward action (Carcasson & Sprain, 2016). This approach avoids the pitfalls and problematic shortcuts of the other methods while creating possibilities for innovation, creativity, and collaboration. Because addressing wicked problems requires constant communication and collaboration, ideally deliberative engagement becomes an ongoing community habit supported by significant embedded local capacity, especially at educational institutions (Carcasson, 2010).

The deliberative mind-set also works to address key issues related to human nature (Carcasson, 2016). This is a broader argument that can be summarized only briefly here. Essentially, the adversarial and expert mind-sets tend to take advantage of and intensify critical flaws in human nature (such as egoism, confirmation bias, the need for simplicity and certainty, and the over-compartmentalization of information), whereas the deliberative mind-set actively works to avoid or mitigate such flaws and alternatively activate or strengthen key positive attributes of human nature (such as creativity, empathy, and social connectivity).

The primary weakness of the deliberative mind-set is that it requires a distinct set of skills and resources that are in short supply. Currently, it is significantly countercultural; because the adversarial and expert models of problem-solving tend to dominate, the skills tied to those approaches are more highly valued. Colleges and universities have the potential to change this balance by becoming critical hubs and capacity builders for deliberative mind-sets and skill sets (Carcasson, 2010). To realize that potential, they must focus on adapting their pedagogical methods, reimagining the campus as a vibrant, deliberative community and reconsidering the impact they can make on their local communities.

The deliberative mind-set highlights five key assumptions about twenty-first-century living that are critical to changing the conversation about problem-solving and recalibrating how we think about education.

1. Wicked problems are inherent, prevalent, and unsolvable, which underscores the importance of understanding tensions and paradoxes and focusing on how to manage them, rather than resolve them.
2. The current dominant problem-solving models (adversarial and expert) are often counterproductive in the face of wicked problems, creating numerous obstacles and distractions.
3. Human nature has clear flaws and strengths, and we need to find ways to mitigate the former and activate the latter in order to address wicked problems effectively.
4. The ability to negotiate among different perspectives is critical for addressing wicked problems, which in turn requires particular communication skills.
5. In the end, deliberative pedagogy supports the development and cultivation of wisdom and judgment in individuals and publics.

The model of deliberative pedagogy presented in this essay builds from these premises. It imagines what would happen if they were utilized as overarching premises for higher education.

Kaner's Model of Participatory Decision-Making

Introduced in *Facilitator's Guide to Participatory Decision-Making*, Sam Kaner's (2014) Diamond of Participatory Decision-Making is a useful concept to think about a wide range of issues relevant to deliberative pedagogy. Kaner developed the diamond for organizational decision-making, but it can also inform broader community contexts, particularly Daniel Yankelovich's (1991) ideas of "working through" while moving from public opinion to public judgment and David Mathews's (1999) focus on work related to choice and trade-offs. Kaner's model essentially has three stages, with the third culminating in a decision point. Each stage requires a different set of processes, skill sets, and forms of communication. The stages are closely connected, however, as successfully navigating one stage essentially creates the central challenge of the subsequent stage. The model is therefore particularly useful because it recognizes both the distinct challenges of each stage and the natural interconnectivity of the stages.

In this section, I walk through each stage, first describing the stage, then examining some of its obstacles, and finally reviewing the processes and skills that can help overcome those obstacles. I explain the model from the perspective of a deliberative practitioner who has utilized the model to organize his work. In the next section, I shift roles to that of a teacher to consider how to apply the lessons learned to the campus setting.

Stage 1: Divergent Thinking

The first step in addressing wicked problems is to work to open up the conversation to make sure multiple perspectives are considered. Kaner connected divergent thinking to actions such as brainstorming, generating alternatives, holding free-flowing and open discussions, gathering diverse points of view, and suspending judgment. This openness is a key aspect of critical thinking and a main concern of many educators, who see the importance both of broad research and of engaging multiple voices and perspectives in making sound decisions. Many decisions are made without consideration of sufficient divergent opinion, however, as leaders, experts, or powerful groups make the decision themselves without seeking input or as status quo, ideology, or tradition simply dominates. Without sufficient divergent opinions, individuals and groups run into the obstacle of *false certainty*. They assume they made the right decision because their perspective was never challenged.

Three forces work against divergent thinking and fuel false certainty. The first is at the individual level. We are subject to psychological forces such as egoism, confirmation bias, selective listening, and cognitive dissonance that have wired us to seek out confirmation of our existing opinions and to avoid or dismiss challenges to our way of thinking (Kahneman, 2013; Cialdini, 2009; DiSalvo, 2011). Simply put, our minds are wired to avoid divergent thinking.

The second major force is tied to group behavior. Sparked by our individual psychology, there is a natural tendency for groups to think simplistically and to polarize. These natural tendencies have become even more problematic with the growth of the Internet, which makes it even easier for us to expose ourselves only to familiar opinions, gather with like-minded choirs, and avoid those that may challenge our views.

The third force is more structural. Many of our current avenues for public discourse and expression are primarily, though unintentionally, geared toward more individualized, entrenched voices. Consider which types of people are likely to approach a microphone and speak at a city council meeting, public hearing, or town hall meeting, or to send a letter to the editor, make a Facebook post, or create or join an interest group. With most issues, the dominant voices are those that are organized and likely focused on narrow aspects of the problem (i.e., they center on one particular value rather than attempting to negotiate multiple competing values). As a result, those who are not so assured of their infallibility are often silent, resulting in deficient divergent thinking. As

Kaner argues, far too often, only the articulate, confident, or powerful are heard or taken seriously; alternative voices are shut down too early as powerful norms that squelch dissent dominate. Many good ideas die or are never heard simply because the people who hold them are absent, quiet, silenced, intimidated, introverted, inarticulate, or dismissed.

Similarly, the voices of many groups (e.g., low-income groups, busy business owners, rural residents, those with limited transportation options, parents with young children, people with language issues) may not be heard because these groups have less access to or a lower comfort level with the available means of communication. In summary, public discourse often suffers from overexposure of the usual suspects and underexposure of many others.

When decisions are made without sufficient voices to inform them, those decisions suffer in multiple ways. They suffer from not having enough input on the front end (therefore better ideas and broader values may have never been considered), as well as from frustration and lack of owner-ship or understanding on the back end. Even if the decision is a good one, lack of understanding or support for it can undermine implementation. As facilitation pioneer Michael Doyle wrote, one of the "lasting lessons of the last 25 years of concerted action research in this field of organi-zational development and change" is that "if people don't participate in and 'own' the solution to the problems or agree to the decision, implementation will be half-hearted at best, probably misunderstood, and, more likely than not, will fail" (2007, p. xi).

Two types of process and communication practices can be utilized to increase divergent think-ing. First, individuals can equip themselves to become better critical thinkers on their own. This may involve simply determining to challenge one's initial assumptions (something that should become more and more automatic with the adoption of a wicked-problem perspective on tough issues). Second, group, organizational, and community processes can be improved to seek out alternative voices, encourage dissent, and challenge dominant perspectives.

Stage 2: Working through the Groan Zone

If the decision-making process avoids or overcomes the obstacle of false certainty and supports sufficient divergent thinking, a new problem arises: dealing with the messiness of multiple com-peting positions Kaner described as the "groan zone." This is why processes that focus solely on divergent opinion and providing opportunities for voice, access, and free speech ultimately fall short. Multiple viewpoints can be very difficult to handle. All of the individual, group, and struc-tural forces that limit divergent thinking come back into play. Social psychology research shows that mere exposure to alternative voices is insufficient and can actually spark further polarization (Nyhan & Reifler, 2010). In the face of expressed opposition, groups will strategically work to push their opinions and undermine opposing views. The structural limitations that favor strong voices exacerbate these natural tendencies. Thus, divergent thinking without a good process to handle it often results in frustration, which in turn leads to increased polarization or cynicism—both of which are counterproductive to democratic decision-making.

Typical public processes tend to bring forth collections of individual opinions rather than interaction among these opinions. For example, offering a microphone to one person at a time for three minutes leads to a steady stream of speakers on any controversial issue but likely results in precious little actual understanding or learning. Letters to the editor, Facebook threads, online message boards responding to newspaper articles, and online petitions all provide similar outlets for voice sans learning. As Michael Briand argues in *Practical Politics*, democracy requires interaction with others and their values:

> Because the things human beings consider good are various and qualitatively distinct; because conflicts between such good things have no absolute, predetermined solution; and because to know what is best requires considering the views of others, we need to engage each other in the sort of exchange that will enable us to form sound personal and public judgments. This process of coming to a public judgment and choosing—together, as a public—is the essence of democratic politics. (1999, p. 42)

Overall, I would argue that due in part to strong support for freedom of speech in the United States and increasing access to the Internet, lack of divergent thinking is often not as much of a problem as the need to deal appropriately with all the noise. We often have plenty of opinions (if you look for them). We simply lack the ability to make sense of them all, develop mutual understanding across these perspectives, surface and work through tensions, and ultimately develop productive responses. As Yankelovich and Friedman (2010) argue, we have a great deal of institutional capacity for introducing new issues and for arguing for our perspective, but little corresponding capacity to work through the issues with fellow citizens. Thus, we may have passed the barrier of false certainty but now fall into *false polarization.*

I label this obstacle false polarization because the lack of understanding across perspectives often exaggerates the conflict on issues. When we focus on providing voice without listening or interacting, natural psychological and group processes lead to situations where people become polarized in their views because they focus on the positives of their own side while processing opposing perspectives through a negative lens that assumes bad motives. False polarization is especially problematic when processes allow a broad range of voices but then move quickly to a decision. Organizers often feel they have done their duty because they have allowed all sides to speak, but when the decision is made, those who disagree are highly dissatisfied. Through their simplistic lens, the point of view they espouse—which was heard but not well addressed—remains clearly superior. At this point, frustration and misinformed rage can erupt, creating more distrust for the decision makers and future processes.

Working through the groan zone therefore involves a set of processes to help transform the cacophony of voices resulting from divergent thinking into mutual understanding, refined opinions, and, ultimately, improved judgment. Kaner explains:

> A period of confusion and frustration is a natural part of group decision-making. Once a group crosses the line from airing familiar opinions to exploring diverse perspectives, *group members have to struggle in order to integrate new and different ways of thinking with their own.* Struggling to understand a wide range of foreign or opposing ideas is not a pleasant experience. Group members can be repetitious, insensitive, defensive, short-tempered—and more! At such times most people don't have the slightest notion of what's happening. Sometimes the mere act of acknowledging the existence of the *Groan Zone* can be a significant step for a group to take. (2014, pp. 18–19)

Working through involves considering all the potential consequences to actions, whether they are positive or negative, intended or unintended. Deliberative practitioners often develop issue maps or frameworks to assist audiences in engaging the tensions among various perspectives. Yankelovich (1991) notes that the working-through process requires genuine interaction and discussion across perspectives, which can be difficult and certainly takes time. Kaner recognizes the need to accept this struggle and the importance of face-to-face interaction to work through it:

> One of the great insights of the 20th century is this: sitting down to work in a small face-to-face group is potentially transformative. . . . We can call it participatory decision-making. We can call it social innovation. We can call it dialogue and deliberation. We can call it cross-functional teams, or multi-stakeholder collaboration. We can call it collective impact. Whatever we call it, we are talking about unleashing the transformative power of face-to-face groups. (2014, pp. xv, xxxvi)

Specific mechanisms to support working through vary widely. Certainly, much deliberative practice is tied to such processes, as are many dialogue and conflict-transformation techniques (National Coalition for Dialogue and Deliberation, 2010).

It is important to point out that working through is not simply about finding ways to negotiate differences and ways to compromise. Wicked problems involve inherent tensions both within and between various perspectives. The between tensions are the primary focus of adversarial processes, but the within tensions are critical to understanding wicked problems. Deliberation is thus a key tool for communities because it recognizes that in the face of wicked problems, we cannot simply focus on negotiating between competing interests or picking winners and losers; rather, we often need to find ways to refine those interests. Fishkin's (2009) work is particularly important here, as he argues that deliberation is critical precisely because it prompts people to transform their opinions in the face of well-framed materials and productive interaction with alternative perspectives. This process helps people recognize and respond to the reality of the situation (i.e., the inherent wickedness of the problem).

Many of our friends in economics and political science tend to assume that politics is best understood as a pitched battle among fixed interests, but deliberative practitioners, informed by their experiences, believe something very different. People may be primarily self-interested, and their interests may be rather steady, but time and again deliberative practitioners have seen interests transform as a result of quality conversations that help participants overcome either false certainty or false polarization and realize that their opponents share many of their values. In general, so many of our conversations are so bad that it doesn't take much in the way of improvement to bring about the common welcome partner to the groan zone: the "aha moment." This is the moment when you might hear, "Oh, *that's* why you think that way. I never understood where you were coming from. That actually makes sense. Hmmm." As many years of Kettering Foundation research has shown, participants may not change their mind about their own views all that much during a deliberative forum, but they often change their views about competing perspectives. Essentially, they shift from assuming that those who disagree with them have negative values (or reject positive values) to recognizing that they simply prioritize alternative positive values. Such a shift—humorously captured in the famous "I disagree with you but I'm pretty sure you're not Hitler" sign from Jon Stewart's 2010 rally—is a critical one for democratic capacity and quality decision-making. Once participants recognize that it's the problem that's wicked (tensions within perspectives) rather than assuming that people with opposing views are the wicked ones (tensions between perspectives), they can begin the process of finding creative ways to integrate their perspectives and address the real wickedness.

Processes that facilitate working through and overcoming false polarization have two key components. The first involves mapping or framing issues deliberatively in order to put key tensions on the table. Essentially, deliberative practitioners often take the raw data (the individual collection of opinions and arguments from various sources) created by the adversarial and expert modes of problem-solving and process it to support the deliberative mode. Good deliberative framing that fairly explains broad views and lays out trade-offs and tensions can help spark mutual understanding and sustain working through. The second component is simply the time and space to deliberate with others. Good facilitation and process design can help encourage shared understanding and integration of new ideas that get people past the frustration. While our communities certainly struggle with finding the time and place for such conversations, one would hope our college campuses would not. Ideally, campuses will model deliberative communities, as well as serving as key resources for the broader community. Too often they do neither.

Stage 3: Convergent Thinking

Once again, however, success breeds a major obstacle. If you have done a good job with divergent thinking and followed that up with overcoming false polarization by working through the groan zone (the combination of which is admittedly rare), then you need processes that help the group begin to move toward some sort of decision. That means clarifying, consolidating, refining, innovating, prioritizing, judging, and choosing among options. In a word, it calls for wisdom—the ability to make good decisions regarding difficult situations under conditions of uncertainty and incomplete information. Wisdom, understood as good judgment, thus comes into play as the most important skill for quality convergent thinking. Without it, groups often get stuck in the groan zone and never actually make a decision.

I call the primary obstacle tied to the lack of sufficient convergent thinking *paralysis by analysis.* This obstacle can arise from many factors, but three are particularly notable. First, once participants realize that an issue is wicked, much of their motivation, passion, and urgency may dissipate. The advantage of adversarial frameworks is that they can be very motivating. A good-versus-evil framework is powerful because people want to see themselves as heroes who defeat evil and ride off into the sunset. The adversarial narrative is intoxicating; once the wishful thinking that dominates it is exposed and the reality sinks in that those with opposing views are motivated by values that you also hold dear, staying involved in the issue and making a decision is much more difficult.

Paralysis by analysis also occurs if the process focuses so much on the importance of open-mindedness—which is critical during divergent thinking—that the necessary closed-mindedness of convergent thinking becomes difficult or seemingly inappropriate. Addressing wicked problems involves accepting the inherent value of all opinions, but not the equal validity or quality of all opinions. The process of convergent thinking, decision-making, and moving to action requires judgment and therefore recognizes the ultimate inequality of ideas and potential actions. The point, after all, is to identify and implement better ideas.

A final cause of paralysis by analysis is tied to an oversaturation of expert perspectives, often combined with the assumption that a technical answer should emerge from research. Many assume that clarity will arise from research and expert consultation, and when it does not, paralysis ensues. The typical reaction is to throw even more research and expertise at the problem, which often escalates the paralysis. An equally damaging reaction is to go in the opposite direction, denigrating expert perspectives and data. An important goal of deliberative practice is to find the right balance in terms of relying on data and experts, recognizing and adapting to the strengths and weaknesses they offer (Carcasson, 2013a). When dealing with wicked problems, data cannot provide a simple solution, but used well it can be a critical tool to support good judgment. Learning more about how to use data well is a critical skill set that warrants more attention.

To avoid or overcome paralysis by analysis and improve convergent thinking, once again better processes and skill sets are critical. As mentioned before, simply acknowledging the difficulty of the work and the inherent nature of the groan zone is an important first step to helping groups manage paralysis by analysis. Adopting the key assumptions regarding wicked problems—that competing underlying values are inherent to all difficult issues, and that at some point tough choices will need to be made between competing ideas—can also work to prepare groups for quality convergent thinking. The bottom line is that if groups and communities have an understanding of the Kaner model, they can be prepared for the obstacles that are likely to arise and therefore somewhat inoculated to them.

In general, moving from the groan zone to a decision point involves two broad steps: discussion of how best to address the wicked problem (what to do) and the move to action (how to do it). The discussion of what to do brings forth a number of important skill sets. Building from the first two stages of the model, it focuses on exploring ways to negotiate tensions as effectively as possible. Creativity and innovation are critical at this stage; the wicked-problem frame helps bring these features out in a way that neither the adversarial nor the expert frame is able to do. Processes that help support, enable, or improve good judgment are also essential. Kaner's (2014) book includes many process design ideas and specific facilitator tactics for this stage. The transition from working through to convergent thinking also connects well with academic scholarship on judgment, practical wisdom, and argumentation (Beiner, 1983; Booth, 2004; Garver, 2004; Fischer & Gottweis, 2012; Willard, 1996). The goal, after all, is to base decisions and the move to action on quality arguments and good judgment that are relevant to broad audiences, rather than on factors such as tradition or the popularity, eloquence, manipulative skill, money, or power of the participants involved.

The focus on quality judgment means that convergent thinking inherently requires consideration of relevant data and evidence, another hallmark of the argumentation perspective. Whereas divergent opinion emphasizes a broad range of voices and expression and working through focuses on developing mutual understanding across perspectives (both of which involve some degree of suspending judgment), convergent thinking must invoke quality controls and therefore a stronger focus on data. Data should not be considered an automatic trump, but as groups review competing perspectives, data can help with the distinctions and choices that need to be made. As a result, conducting research (i.e., finding or producing relevant data) and understanding what distinguishes quality data are two additional critical skill sets. As noted earlier, however, data must be viewed as a useful tool for contributing to the ongoing conversation and managing wicked problems, rather than as an end in itself or a means of finding a technical solution.

The second step of convergent thinking—the move to action (how to do it)—focuses on considering the broad range of actors and actions designed to address the wicked problem. Collaborative skills are paramount, and at the community level, interaction across public, private, and nonprofit lines is critical. Action here is defined broadly, ranging from changes in individual behavior to official legislation, with many levels in between. At this stage, the concepts of collaborative and democratic governance become exceedingly relevant (Boyte, 2005; Bingham, Nabatchi & O'Leary, 2005).

Based on these ideas, two adjustments to the Kaner model regarding convergent thinking are necessary to better fit the reality of wicked problems. One concerns the narrowing of convergent thinking to a single decision point. That may occur in an organizational setting, but in a broader community setting, the decision point or the move to action may take many different forms. Yes, in some cases one decision may be made, either by vote or by some sort of authority, but rarely would such a decision be based on consensus. With community decision-making, deliberative processes often result in multiple decisions and actions.

The second adjustment is recognizing that tackling wicked problems is not a linear process and will always be ongoing. The Kaner model shows time proceeding from left to right, but in certain situations the flow will not necessarily be one way. So at the end of the diamond, the decision point is more of a milestone than a conclusion. In many ways, the process begins anew as soon as it ends; gathering divergent reactions to the decisions or actions is necessary for implementation, evaluation, and assessment, and eventually groups will need to gather again to work through the issue and make another set of adjustments. This notion connects with both the cycle of deliberative inquiry (Carcasson & Sprain, 2016) and with John Dewey's (1929) construct of democracy as an ongoing conversation and a way of life rather than simply a mechanism for decision-making.

Application to Deliberative Pedagogy in Higher Education

Many current pedagogies are focused on or effective at individual stages within the model, but pedagogies that see the big picture and link the stages are unfortunately uncommon. As a result, students are often left to their own devices to build connections among the skill sets they are developing, and generally it simply doesn't happen. Students may pick up valuable individual skills and be motivated to complete certain actions, but too often they leave campus unequipped for the wicked problems they will face in their organizations and their communities.

It is worth noting that while the Kaner model is clearly a group model, it nonetheless provides insights regarding individual skills that are relevant to the overall process. Individuals can certainly learn to seek out divergent opinions and develop skills to complement the working-through and convergent-thinking processes. That said, although some individuals with significant research and other skills can essentially work through and make quality judgments on their own, addressing wicked problems well must generally be considered a group process.

Table 1 shows an initial foray into outlining how a wide variety of concepts and skills can be mapped onto the three main stages of the Kaner model. Building from the analysis of the obstacles

Table 1. Key Concepts and Skills Mapped onto the Kaner Model

	DIVERGENT THINKING	WORKING THROUGH	CONVERGENT THINKING
KEY TERMS/CONCEPTS	Voice, discovery, analysis, inclusion, open-mindedness, ability to look beyond the usual suspects, diversity, deconstruction, criticism	Listening, dialogue, mutual understanding, identifying and addressing tensions/ trade-offs/ tough choices/paradoxes, issue framing/mapping	Judgment, prioritization, evaluating arguments, criticism, action planning with a broad range of stakeholders, creativity/innovation, balancing/transcending tensions, making choices
INDIVIDUAL SKILLS	Speaking, writing, self-expression, research, interviewing, perspective taking, curiosity	Listening, empathy, dialogue, asking questions	Judgment, decision-making, prioritization, discernment, action planning, collaboration, project management, argument evaluation
NECESSARY COMMUNITY/ ORGANIZATIONAL-LEVEL CAPACITIES	Culture of freedom of speech and dissent, inclusion of diverse voices in the public conversation, ready access to means of communication by all	Safe places for gathering of non-like-minded people, time to work through properly, quality facilitators to support smaller groups, quality framing and process design	Collaborative capacity, legitimate conveners, mediating institutions/ backbone organizations, data evaluation

inherent to each stage, it's clear that many of the most critical skills are those required to overcome obstacles and avoid faulty thinking. Inoculating our students against common pitfalls is therefore a big part of the work of supporting deliberative pedagogy. This concept is derived in particular from the work of Charles Lindblom, who argued in *Inquiry and Change*:

> Improving the quality of inquiry by citizens and functionaries does not rest on improbable or improbably successful positive efforts to promote better probing. . . . It rests on what might be called negative reforms—reducing impairment, getting the monkey of impairment off the citizen's back. Societies do not need to urge citizens to probe; they need only to permit them to do so. They need only to reduce the disincentives to probe, the diversions and obfuscations that muddle or dampen probing, the misinformation and indoctrinations that misdirect it, and the intimidations and coercions that block it. (1990, p. 230)

In order to lay out my analysis clearly, I will walk back through the stages to consider how they relate to pedagogy, and then examine how the model can help us identify and overcome some of the common problems of current practice.

Divergent Thinking on Campus

In many ways we are already doing a nice job of providing opportunities for divergent thinking on our campuses. In general, campuses tend to be places where varied opinions abound, freedom of speech receives widespread support, and students have their initial beliefs and assumptions challenged. That is not to say that we don't face challenges in this regard. Students have certainly been known to defer too much to their professors, fail to think for themselves, or feel uncomfortable dissenting. What Paulo Freire (1970) calls the "banking" model of education—which he criticizes for overemphasizing teachers' authority and relegating students to passively receiving knowledge—may be less pervasive today, but it has not disappeared. Professors have more power than most discussion leaders to discourage dissent, given that they control grading, which is often a primary student motivation. In addition, some majors (e.g., in the hard sciences, some of the more rigorous social sciences, and the more professionally oriented majors) may not support sufficient divergence. And if campuses continue to professionalize, with students increasingly focusing on specific vocational majors while core curriculum classes fade away, the capacity for divergent thinking will decline. (The full-fledged university can be a bastion of divergent thinking; the university as a job-training mecca, not so much.)

As a rule, however, one of the inherent benefits of the college years is exposure to a broad range of opinions. In other words, we often successfully negotiate the first obstacle of false certainty on our campuses to get through the divergent thinking stage of Kaner's model. Many of the concepts and skills connected to divergent thinking on Table 1 are common on campus. Students are provided opportunities learn about other perspectives, and classrooms often support multiple viewpoints. Campuses typically boast students and faculty from diverse backgrounds and offer ample chances to make connections across cultures and perspectives. Where we struggle more is taking true advantage of the latent diversity on campus, which implicates the later stages of Kaner's model.

Working Through on Campus

Whereas our campuses seem to do a decent job of providing access to divergent thinking, lack of working through is a major flaw in our campus pedagogies. I see two particular causes for this deficiency. Foremost, the dominant epistemological perspectives on campus favor the search for certainty through scientific methods. Most major universities are still dominated by the hard sciences and the social sciences that strive to emulate the scientific model. As Gerald Hauser (2004) has noted, in the early twentieth century, American higher education shifted its focus to the German model of education, with its emphasis on discovering new knowledge, and away from the engaged and civic-minded model that came from Athens. The German model privileges empiricism, narrowly defined subject areas, and the banking model of pedagogy, all three of which are a poor fit for wicked problems, systemic thinking, and deliberative pedagogy. Essentially, such a perspective responds to divergent opinions through specialization and focus. A particularly damaging consequence of such a model is the overcompartmentalization of knowledge, with disciplines often operating as silos with their own majors, buildings, vocabulary, and specialized journals. The model also tends to favor pure research over applied research. For most faculty, publishing in the top journals in their field (meaning narrow journals focused on their specific subdiscipline) is their most incentivized responsibility, dwarfing both teaching and service to their community. Students thrust into that world typically are given few opportunities to actively work through tough issues and explore the intersections among disciplines and ideologies.

The liberal arts can serve as one counterbalance to the empirical, knowledge-focused epistemology. Yet liberal arts programs often fall into their own problematic patterns that limit their impact on deliberative pedagogy, and in particular their support for the working through stage. While liberal arts programs seek to take on the critical questions of values and ethics that empirical programs tend to avoid, the degree to which they truly equip students for judgment and deliberative decision-making is unclear. Too often, students are exposed to numerous perspectives and ideologies through their liberal arts education without learning how to address the conflicts and tensions between them (Graff, 1992). Divergent perspectives certainly exist, but the problem is that the divergence is often between classes rather than within them, leaving students disconnected and ill equipped. As Lanham quipped, students are often asked to "change intellectual worlds every hour on the hour" (1993, p. 159). They may be exposed to Marxism by one professor, feminism by another, and free-market ideology by a third without ever seeing those various perspectives in relationship to each other.

Consider, for example, the types of assignments students are asked to complete in many liberal arts classes. We often focus on teaching students to express their opinions or make an argument without necessarily asking for or equipping them to complete sufficient divergent thinking or working through. Students will give multiple presentations and write numerous papers over their college careers. Too often papers and presentations are much more in the adversarial model, starting with a conclusion and then cherry picking evidence and arguments to support that conclusion. Such an assignment is similar to a process with minimal divergent thinking that jumps to a decision point. Students need to learn how to make a persuasive case, but with the current information overload, supporting a preset opinion with strategically narrow research is not particularly skillful. As a response, Graff (1992) calls for universities to focus more on "teaching the conflicts." This can essentially be interpreted as the need to put students in the groan zone and have them work through the differences among various perspectives rather than simply exposing them to those perspectives separately.

Students may also take part in various opportunities on campus to engage or serve, but those opportunities are similarly often tied to particular perspectives and causes rather than struggling with the tensions among different viewpoints. Most campus political groups and service-learning opportunities, for example, begin with entrenched opinions or offer opportunities to engage and organize only with others who are like-minded. Oddly, even though the dominant scientific epistemology and the liberal arts counterpush are opposites in many ways, they both lead to disconnected perspectives and therefore undermine or limit deliberative pedagogy.

So the question remains, to what extent do our campuses both provide opportunities to experience groan zones and help students develop the skill sets needed to work through them? Some professors are very skilled at creating a deliberative environment in their classrooms, asking good questions and serving as facilitators for having students explore different sides of an issue, challenge their assumptions, and develop mutual understanding across perspectives. (The smaller the class size, the better such experiences can be—it's questionable whether a 150-student class can be truly deliberative.) Both K–12 and higher education offer students multiple opportunities to hone their skills in writing and public speaking, but to what degree do they build competence in listening and asking good questions, two critical deliberative skills? Projects, paper assignments, and even essay questions on exams can ask students to work through a tough issue and struggle with tough choices that don't have clear answers. But such experiences are generally individual, limiting their deliberative potential. Classes in dialogue, conflict management, and deliberation may be increasing in popularity, but they are not quite common yet and certainly not required. These are essential skills for any sort of collaborative problem-solving process, but they rarely seem to be an official part of any curriculum.

Convergent Thinking on Campus

The need for convergent thinking on campus is somewhat limited because classroom instruction inherently focuses on education rather than action. Thus, the first step of convergent thinking (what to do) is more relevant than the second (how to do it). Groups tend not to have to make decisions or move to action in an educational setting; conversation for the sake of conversation and improved understanding is often sufficient, and grading is often individual. Herein lies the importance of applied learning, considering the campus as a community in itself, and strengthening campus connections to the local community so students have more exposure to all the relevant skill sets. Students may get some exposure to more individual convergent thinking as they complete projects and papers, and some of those may be group projects, but rarely do they involve larger groups or community-level decisions.

The exciting potential is for college students to work on projects, influenced by the deliberative mind-set, that focus on turning the broader noise in the community about tough issues into clearer issue maps and frameworks. This is a clear win-win situation in which communities likely lack the capacity for completing this hard work on their own and college students desperately need the practice.

Several additional concerns arise when considering the extent of convergent thinking on campus. First, the dominant positivistic epistemology tends to assume that convergent thinking is driven by rigorous analysis and research. As explained earlier, such epistemological views remain disconnected from the notion of wicked problems and their competing underlying values, and thus do not recognize the importance of working through or convergent thinking. The assumption is that there is one right answer, and convergence will occur naturally. Such an assumption may work with scientific questions, but not with wicked problems.

Similarly, the strongly entrenched ideological perspectives that can at times emanate from liberal arts perspectives can be problematic for convergent thinking. This problem can be better described as a lack of divergent thinking, which often occurs within a specific class, that then precludes the need for working through and convergent thinking. Narrow perspectives limit the need for judgment, therefore undermining the need for teaching such skills. Considered a different way, the liberal arts on our campuses often tend to be either overly ideological (supporting one particular way of thinking) or overly open-minded (supporting all ways of thinking indiscriminately). The problems with narrow ideological views are clear, but the perils of unfettered open-mindedness are often less understood. Open-mindedness is certainly important for divergent thinking, but extreme open-mindedness can be as problematic as closed-mindedness for judgment and deliberative decision-making.

Overall, these concerns call for the need for deliberative engagement that can negotiate tensions on two separate axes, as seen in a model that I introduced in an earlier Kettering report (figure 1) (Carcasson, 2013a). Wicked problems call for convergent thinking to negotiate among perspectives that focus too much on data and expertise and those that focus too little on them (the vertical axis), as well as among perspectives that are too close-minded and those that are too open-minded (the horizontal axis). Campuses have plenty of examples of pedagogy from all over the map; deliberative pedagogies should be designed to explore how these pedagogies relate to each other.

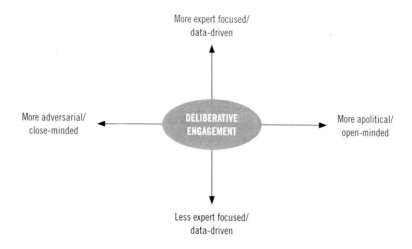

Carcasson, 2013a.

Conclusion: Improving Deliberative Pedagogy

Each of the three stages of the Kaner model—divergent thinking, working through the groan zone, and convergent thinking—calls for highly developed mind-sets and skill sets in order to avoid or overcome the key obstacles of false certainty, false polarization, and paralysis by analysis. Perhaps most important, the Kaner model brings all these diverse skills in connection with each other and highlights the paradox of how success at one stage sparks the challenge of the next.

The Kaner model also provides a number of insights regarding the limits and possibilities of pedagogy in higher education. My analysis points in particular to the problematic disconnects evident on our campuses, while also recognizing that all the necessary components of a robust deliberative pedagogy are typically present. The problem is that examples of those components coming together are often episodic, disconnected, underfunded, less prestigious, and/or voluntary. Following are suggestions for improving the quality of deliberative pedagogy on our campuses as well as further steps for analysis.

Perhaps the simplest and most effective change that could improve deliberative pedagogy is to give students a clear introduction to wicked problems and the deliberative mind-set. I imagine here a freshman course based on wicked problems and the Kaner model that would, from the beginning, provide students with an overarching epistemological framework for putting many of their other classes into a broader context. It would essentially provide students with a map on which to situate all the experiences they have on campus, whether curricular, cocurricular, or extracurricular. Such a framework would also offer a broader view of the relevant skill sets for complex decision-making in the communities and organizations they will be involved with moving forward.

A broader potential move is to focus more on the campus as a community in itself. Colleges and universities have real issues that require difficult conversations every day. The interactions between administration, faculty, staff, students, and the local community can and should be more deliberative. To what degree is the faculty senate or student government a model of deliberative excellence? Reimagined as a deliberative community, the campus can ideally become a model of participatory decision-making, while at the same time helping students build the skill sets needed to address wicked problems.

Colleges and universities should also create and support campus centers that focus on deliberative pedagogy and practice. Such centers can serve not only as important "hubs of democracy" for the community (Carcasson, 2010) but also as critical on-campus hubs of deliberative pedagogy. Similar to writing centers and speech centers, deliberation centers can support "deliberation across the curriculum" initiatives by offering resources, providing training and consulting services to help faculty incorporate deliberative projects and concepts into their courses, training student facilitators for in-class deliberations, and supporting specialized deliberation classes of their own. Teacher training is particularly important, since most faculty receive sparse instruction in this area in graduate school, and the training they do have most likely comes from a narrow epistemological perspective. The argument here is not that all teaching needs to be deliberative, but rather that enough of a deliberative frame needs to exist for students to be more likely to make necessary connections.

Ideally, in the coming years more faculty positions will be developed with a focus on deliberation, whether they are housed in communication studies, political science, sociology, environmental studies, education, or related fields. The more faculty working on deliberative theory and practice on our campuses, the more the latent resources for a robust deliberative pedagogy may be ignited. With dedicated faculty will come dedicated courses, another critical step forward.

From a theoretical perspective, two issues raised in this chapter warrant deeper analysis moving forward. The first is improving how we understand, engage, and ultimately respond to tensions during the working-through and convergent-thinking stages of participatory decision-making. In the end, deliberative pedagogy can perhaps be best understood as pedagogy whose focus is to help students negotiate the important tensions and polarities that are inherent to democratic living and creative problem-solving. Some key tensions are those that exist between these factors:

- Complexity and simplicity (i.e., unconstrained divergence versus abrupt convergence).
- Individual rights and community good (also conceptualized as the tension between freedom and other key American values such as security and equality).
- Closed-mindedness and open-mindedness (see figure 1).
- Data-dominated focus and data-deficient focus (see figure 1).

Each of these pairs represents polarities in which each pole has positive values but holds an inherent tension with the opposing pole. As Barry Johnson (1996) argues in *Polarity Management*, difficulties arise when we focus too much on one pole and dismiss the opposing pole. These polarities are not problems to solve but rather relationships to manage. Doing so is a key feature of deliberative pedagogy that is often not directly addressed on our campuses.

The second theoretical issue that warrants further examination is a familiar one: the need to understand more fully the connections between deliberation and decision-making/moving to action. The Kaner model provides a new way of thinking about these connections in terms of how deliberative processes can encourage convergent thinking and judgment. As mentioned earlier, the goal is to ensure that decisions and the move to action are based on quality arguments and good judgment that are relevant to broad audiences, rather than on tradition or on the popularity, eloquence, manipulative skill, money, or power of the individuals involved. To do so, however, we need to develop a better understanding of what good arguments are and how to sharpen judgment, two topics that do not receive enough attention on our campuses. Ultimately, processes will tend to revert to some combination of those less deliberative options, but deliberative practitioners will continue to strive toward that noble, though likely unattainable, ideal. If we can elevate deliberative pedagogy and improve how we equip students for all three of the stages of Kaner's model, campuses will be able to provide strong support for that ongoing quest.

REFERENCES

Beiner, R. (1983). *Political judgment*. Chicago: University of Chicago Press.

Bingham, L. B., Nabatchi, T., & O'Leary, R. (2005). The new governance: Practices and processes for stakeholder and citizen participation in the work of government. *Public Administration Review*, 65(5), 547–58.

Booth, W. C. (2004). *The rhetoric of rhetoric: The quest for effective communication*. Malden, MA: Blackwell.

Boyte, H. C. (2005). Reframing democracy: Governance, civic agency, and politics. *Public Administration Review*, 65(5), 536–46.

Briand, M. K. (1999). *Practical politics: Five principles for a community that works*. Urbana: University of Illinois Press.

Carcasson, M. (2010). Developing democracy's hubs: Building local capacity for deliberative practice through passionate impartiality. *Connections*, 9–11.

Carcasson, M. (2013a). Rethinking civic engagement on campus: The overarching potential of deliberative practice. *Higher Education Exchange*, 37–48.

Carcasson, M. (2013b). Tackling wicked problems through deliberative engagement. *Colorado Municipalities*, October, 9–13.

Carcasson, M. (2016). *Process Matters: Human Nature, Democracy, and a Call for Rediscovering Wisdom*. Research report. Kettering Foundation.

Carcasson, M., & Sprain, L. (2016). Beyond problem solving: Reconceptualizing the work of public deliberation as deliberative inquiry. *Communication Theory*, 26(1), 41–63.

Cameron, K. S. & Quinn, R. E. (1988). Organizational paradox and transformation. In R. E. Quinn & K. S. Cameron (Eds.), *Paradox and transformation: Toward a theory of change in organization and management* (pp.1–18). Cambridge, MA: Ballinger.

Cialdini, R. B. (2009). *Influence: Science and practice* (5th ed.). Boston: Pearson.

Dewey, J. (1929). *The quest for certainty: A study of the relation of knowledge and action*. New York: Putnam.

DiSalvo, D. (2011). *What makes your brain happy and why you should do the opposite*. Amherst, NY: Prometheus Books.

Doyle, M. (2007). Foreword. In S. Kaner, *Facilitator's guide to participatory decision-making*. San Francisco: Jossey-Bass.

Fischer, F., & Gottweis, H. (Eds.). (2012). *The argumentative turn revisited: Public policy as communicative practice*. Durham, NC: Duke University Press.

Fishkin, J. S. (2009). *When the people speak: Deliberative democracy and public consultation*. New York: Oxford University Press.

Freire, P. (1970). *Pedagogy of the oppressed* (M. B. Ramos, Trans.). New York: Continuum.

Garver, E. (2004). *For the sake of argument: Practical reasoning, character, and the ethics of belief*. Chicago: University of Chicago Press.

Graff, G. (1992). *Beyond the culture wars: How teaching the conflicts can revitalize American education*. New York: Norton.

Hart Research Associates. (2013). *It takes more than a major: Employer priorities for college learning and student success*. Https://www.aacu.org.

Hauser, G. A. (2004). Teaching rhetoric: Or why rhetoric isn't just another kind of philosophy or literary criticism. *Rhetoric Society Quarterly, 34*(3), 39-53.

Johnson, B. (1996). *Polarity management: Identifying and managing unsolvable problems*. Amherst, MA: HRD Press.

Kadlec, A. (2007). *Dewey's critical pragmatism*. Lanham, MD: Rowman & Littlefield.

Kahneman, D. (2013). *Thinking, fast and slow*. New York: Farrar, Straus and Giroux.

Kaner, S. (2014). *Facilitator's guide to participatory decision-making* (3rd ed.). San Francisco: Jossey-Bass.

Lanham, R. A. (1993). *The electronic word: Democracy, technology, and the arts*. Chicago: University of Chicago Press.

Lindblom, C. E. (1990). *Inquiry and change: The troubled attempt to understand and shape society*. New Haven, CT: Yale University Press.

Mathews, D. (1999). *Politics for people: Finding a responsible public voice*. (2nd ed.). Urbana: University of Illinois Press.

National Coalition for Dialogue and Deliberation. (2008). *Resource guide on public engagement*. http://www.ncdd.org/files/NCDD2010_Resource_Guide.pdf.

Nyhan, B., & Reifler, J. (2010). When corrections fail: The persistence of political misperceptions. *Political Behavior, 32*(2), 303-30.

Quinn, R. E. (1988). *Beyond rational management: Mastering the paradoxes and competing demands of high performance*. San Francisco: Jossey-Bass.

Rittel, H. W. J., & Webber, M. M. (1973). Dilemmas in a general theory of planning. *Policy Sciences, 4*(2), 155-69.

Senge, P. M. (2006). *The fifth discipline: The art and practice of the learning organization*. New York: Doubleday.

Smith, W. K., & Lewis, M. W. (2011). Toward a theory of paradox: A dynamic equilibrium model of organizing. *Academy of Management Review, 36*(2), 381-403.

Willard, C. A. (1996). *Liberalism and the problem of knowledge: A new rhetoric for modern democracy*. Chicago: University of Chicago Press.

Yankelovich, D. (1991). *Coming to public judgment: Making democracy work in a complex world*. Syracuse: Syracuse University Press.

Yankelovich, D., & Friedman, W. (2010). *Toward wiser public judgment*. Nashville: Vanderbilt University Press.

Democracy and Education: Historical Roots of Deliberative Pedagogy

Timothy J. Shaffer

While the phrase *deliberative pedagogy* has been used only sparingly and in distinct ways in recent years (e.g., Dedrick, Grattan & Dienstfrey, 2008; Doherty, 2012; Longo, 2013; Roth, 2008a, 2008b; Shaffer, 2016b), the concept is situated in a growing literature that explores the experiences, possibilities, and promise of integrating deliberative democracy into educational settings, and specifically into higher education (Shaffer, 2014b; Thomas, 2010; Thomas & Carcasson, 2010; Thomas & Levine, 2011). It is not surprising that deliberation has often been aligned with the idea of educational settings as centers of collective learning, rather than as venues for transferring information from teacher to student—what Paulo Freire (2000) referred to as the "banking" model of education. But for higher education, deliberation has long-established but often-forgotten roots that trace back centuries.

In both classroom and community settings, democratic—and often deliberative—practices have shaped teaching and learning in the United States since before the country's inception, although these practices have often been overshadowed by a paradigmatic approach that positions teachers as disseminators of knowledge and students as passive recipients of their expertise. This chapter introduces some of the historical antecedents to today's conceptualization of deliberation in civic and higher education settings in order to provide context for current efforts. It does not explore the broader historical development of deliberative democracy (e.g., Gastil & Keith, 2005; Gustafson, 2011), although it is important to look to what preceded the "deliberative turn" that emerged in political theory in recent decades in order to understand what helped to shape and inspire this turn (Barker, McAfee & McIvor, 2012; Dryzek, 2000). While deliberative practices have historical roots in diverse cultural contexts (e.g., Marin, 2006), this chapter focuses on the development of deliberative pedagogy in the United States. A focused chapter on the historical development of the intersection of democracy and education through deliberation helps to illuminate the diverse wells from which today's scholars and practitioners draw insight and inspiration—knowingly or not. A global survey of the historical development of deliberative pedagogy is a worthwhile pursuit, but it is beyond the scope of this chapter and project, more broadly.

In exploring deliberation in and through higher education, we must situate deliberative approaches to teaching and learning within their social and political settings. While most of this volume describes contemporary experiments with deliberative pedagogy, this chapter focuses on some of the earlier manifestations of deliberation and group discussion in educational settings.

Historical Roots: Town Meetings, Lyceums, and Chautauqua

The ideas of deliberative dialogue, public forums, and participatory democracy trace to the earliest days of European settlement of what would become the United States of America. In colonial America and later, deliberation was practiced in informal gatherings and town meetings, as well as in state capitals and Congress, drawing on classic republican thought (Bailyn, 1967; Gustafson, 2011, pp. 15–29; Pangle, 1988). For example, in 1727 Benjamin Franklin founded the Junto, a "club for the discussion of scientific and other subjects," a significant milestone for adult education in this early American period (Cartwright, 1945, p. 284). While Philadelphia's urban population experienced the Junto—or as one scholar put it, "Ben Franklin's Friday night discussion group"—rural communities also embraced the idea of discussion-based adult education as a means of educating people about the challenges of the day (Lang, 1975, p. 43).

In New England, town meetings had already been established before the eighteenth century. David Mathews calls the birth of the town meeting a story that "begins in 1633, not 1787"; this approach to local governance and problem-solving grew out of the public issue of "*how to decide*" the best ways to protect public green spaces in the face of competing interests (Mathews, 1988, p. 1). While the New England town meeting did not survive as a principal means of governing, it shaped political discourse and, importantly, provided a way to think about and conceptualize education's role in a democratic society. As Morse A. Cartwright put it, "the New England town meeting [was] a truly democratic educational agency for adults" (1945, p. 284).

The intersection of adult education and democracy continued throughout the 1800s through efforts such as lyceums, the Chautauqua Institution and the entire chautauqua movement, and public lectures. To many, the New England town meeting of the seventeenth century, which "formed the initial adult education venture" in North America, was viewed as an ideal that was often evoked for engaging communities around important social and political issues (Cartwright, 1935, p. 8). This ideal has remained, as William Keith has noted, even though we know little about what actually went on at these meetings (Keith, 2007, p. 222).

The first lyceum, an early form of organized adult education, was established in Massachusetts in 1826. It was formed as a voluntary association of farmers and mechanics "for the purpose of self-culture, community instruction and mutual discussion of common public interests" (Cartwright, 1935, p. 9). Lyceums were called by one commentator a "particularly American institution" that were first formed as "associations of local townsfolk for the mutual study and discussion of educational matters and public affairs" (Frank, 1919, pp. 405, 407). By 1839, more than three thousand town lyceums were in existence.

With the example of the lyceum movement as a model, Bishop John J. Vincent and colleagues established what would become the Chautauqua Institution, expanding a Sunday school association into a general adult education venture that resulted in the development of commercial and lyceum forums that expanded across the country. Chautauqua and the movement it spawned retained a strong religious feel, including "revival preaching, . . . sing-alongs, [and] devotional reading," although they outgrew their "Sunday-school mission" and the "mix of education and worship became weighted toward education" (Keith, 2007, pp. 222, 223). At Mother Chautauqua this "gradual and orderly incorporation of other studies, and a few carefully selected items of entertainment" culminated in a "fully rounded and comprehensive program of sterling appeal to mind and heart; a veritable popular university of informal method and ideal concept" (Orchard, 1923, p. 13). It was this vision for an educational environment built upon informal learning, discussion, and engagement that continues to be the cornerstone of the Chautauqua Institution.

While not directly connected with policy decisions, the Chautauqua movement spurred informed discussion and reflective citizens, reaching its crest of popularity in the late nineteenth and early twentieth centuries (Lyman, 1915, p. 3; Orchard, 1923). Former president Theodore Roosevelt was quoted as saying that Chautauqua was "the most American thing in America" (Carlisle, 2009, p. 127). While the Chautauqua Institution remains active with programming continuing today in rural western New York, the chautauqua movement lost its prominence because of numerous cultural and technological developments. Increased mobility as well as the widespread use of radio for leisure and entertainment replaced the need to attend a presentation by a circuit lecturer.

Adult education played a pivotal role in meeting the developing needs and interests of citizens as they sought to better understand issues they faced and, more broadly, to become enlightened about the world around them. An important transformation was taking place in the United States. Growing urban centers were overtaking the agrarian roots of America's past. The nineteenth century had been a period of massive change during which "geographic, political, social, economic, and technological developments had affected every American citizen and every aspect of life" (Burt, 2004, p. 135). Between 1880 and 1910, the number of Americans living in cities rose from fifteen million to forty-five million (Gould, 1974, p. 3). Developments in transportation, communication, medicine, and industry were lauded as "the positive and inevitable progress of civilization" (Burt, 2004, p. 136). The modern world was changing how people lived, interacted, and learned. The need for an educated populace was even more critical for the country's continued development. The growth of venues for public forums helped to meet this aspiration.

Public Forums: Teaching Democracy through Civic Engagement

In the midst of the technological and scientific transformations at the beginning of the twentieth century, people were drawn to and demanding greater forms of democratic participation in their communities through both formal and informal channels. Local urban governments made efforts to establish ongoing and robust opportunities for men and women to deliberate with one another about various public issues (Mattson, 1998). Similarly, civic organizations cultivated spaces for deliberation. As John Gastil and William Keith put it, "Settlement houses and community centers sponsored debate clubs and forum series, and granges provided places where farmers could discuss the issues of the day" (2005, p. 10).[1] The open forum movement (in contrast with private clubs) built on the model established by Chautauqua and the lyceum movement by having speakers present material to be followed up by discussion among attendees. These discussions did not directly affect legislation or policies, "but they embodied the spirit of deliberation in a public setting" (p. 11).

One of the most popular examples of the open forum movement was the Ford Hall Forum in Boston and the forums that developed across the United States in the style of talks that moved away from the religious topics of the Chautauqua and lyceum forums to more intellectual and civic topics. Arthur S. Meyers refers to the open forum movement as an "innovative direction in community learning" that was a "decentralized, locally planned, non-partisan, non-sectarian assembly of citizens discussing matters of public interest, always under the guidance of leaders but with full audience participation" (2012, pp. 3–4). Because they addressed a broader slate of topics, open forums brought together diverse audiences comprising "recent immigrants, long-time residents, working people, union leaders, and business owners" (p. 6). As Maureen A. Flanagan writes, open forums were necessary because a "truer democracy requires places where ordinary people could gather together and discuss the problems of society, and such places were in short supply" (2007, p. 39). Over the following decades, the use of forums would spread across the United States. As Rollo Lyman wrote in 1915, "The forum must find its place in the useful, the practical, the tool aspects of the educative process" (p. 5). Forums were, in his view, settings in which people could form "sound judgments on accurate data," and not simply about a single issue: "It is the habit of forming sound judgment which we desire to foster" (pp. 5, 6).

One of the most prominent examples of public forums being used for citizen engagement came about through the work of John W. Studebaker, an educator who served as the U. S. commissioner of education from 1934 to 1948. Studebaker's work led to the use of public schools as sites for forum-based adult education. In *The American Way*, Studebaker argued that the most important problem facing the United States was "to save the democracy of free learning and to make possible, through it, intelligent choices at the happy medium between the old democracy of rugged economic individualism and the new democracy of cooperative effort" (1935a, p. 7). He observed that "our common problems have become so complex that the ordinary citizen begins to despair of his ability to understand them—and more important still, of his ability to retain, and adequately to discharge, responsibility for their solution," noting that a possible solution was the use of public forums as a means of preserving democratic ideals (p. 14). He believed that the interest in public discussion expressed through the forum movement was "neither a passing fad nor a temporary excrescence of political or economic unrest" (Studebaker, 1937, p. 393).

As an advocate for forums in urban neighborhoods, Studebaker championed group discussion because he believed that "good democratic action" was foundational to the capacity to engage "all issues and problems which affect our group life" (Studebaker, 1935b, p. 43). His efforts to revive neighborhood discussions as they were experienced in the previous decades received national press coverage, but financial support was limited (Hill, 1935).

While superintendent of the Des Moines, Iowa, public school system, Studebaker used public schools as sites for forums where citizens could learn about problems through discussion with others. The response to these forums was hugely positive: in their first year (January 1933 to January 1934), 13,404 individuals attended, and in the second year attendance rose to 70,000 (Hilton, 1982, p. 5). Importantly, those who participated in these forums represented a highly educated demographic. Studebaker noted that "Almost 55 percent of the adults with more years of schooling than are required to complete college attended the forums" (Studebaker, 1935a, p. 104). He also found a similar issue to current challenges of reaching diverse audiences: "It is apparent that a much larger proportion of persons living in the better residential neighborhoods attended forums than was the case in inferior neighborhoods. In other words, forum attendance and socioeconomic status as indicated by residential areas are directly related" (p. 105).

The interest in public forums continued, and Studebaker, along with Chester Williams in 1939, published a handbook for educators and civic leaders interested in organizing local forums (Studebaker & Williams, 1939).[2] Studebaker eventually secured funding to establish ten federal forum demonstration sites—in cities and counties from Portland, Oregon, to Monongalia County, West Virginia—beginning in 1936 and lasting until 1941. Building on the forums in Des Moines, the Federal Forum Project would expand into a national system of forums "touch[ing] the lives of millions of Americans" (Keith, 2007, p. 277).

The project established Cooperative Forum Centers and Forum Counseling Programs in partnership with state universities and departments of education. During a period when agricultural extension education was the primary vehicle for universities engaging citizens, the Federal Forum Project similarly tapped audiences that were otherwise disconnected from higher education. As Christopher Loss notes, however, the forum movement never achieved the hoped-for status of a "training ground for national citizenship" (2012, p. 83). Nevertheless, it did encourage an estimated 2.5 million citizens who participated in one of the project's twenty-three thousand discussion sessions between 1936 and 1941 to think of citizenship as more than voting. As Loss explains further, the forum program was "eventually eclipsed by wartime exigencies and the availability of new mass communications" (Loss, 2012, pp. 83, 85). The emergence of television and the broadening reach of radio reduced the need for and interest in face-to-face communication.

Higher Education and Deliberative Pedagogy: Disciplines and Deliberation

In addition to hosting public forums, higher education has served as a hub for the intersection for education and democracy in a variety of ways. In the last quarter of the nineteenth century, disciplinary specialization took hold of American higher education, leading to the professionalization of fields of study and corresponding academic societies and journals. The Modern Language Association, the American Historical Association, and the American Psychological Association started in 1883, 1884, and 1892, respectively (Berelson, 1960; Schuster & Finkelstein, 2006, pp. 25–26). In similar fashion, in 1914 a "group of ten members of the Public Speaking Section of the National Council of Teachers of English met for a day . . . and so founded their own professional association, the National Association of Academic Teachers of Public Speaking (NAATPS)" (Keith, 2008, p. 241).[3] The emergence of a professional association put the academic field of speech communication on par with other disciplines, carving out its place and identity within the academy (Gehrke & Keith, 2015, pp. 3–7). Within a number of years the discipline saw the emergence of courses based on discussion rather than only debate, focusing on "cooperative small group problem solving" sometimes as an outgrowth from and sometimes as an alternative to courses in debate (Gastil & Keith, 2005, p. 11).[4] Parallel to the expansion of group discussion in public and adult education settings, colleges and universities looked at their own institutions as sites ripe for teaching and research focused on group discussion and pedagogy rather than concentrating exclusively on debate as a way of addressing issues.[5]

Much of this shift to discussion was based on the philosophical and pedagogical writings of John Dewey. In 1897, Dewey published *My Pedagogic Creed*, a brief seventeen-page document outlining his beliefs about education, in which he states that "all education proceeds by the participation of the individual in the social consciousness of the [human] race" (Dewey, 1897, p. 3). Throughout his body of work, Dewey defined education as the opportunity for discovery and experience rather than the "traditional scheme" of education, described as the "imposition [of ideas] from above and outside" (Dewey, [1916] 1997, pp. 159–60; [1938] 1997, p. 18). Dewey's prominent role at Columbia University's Teachers College meant his sphere of influence reached across the country as students such as John Studebaker and others put into practice the democratic- and discussion-based approaches to understanding and addressing public problems he championed (Keith, 2007, pp. 100–101).[6]

While Dewey was situated in the field of education, much of the early work related to dialogue and discussion emerged from the field of communication—tracing roots to departments of speech, public speaking, oratory, or rhetoric—in which students were trained and educated as speakers and as individuals capable of understanding, assessing, and criticizing the speech of others (Cohen, 1994; Keith, 2007, pp. 89–191). Early on, speech teachers drew on Dewey's book *How We Think* (1910) because he "deftly wove the experimental method of science together with everyday practical concerns, and succeeded in moving 'thinking' out of peoples' heads and into the predicaments in which they find themselves" (Keith, 2007, p. 93). This book would prove to be foundational for scholars concerned about teaching discussion (Gouran, 1999, pp. 4–5; Johnson, 1943, pp. 83–84).

The study of group communication and improving group discussion as a central tool in promoting democracy was introduced by A. D. Sheffield's *Joining in Public Discussion* (1922) and expanded upon by others over the next decade and beyond (Barge, 2002, p. 159; Gouran, 1999, p. 4). Within the academy there was an acknowledgement of the need to connect course content with the growing national movement toward discussion. Significantly, this required a change in pedagogical approach; as Keith puts it, "educators understood that the *form* of speech pedagogy needed to be brought into line with a correct understanding of the *political function* of speech in a democracy" (2007, pp. 151, 152).

Scholars in fields such as communication, political science, adult education, and sociology engaged questions about the role that groups and group discussion played in what Mary Parker Follett (1924, p. 30) referred to as a "process of cooperating experience" within a broader social process inclusive of both experts and broader populations.[7] Dwight Sanderson, a rural sociologist, wrote extensively about communities and placed communication at the heart of social relations: "Without communication there would be no community and no civilization" (1922, p. 37). Throughout the 1910s, 1920s, and 1930s, disciplines explored groups and their interactions from multiple vantage points (Lindeman, 1924; Sanderson, 1938). In 1940, J. V. Garland and Charles F. Phillips of Colgate University published *Discussion Methods Explained and Illustrated*, an extensive collection of diverse group discussion methods intended to serve as a resource for those studying group discussion. In their preface, the editors wrote about the goal of the book: "In the use of this book, as well as in the use of other aids, the student will do well to forgo the temptation to seek ready-made answers to all his problems, and to remember that discussion is a constantly changing and shifting field where the 'rules' are largely descriptions of practice" (Garland & Phillips, 1940, pp. 3–4). This publication, like others, emphasized the need to see discussion as a way to overcome the appeal of easy answers and instead to engage complexity in responding to and addressing issues.

One of the few examples from that period of scholarship on group discussion and college students comes from a 1941 study by Karl F. Robinson who defined group discussion as "the reflective deliberation of problems by persons thinking and conversing together cooperatively in face-to-face or co-acting groups under the direction of a leader" (1941, p. 34).[8] Robinson also drew explicitly on Dewey's concept of reflective thinking and the idea that discussion is a cooperative activity meant to allow participants both to understand a problem and, if possible, "reach some consensus of opinion" (Robinson, 1941, pp. 34–35). For our concerns about deliberative pedagogy, it is worthwhile to include an extended quote from Robinson's study of college students and group discussion:

> Participants are urged to "consider the common good," "assume their share of group responsibility," "contribute objectively," "listen to understand." Whereas a debate is a competition between opposing or logically incompatible outcomes of thought on a given problem, discussion is a cooperative effort to solve such a problem. Its purpose is inquiry rather than advocacy.
>
> The typical situation for discussion is the face-to-face group with the participants seated in a circle or at least arranged so that every person can readily see and hear every other person without moving to the front of the room. (p. 35)

Robinson (1941) found through a number of experiments that participants who engaged in discussions about public issues showed significant changes in attitude, in contrast to those who did not engage in discussion. William E. Utterback, a prolific author on group discussion, published *Group Thinking and Conference Leadership: Techniques of Discussion* in 1950 and included a chapter on discussion in the classroom. He noted how, "Though widely accepted on theoretical grounds, the use of genuine discussion in the classroom is rare" (Utterback, 1950a, p. 136). His rationale for this statement was that the literature on discussion in classrooms "stresses the philosophy of group thinking without suggesting procedures for its application" (p. 136). In the pages that followed, Utterback offered concrete examples for multiple disciplines to include discussion. He also warned against "simulated impartiality" on the part of a teacher and how, "In the long run it is sounder to regard as frankly controversial any matter upon which difference of opinion actually exists" (p. 145). Noteworthy was Utterback's interest in the relationship between discussion and debate and the importance to offer more opportunities for group discussion in educational and public settings (Utterback, 1950b, 1956, 1958).

While the study by Robinson, alongside a small number of other studies, had positive results, a community of research-oriented scholars focusing on this process did not begin to develop until the 1950s in the field of communication as highlighted by the work of Utterback (Gouran, 1999, pp. 3–4). Importantly, as Henry L. Ewbank and J. Jeffery Auer note at the beginning of their 524-page tome on the place and role of discussion and debate in democracy, "Discussion and debate are not simply courses in a college curriculum. They are the essential tools of a democratic society"

(1941, p. 3). It is with this in mind that we turn our attention to focus more explicitly on democratic society, with land-grant universities playing a critical role in this work.[9]

Adult Education, Farmer Discussion Groups, and Schools of Philosophy

Dewey, Follett, and others were critical figures in the development, maturation, and expansion of the idea that discussion was foundational of democratic society, influencing people like M. L. Wilson, who helped to create one of the most robust examples of higher education institutions engaging in deliberative democracy through adult education programs (Ansell, 2011, pp. 9–14; Gilbert, 2000, p. 169; 2015, p. 18). A major facet of this effort was a partnership between the U.S. Department of Agriculture (USDA), land-grant universities, and the Cooperative Extension Service through which higher education played a critical role in creating and facilitating discussion groups. Cooperative Extension, established in 1914 as the outreach and engagement arm of land-grant universities, was traditionally based on a demonstration model of education to "aid in the diffusing among the people of the United States useful and practical information on subjects relating to agriculture and home economics" (Smith & Wilson, 1930, p. 365). This is an oversimplification of a highly complex and nuanced organization (see Peters, 2014), but it was against the backdrop of this model of education that extended university expertise that democratic discussion and adult education emerged as important dimensions that embraced not only the improvement of agricultural production, but also the "improved utilization of resources within the family, personal development, improved quality of life, and the improvement of the total community" (Warner & Christenson, 1984, p. 126). Cooperative Extension played a critical role in communities, offering education opportunities for men, women, and children that included expert knowledge as well as cultural and social experiences and opportunities.

While the use of public forums was expanding in cities across the country, leaders in the USDA were developing their own experiment with the use of discussion forums as a space for adult education alongside the USDA's other efforts in rural communities. As Jess Gilbert puts it: "Probably the most unusual innovation in the New Deal USDA aimed to advance democracy through adult or continuing education" (2015, p. 142). USDA Secretary Henry A. Wallace called for a "Forum on Forums" in order to look at the possibilities of using forums, panels, and group discussion in the agency's educational work, complementing its existing action programs. Those in attendance at the first meeting on December 7, 1934, included staff members from the USDA, John W. Studebaker (then U.S. commissioner of education), and representatives from various other agencies. After more meetings, the outcome was a decision to conduct an experiment in adult education during the winter and early spring months of 1935. To lead this effort, Wallace selected M. L. Wilson, who would later bring on Carl F. Taeusch to run the day-to-day operations of this initiative (Gilbert, 2015, p. 149).

This new "pillar" of the national agricultural policy was distinct from other programs within the USDA. Wilson and Wallace did not want the discussion groups to be "forums for the dissemination of the USDA's propaganda"; instead, they were meant to "provide a means for the expressing of all points of view" (McDean, 1969, p. 415). The effort was designed to help rural communities exchange information and viewpoints while also testing and challenging positions by subjecting various topics to group discussion and analysis. According to Wilson, the federal government made no attempt to control discussion, but it did have an interest in guaranteeing that the "facts [were] set forth correctly" (1941, p. 8). The role of the USDA in this setting was to prepare discussion guides and outlines. While the USDA would produce such documents and disseminate them widely, "the handling of the discussion programs [was] entirely up to the States," meaning that local actors were critical to its success (Wilson, 1935b, p. 33). Wilson was emphatic that the USDA would not advocate for anything other than the opportunity for citizens to learn about the issues facing them during this time of transformation. The agency's leaders "counted themselves among a 'great democratic movement' that had education at its core" (Gilbert, 2015, p. 143), as Wilson believed that "free and full discussion is the archstone of democracy" (Wilson, 1935a, p. 145).

Over the next few years, discussion-based continuing education opportunities for men and women blossomed into two interrelated programs, overseen by a body called the Program Study and Discussion (PSD) unit: first, discussion groups that were organized and facilitated by local Cooperative Extension agents from land-grant universities with rural men and women; and second, multiday training and educational opportunities known as Schools of Philosophy for Extension Workers that were organized and facilitated by USDA staff and distinguished scholars (Gilbert, 2015; Jewett, 2013; Shaffer, 2013, 2014a, 2016a; Taeusch, 1941). From 1935 until the PSD closed in 1946, these programs created discussion group materials for more than forty wide-ranging topics, such as those used during the 1936–37 and 1937–38 seasons (Shaffer, 2014a, pp. 301–2):

- What Should Be the Farmers' Share in the National Income?
- How Do Farm People Live in Comparison with City People?
- Should Farm Ownership Be a Goal of Agriculture Policy?
- Exports and Imports—How Do They Affect the Farmer?
- Is Increased Efficiency in Farming Always a Good Thing?
- What Should Farmers Aim to Accomplish Through Organization?
- What Kind of Agriculture Policy Is Necessary to Save Our Soil?
- What Part Should Farmers in Your County Take in Making National Agriculture Policy?
- Taxes: Who Pays, What For?
- Rural Communities: What Do They Need Most?
- Soil Conservation: Who Gains By It?
- Co-ops: How Far Can They Go?
- Farm Finance: What Is a Sound System?
- Crop Insurance: Is It Practical?
- Reciprocal Trade Agreements: Hurting or Helping the Country?
- Farm Security: How Can Tenants Find It?

In addition to materials for these topics, the PSD created methodology pamphlets for group discussion leaders to utilize when planning and conducting forums, providing diagrams for encouraging discussion flow among diverse members of a group rather than having conversations take place between a select few (Bureau of Agricultural Economics, 1942; U.S. Department of Agriculture, The Extension Service & Agricultural Adjustment Administration, 1935).

The PSD prepared and distributed copies of these topic-based discussion guides. Participation figures, as complete as possible, suggest that more than three million rural men and women participated in discussion groups, sixty thousand discussion leaders received training, and tens of thousands of extension workers and other rural community leaders attended more than 150 Schools of Philosophy (Gilbert, 2015, p. 142; Shaffer, 2014a, p. 264; Taeusch, 1952, p. 41; Vogt, 1940, p. 6). With a modest staff, it engaged communities across the entire nation—men, women, and children—in civic education that was based on deliberation about a range of issues facing rural communities.

In the end, those with a vested interest in large-scale agriculture who viewed this citizen-centered deliberation work and the more popular land-use planning work as deviations from the USDA's more traditional work succeeded in shuttering these programs. Other efforts within the agency faced a similar fate (Roberts, 2015). Obstructing actions beginning in 1942 and continuing for four years—led by the American Farm Bureau Federation, sympathetic supporters in Congress, and some within the land-grant colleges who felt the USDA should provide statistical information and not engage in the planning and educational work as had been done since the mid-1930s—brought this democratic initiative to an end.[10] The rise of the research university after World War II and the establishment of the National Science Foundation helped to push these community-based educational opportunities to the back of institutional memories as basic research aimed at solving the world's problems replaced the open-endedness of discussion about public problems (Vest, 2007, p. 24). The place for political ideals and principles, as well as a problem-solving approach in the land-grant university (and the Cooperative Extension Service), was and is a complicating factor when thinking about universities as primarily technocratic in their approach and purpose (Peters, Alter & Schwartzbach, 2010, pp. 19–62; Peters, 2015, p. 48).

Reclaiming Our Roots

Higher education has long-established but often-forgotten roots connecting previous deliberation and discussion initiatives with today's efforts to cultivate opportunities for faculty and students to use deliberation in their classrooms and in communities. Broadly defined, education played a key role in shaping cultural and political narratives about the United States as a place where people could learn about public issues and determine what to do about them as civic actors. Through town meetings, adult education, and public forums, citizens had opportunities to learn alongside others about larger social issues that affected not only individual communities, but also entire regions and the country as a whole. As William Keith and Paula Cossart put it, "as people attempted to enact their role as citizen deliberators, they developed norms and practices that embodied a vision of rational, discursive citizenship. . . . participation allowed people to speak *as citizens* to other citizens, and so constitute a civic identity" (2012, pp. 46, 58). These examples of public deliberation highlight the importance of the robust educational foundations that shaped these forums and meetings, even though they did not always bear titles that explicitly framed them as being educational. It is essential to recognize informal and nonformal learning that takes places in public discussions.

The role of discussion and deliberation has also been essential to the history of American higher education. In the early twentieth century, the development of disciplines within the university created the space—and need—for departments to focus on the ways people interacted and engaged one another in group settings. The field of communication was a natural disciplinary home for many of the early efforts to engage in group discussion in higher education settings, but the idea that informed citizens should make decisions transcended disciplinary boundaries. Drawing from John Dewey, Mary Parker Follett, and others, scholars and practitioners from political science, education, sociology, and other disciplines helped articulate the idea that while deliberation and discussion were topics to learn about and understand in courses, they were also significant because of the critical role they played in democratic society. The USDA's deliberative democracy and adult education initiative, which existed because university faculty and extension agents engaged citizens in communities as facilitators for community discussions, brought together millions of rural citizens and points to what role higher education can play in convening democratic publics to discuss and understand complex social issues.

These historical examples give scholars who are interested and engaged in deliberative pedagogy not only a strong precedent but also tangible models for using group discussion—in both institutional and community settings—as a basis for educating for democracy. These early manifestations of higher education as a catalyst for group discussion and cooperative decision-making processes point to the possibility of what can be done by colleges and universities for students and communities today. Educating for democracy is woven into our history. We would be served well to reclaim our past for moving toward and shaping our future.

NOTES

1. See also Carson (1990), Levine (2000), Longo, (2005).
2. For Studebaker's own writing, see Studebaker (1935a, 1935b, 1937, 1942), Studebaker & Cartwright (1936), Studebaker & Williams (1938, 1939). For scholarship on Studebaker and the Federal Forum Project, see Hilton (1981, pp. 98–121), Keith (2007, pp. 213–329), Loss (2012, pp. 79–86).
3. For a more thorough account of the founding of what would become the National Communication Association, see Gehrke & Keith (2015).
4. Examples of texts from the period include Fansler (1938a, 1938b), Judson & Judson (1938), McBurney & Hance (1939), McCabe (1938), Pellegrini & Stirling (1936), Sanderson (1938). The connection between group communication and democracy continued throughout the twentieth century; see Barge (2002, p. 159). One particular example of how scholars saw the complementarity of discussion and debate as essential elements of democracy is Ewbank & Auer (1941).
5. William Keith (2007) offers the most extensive treatment of the development of discussion-based courses and programs as opposed to exclusively debate-oriented programs.
6. Dewey has remained a central figure at the intersection of study about democracy and education. See, for example, Kadlec (2007), Keith (2007, pp. 89–110), Westbrook (1991).
7. A more recent study of cooperation is Sennett (2012).
8. For other studies from this period, see Utterback (1964, p. 374 n. 1).
9. While scholars have written about this period, the focus has been on Studebaker's forums. See Goodman (2004), Loss (2012).

10. The most thorough overviews of this chapter of the USDA's democratic efforts are Gilbert (2015), Kirkendall (1966).

REFERENCES

Ansell, C. K. (2011). *Pragmatist democracy: Evolutionary learning as public philosophy*. New York: Oxford University Press.

Bailyn, B. (1967). *The ideological origins of the American revolution*. Cambridge, MA: Harvard University Press.

Barge, J. K. (2002). Enlarging the meaning of group deliberation: From discussion to dialogue. In L. R. Frey (Ed.), *New directions in group communication* (pp. 159–79). Thousand Oaks: SAGE Publications.

Barker, D. W. M., McAfee, N., & McIvor, D. W. (2012). Introduction: Democratizing deliberation. In D. W. M. Barker, N. McAfee & D. W. McIvor (Eds.), *Democratizing deliberation: A political theory anthology* (pp. 1–17). Dayton, OH: Kettering Foundation Press.

Berelson, B. (1960). *Graduate education in the United States*. New York: McGraw-Hill.

Burt, E. V. (2004). *The progressive era: Primary documents on events from 1890 to 1914*. Westport, CT: Greenwood Press.

Carlisle, R. P. (2009). *The gilded age: 1870 to 1900*. New York: Facts on File.

Carson, M. J. (1990). *Settlement folk: Social thought and the American settlement movement, 1885–1930*. Chicago: University of Chicago Press.

Cartwright, M. A. (1935). *Ten years of adult education: A report on a decade of progress in the American movement*. New York: Macmillan.

Cartwright, M. A. (1945). The history of adult education in the United States. *Journal of Negro Education*, 14(3), 283–92.

Cohen, H. (1994). *The history of speech communication: The emergence of a discipline, 1914–1945*. Washington, DC: National Communication Association.

Dedrick, J. R., Grattan, L., & Dienstfrey, H. (Eds.). (2008). *Deliberation and the work of higher education: Innovations for the classroom, the campus, and the community*. Dayton, OH: Kettering Foundation Press.

Dewey, J. (1897). *My pedagogic creed*. Washington, DC: The Progressive Education Association.

Dewey, J. (1910). *How we think*. Boston: D. C. Heath.

Dewey, J. ([1916] 1997). *Democracy and education: An introduction to the philosophy of education*. New York: Free Press.

Dewey, J. ([1938] 1997). *Experience and education*. New York: Simon & Schuster.

Doherty, J. (2012). Deliberative pedagogy: An education that matters. *Connections*, 24–27.

Dryzek, J. S. (2000). *Deliberative democracy and beyond: Liberals, critics, contestations*. New York: Oxford University Press.

Ewbank, H. L., & Auer, J. J. (1941). *Discussion and debate: Tools of a democracy*. New York: F. S. Crofts.

Fansler, T. L. (1938a). *Effective group discussion: A guide for group members*. (Rev. ed.). New York: New York University.

Fansler, T. L. (1938b). *Teaching adults by discussion*. New York: New York University.

Flanagan, M. A. (2007). *America reformed: Progressives and progressivisms, 1890s–1920s*. New York: Oxford

University Press.

Follett, M. P. (1924). *Creative experience*. New York: Longmans, Green.

Frank, G. (1919). The parliament of the people. *The Century*, July, 401–16.

Freire, P. (2000). *Pedagogy of the oppressed* (M. B. Ramos, Trans.; 30th anniversary ed.). New York: Continuum.

Garland, J. V., & Phillips, C. F. (Eds.). (1940). *Discussion methods explained and illustrated* (Rev. ed.). New York: H. W. Wilson Company.

Gastil, J., & Keith, W. M. (2005). A nation that (sometimes) likes to talk: A brief history of public deliberation in the United States. In J. Gastil & P. Levine (Eds.), *The deliberative democracy handbook: Strategies for effective civic engagement in the twenty-first century* (pp. 3–19). San Francisco: Jossey-Bass.

Gehrke, P. J., & Keith, W. M. (2015). Introduction: A brief history of the National Communication Association. In P. J. Gehrke & W. M. Keith (Eds.), *A century of communication studies: The unfinished conversation* (pp. 1–25). New York: Routledge.

Gilbert, J. (2000). Eastern urban liberals and Midwestern agrarian intellectuals: Two group portraits of progressives in the New Deal Department of Agriculture. *Agricultural History*, 74(2), 162–80.

Gilbert, J. (2015). *Planning democracy: Agrarian intellectuals and the intended New Deal*. New Haven, CT: Yale University Press.

Goodman, D. (2004). Democracy and public discussion in the progressive and New Deal eras: From civic competence to the expression of opinion. *Studies in American Political Development*, 18(2), 81–111.

Gould, L. L. (1974). Introduction: The progressive era. In L. L. Gould (Ed.), *The progressive era* (pp. 1–10). Syracuse, NY: Syracuse University Press.

Gouran, D. S. (1999). Communication in groups: The emergence and evolution of a field of study. In L. R. Frey, D. S. Gouran & M. S. Poole (Eds.), *The handbook of group communication theory and research* (pp. 3–36). Thousand Oaks: SAGE Publications.

Gustafson, S. M. (2011). *Imagining deliberative democracy in the early American republic*. Chicago: University of Chicago Press.

Hill, F. E. (1935). Back to "town meetings." *New York Times Magazine*, September 15, p. SM9.

Hilton, R. J. (1981). The short happy life of a learning society: Adult education in America, 1930–39. PhD dissertation, Syracuse University.

Hilton, R. J. (1982). *Humanizing adult education research: Five stories from the 1930's*. Syracuse, NY: Syracuse University.

Jewett, A. (2013). The social sciences, philosophy, and the cultural turn in the 1930s USDA. *Journal of the History of the Behavioral Sciences*, 49(4), 396–427.

Johnson, A. (1943). An experimental study in the analysis and measurement of reflective thinking. *Speech Monographs*, 10(1), 83–96.

Judson, L. S., & Judson, E. M. (1938). *Modern group discussion: Public and private*. New York: H. W. Wilson.

Kadlec, A. (2007). *Dewey's critical pragmatism*. Lanham, MD: Lexington Books.

Keith, W. M. (2007). *Democracy as discussion: Civic education and the American forum movement*. Lanham, MD: Lexington Books.

Keith, W. M. (2008). On the origins of speech as a discipline: James A. Winans and public speaking as practical democracy. *Rhetoric Society Quarterly*, 38(3), 239–58.

Keith, W. M., & Cossart, P. (2012). The search for "real" democracy: Rhetorical citizenship and public deliberation in France and the United States, 1870–1940. In C. Kock & L. S. Villadsen (Eds.), *Rhetorical citizenship and public deliberation* (pp. 46–60). University Park: Penn State University Press.

Kirkendall, R. S. (1966). *Social scientists and farm politics in the age of Roosevelt*. Columbia: University of Missouri Press.

Lang, C. L. (1975). A historical review of the forces that contributed to the formation of the Cooperative Extension Service. PhD dissertation, Michigan State University.

Levine, P. (2000). *The new progressive era: Toward a fair and deliberative democracy*. Lanham, MD: Rowman & Littlefield.

Lindeman, E. C. (1924). *Social discovery: An approach to the study of functional groups*. New York: Republic Publishing.

Longo, N. V. (2005). *Recognizing the role of community in civic education: Lessons from Hull House, Highlander Folk School, and the Neighborhood Learning Community*. (Circle Working Paper 30.) College Park: School of Public Policy, University of Maryland.

Longo, N. V. (2013). Deliberative pedagogy in the community: Connecting deliberative dialogue, community engagement, and democratic education. *Journal of Public Deliberation*, 9(2), Article 16.

Loss, C. P. (2012). *Between citizens and the state: The politics of American higher education in the 20th century*. Princeton, NJ: Princeton University Press.

Lyman, R. L. (1915). The forum of educative agency. *Quarterly Journal of Speech*, 1(1), 1–8.

Marin, I. (Ed.) (2006). *Collective decision making around the world: Essays on historical deliberative practices*. Dayton, OH: Kettering Foundation Press.

Mathews, D. (1988). *The promise of democracy: A source book for use with National Issues Forums*. Dayton, OH: Kettering Foundation.

Mattson, K. (1998). *Creating a democratic public: The struggle for urban participatory democracy during the progressive era*. University Park: Penn State University Press.

McBurney, J. H., & Hance, K. G. (1939). *The principles and methods of discussion*. New York: Harper & Brothers.

McCabe, M. R. (1938). Annotated bibliography: Discussion groups and the public forum. *Phi Delta Kappan*, 21(3), 88–90.

McDean, H. C. (1969). M. L. Wilson and agricultural reform in twentieth-century America. PhD dissertation, University of California, Los Angeles.

Meyers, A. S. (2012). *Democracy in the making: The Open Forum lecture movement*. Lanham, MD: University Press of America.

Orchard, H. A. (1923). *Fifty years of Chautauqua: Its beginings, its development, its message and its life*. Cedar Rapids, IA: Torch Press.

Pangle, T. L. (1988). *The spirit of modern republicanism: The moral vision of the American founders and the philosophy of Locke*. Chicago: University of Chicago Press.

Pellegrini, A. M., & Stirling, B. (1936). *Argumentation and public discussion*. New York: D. C. Heath.

Peters, S. J. (2014). Extension reconsidered. *Choices: The Magazine of Food, Farm and Resource Issues*, 29(1), 1–6.

Peters, S. J. (2015). A democracy's college tradition. In H. C. Boyte (Ed.), *Democracy's education: Public work, citizenship, and the future of colleges and universities* (pp. 44–52). Nashville: Vanderbilt University Press.

Peters, S. J., Alter, T. R., & Schwartzbach, N. (2010). *Democracy and higher education: Traditions and stories of civic engagement.* East Lansing: Michigan State University Press.

Roberts, C. K. (2015). *The Farm Security Administration and rural rehabilitation in the South.* Knoxville: University of Tennessee Press.

Robinson, K. F. (1941). An experimental study of the effects of group discussion upon the social attitudes of college students. *Speech Monographs*, 8(1), 34–57.

Roth, K. (2008a). Deliberative pedagogy and the rationalization of learning. *Education and Society*, 26(3), 73–85.

Roth, K. (2008b). Deliberative pedagogy: Ideas for analysing the quality of deliberation in conflict management in education. *Studies in Philosophy and Education*, 27(4), 299–312.

Sanderson, D. (1922). *The farmer and his community.* New York: Harcourt, Brace.

Sanderson, D. (1938). Group description. *Social Forces*, 16(3), 309–19.

Schuster, J. H., & Finkelstein, M. J. (2006). *The American faculty: The restructuring of academic work and careers.* Baltimore: Johns Hopkins University Press.

Sennett, R. (2012). *Together: The rituals, pleasures and politics of cooperation.* New Haven: Yale University Press.

Shaffer, T. J. (2013). What should you and I do? Lessons for civic studies from deliberative politics in the New Deal. *The Good Society*, 22(2), 137–50.

Shaffer, T. J. (2014a). Cultivating deliberative democracy through adult civic education: The ideas and work that shaped farmer discussion groups and schools of philosophy in the New Deal Department of Agriculture, land-grant universities, and Cooperative Extension Service. PhD dissertation, Cornell University.

Shaffer, T. J. (2014b). Deliberation in and through higher education. *Journal of Public Deliberation*, 10(1), Article 10.

Shaffer, T. J. (2016a). Looking beyond our recent past. *National Civic Review*, 105(3), 3–10.

Shaffer, T. J. (2016b). Teaching deliberative democracy deliberatively. *eJournal of Public Affairs*, 5(2), 92–114.

Sheffield, A. D. (1922). *Joining in public discussion: A study of effective speechmaking for members of labor unions, conferences, forums, and other discussion groups.* New York: George H. Doran.

Smith, C. B., & Wilson, M. C. (1930). *The agricultural extension system of the United States.* New York: John Wiley & Sons.

Studebaker, J. W. (1935a). *The American way: Democracy at work in Des Moines forums.* New York: McGraw-Hill.

Studebaker, J. W. (1935b). What I mean by public forums. *Yearbook of the National Association of Secondary-School Principals*, 19(58), 43–44.

Studebaker, J. W. (1937). Public forums: An evaluation. *Journal of Adult Education*, 9(4), 393–95.

Studebaker, J. W. (1942). Beacon lights in a murky world. In W. L. Slate (Ed.), *Proceedings of the Association of Land-Grant Colleges and Universities: Fifty-fifth annual convention, Chicago, Illinois, November 10–12, 1941* (pp. 68–78). New Haven, CT: Quinnipiack Press.

Studebaker, J. W., & Cartwright, M. A. (1936). *Plain talk.* Washington, DC: National Home Library Foundation.

Studebaker, J. W., & Williams, C. S. (1938). *Choosing our way: The story of a forum program sponsored by the Office of Education and the results of a survey of 431 forums under various sponsorships.* Washington,

DC: U.S. Government Printing Office.

Studebaker, J. W., & Williams, C. S. (1939). *Forum planning handbook: How to organize school-administered forums.* Washington, DC: American Association for Adult Education; U. S. Department of the Interior, Office of Education.

Taeusch, C. F. (1941). *Report on the schools of philosophy for agricultural leaders.* Washington, DC: U.S. Bureau of Agricultural Economics.

Taeusch, C. F. (1952). Freedom of assembly. *Ethics,* 63(1), 33–43.

Thomas, N. L. (Ed.) (2010). *Educating for deliberative democracy.* San Francisco: Jossey-Bass.

Thomas, N. L., & Carcasson, M. (2010). Editors' introduction: Special issue on higher education. *Journal of Public Deliberation,* 6(1), Article 11.

Thomas, N. L., & Levine, P. (2011). Deliberative democracy and higher education: Higher education's democratic mission. In J. Saltmarsh & M. Hartley (Eds.), *"To serve a larger purpose": Engagement for democracy and the transformation of higher education* (pp. 154–76). Philadelphia: Temple University Press.

U. S. Bureau of Agricultural Economics. (1942). *Group discussion and its techniques: A bibliographical review.* Washington, DC: U.S. Government Printing Office.

U.S. Department of Agriculture, The Extension Service & Agricultural Adjustment Administration. (1935). *Discussion: A brief guide to methods.* Washington, DC: U.S. Government Printing Office.

Utterback, W. E. (1950a). *Group thinking and conference leadership: Techniques of discussion.* New York: Rinehart.

Utterback, W. E. (1950b). The influence of conference on opinion. *Quarterly Journal of Speech,* 36(3), 365–70.

Utterback, W. E. (1956). Measuring the outcome of an intercollegiate discussion conference. *Journal of Communication,* 6(1), 33–37.

Utterback, W. E. (1958). Evaluation of performance in the discussion course at Ohio State University. *The Speech Teacher,* 7(3), 209–15.

Utterback, W. E. (1964). Radio panel vs. group discussion. *Quarterly Journal of Speech,* 50(4), 374–77.

Vest, C. M. (2007). *The American research university from World War II to World Wide Web: Governments, the private sector, and the emerging meta-university.* Berkeley: University of California Press.

Vogt, P. L. (1940). Study clubs and citizenship. *Mountain Life and Work,* 15(4), 4–7.

Warner, P. D., & Christenson, J. A. (1984). *The cooperative extension service: A national assessment.* Boulder, CO: Westview Press.

Westbrook, R. B. (1991). *John Dewey and American democracy.* Ithaca, NY: Cornell University Press.

Wilson, M. L. (1935a). Discussion time is here. *Extension Service Review,* 6(10), 145.

Wilson, M. L. (1935b). Farm folk talk over national affairs. *Extension Service Review,* 6(4), 33, 34.

Wilson, M. L. (1941). *A theory of agricultural democracy.* (Extension Service Circular 355.) Washington, DC: Extension Service, U.S. Department of Agriculture.

Talking Out of School: Using Deliberative Pedagogy to Connect Campus and Community

Nicholas V. Longo and Cynthia M. Gibson

Significant shifts happen when citizens—as opposed to experts—are at the center of decision-making. No one knows this better than public officials, school administrators, and other traditional decision makers who are realizing that public problems are too complex for them to resolve alone. That's why they are increasingly reaching out and convening diverse groups of community residents and organizations to identify pressing issues, develop strategies to address those issues, and implement solutions.

This kind of engagement goes beyond simply asking residents for input or involving only select groups of people in decision-making processes. Instead, it is intentional about seeing residents as active and equal partners in all facets of planning, implementing, assessing, and improving efforts to strengthen communities. It is an approach that melds top-down and bottom-up strategies for decision-making, and it is inherently democratic.

A growing number of urban-planning, civic, political, educational, and environmental groups globally are exploring and advocating citizen-centered approaches to a wide range of public problems, from community revitalization to clean air campaigns. In communities across the globe, groups have convened citizen-led deliberations that have produced a set of public priorities that local communities are now taking steps to enact. These localities are opening the doors of their firehouses and school gyms to bring together people—including those who disagree—to negotiate their diverse interests and identify the common good. These efforts are occurring not only in physical settings but in digital spaces as well, thanks to technology's ability to connect people at the touch of a keypad.

Now this approach is being applied to a promising new form of civic education: deliberative pedagogy. Deliberative pedagogy connects a broad range of studies with civic learning, offers new approaches for teaching and learning, and provides avenues for more seamless multicultural and cross-disciplinary education strategies. As the approach gains recognition, we believe it has the potential to transform teaching and learning in a way that has powerful implications for civic

37

education, community problem-solving, and democracy (Dedrick, Grattan & Dienstfrey, 2008; Nabatchi, Gastil, Leighninger & Weiksner, 2012).

Deliberative pedagogy also complements public engagement pedagogies like service-learning and community engagement, which help students learn civic responsibility through reciprocal partnerships that occur outside campus borders. These approaches have become widespread across higher education. According to the Higher Education Research Institute, 65 percent of college freshmen report that their college or university offers opportunities for community service or community service-learning. An array of campus and national structures support this work. For example, some 94 percent of Campus Compact's 1,100 member colleges and universities have service-learning and civic-engagement centers (Campus Compact, 2008); Campus Compact itself is a national consortium that supports the civic mission of higher education. In addition, new campus programs allow students to major or minor in civic engagement, and a new career track exists for directors of community engagement in higher education (Butin & Seider, 2012).

But these and other civic engagement practices in higher education often seem to be on a separate trajectory from each other—another example of the "ships passing in the night" phenomenon that David Mathews (2009) found between academic institutions and citizens. Publicly engaged pedagogies often simply mirror the silo mentality that permeates academia. There are separate conferences, academic journals, funding streams, and offices to promote what could and should be complementary approaches.

Now, however, many programs and practices are starting to break new ground in bridging pedagogical divides by being more intentional about connecting deliberative dialogue with education in the community. Deliberative pedagogy is an approach that takes in-class discussions and learning into the community and involves students in deliberative conversations with community members to identify actions they can take collaboratively to address public problems.

Deliberative Pedagogy in the Community

We define public deliberation as a process through which a range of constituencies come together to share ideas and perspectives and then make collective decisions that form the basis for public action. The efficacy of this process in resolving complex issues has led to its replication in domains beyond the public policy or political sphere. One of the most prominent of these areas is education—specifically, deliberation as an integral part of pedagogy. The difference between *deliberative politics* and *deliberative pedagogy* is that the former integrates deliberative decision-making with public action (Mathews, 2012) and the latter integrates deliberative decision-making with teaching and learning.

What we are calling *deliberative pedagogy in the community* is a collaborative approach that melds deliberative dialogue and community engagement. This approach is especially timely as a growing number of institutions involve college students in deliberative conversations outside of their college campus bubble. Specifically, students are stepping outside the classroom and connecting theory with real-world problem-solving in the community through structures such as intergenerational learning circles with new immigrants, forums with community members on public issues, and multiyear civic-engagement courses. Faculty and students are cocreating shared spaces for dialogue and collaborative action in the community and rethinking long-held power dynamics between the campus and the community.

While deliberative pedagogy is not without its challenges, it holds enormous promise in promoting the civic mission of higher education through more collaborative approaches to teaching and learning that respond to important and rapidly shifting contextual trends: increasing cultural diversity, new technologies that promote transparency and collaboration, and the ardent desire of young people to make a difference through concrete social action. It moves the academy from the more traditional teaching-to-learning dynamic toward a model of collaborative engagement (Longo & Gibson, 2016) in which knowledge is more genuinely cocreated through reflective public action. This shift toward collaboration also helps illuminate the civic dimensions of teaching and learning that increasing numbers of students are demanding and that the communities in which higher education institutions are located are seeking.

Education in the Community

Throughout our nation's history, education has been linked to the promise of democracy. Deliberative pedagogy is often used as a vehicle to make this connection in classrooms of all types, from kindergarten through higher education. For instance, a teacher might use public deliberation to help students understand the nature of public policy choices, develop skill in group communication, or learn about a range of complex public issues such as immigration, federal debt, or educational reform. These approaches to public deliberation tend to be important examples not only of civic learning but also of engaged teaching and learning.

Yet too often over the past century, the connection between democracy and education has been confined to a classroom. This makes civic learning a more theoretical exercise and tends to value civic knowledge and attitudes above more action-oriented priorities, such as civic practices and public skills. It can also be constrictive because it overlooks the many assets neighborhood and community institutions can bring to the education table. "The American tendency to equate education and schooling and make schools the instrument for satisfying our wants and alleviating our malaise takes attention from our circumstances," writes John Goodlad. "We beat on schools, leaving the contextual circumstances unaddressed" (1997, p. 41).

Schooling and communities are inextricably linked; solutions to the problems in each must be addressed by harnessing the many talents in the entire "ecology of education" (Cremin, 1976, p. 25). Thus, community centers, places of worship, libraries, local businesses, coffee shops, and the networks of other community institutions can be seen as part of the learning ecosystem.

Drawing on the education philosophies and practices of Jane Addams, John Dewey, Elsie Clapp, Myles Horton, Lawrence Cremin, and others (Longo, 2007), a growing number of educators are recognizing the power of the community in advancing civic learning. These educators assert that thinking more broadly about where and how learning takes place is just as important as what is learned. It also unleashes a vast set of resources for learning—what Addams ([1902] 2002) referred to as "free[ing] the powers" (p. 80) of people to contribute to public life—and allows education to be more connected to democratic engagement.

Education in the community is active learning that takes place outside of, but is often connected with, the classroom. It involves more than a short-term community-service project; it means intentionally putting education in the context of sustained community-building efforts. It is most often place-based, using a collaborative, integrated, problem-solving approach (Smith, 1992; Stein, 2001).

In higher education, the role of community typically gets recognized as part of student internships, practicums, international immersion, and especially service-learning courses. An additional strand of education in the community includes public deliberation. This focus, which is the crux of the approach outlined in this chapter, is used in a growing number of courses and programs, several of which are described below. In these programs, students become involved in public deliberation in community-based settings in a way that goes well beyond "Deliberation 101."

Today, students are involved in a variety of deliberative projects that ask them to take on leadership roles in their local communities. Students lead dialogues about complex issues with campus and community stakeholders and guide reflection sessions for service-learning courses. Students spearhead efforts to magnify the voices of young people on public issues and to capture the stories of the elders in a community. They use not only speaking forums but also photography, dance, film, poetry, and other media to facilitate community deliberations.

Deliberative pedagogy in the community takes community-based learning one step further and offers an opportunity to address common criticisms of both deliberative dialogue and community engagement. For instance, the major criticism of deliberative dialogue is that it's all talk and no action—or, as critics described deliberation at Highlander, the well-regarded community education center during the labor movement of the 1930s–1940s and the civil rights movement in the 1950s–1960s: "All you do is sit there and tell stories" (Horton & Freire, 1990, p. 99). Deliberative, community-based pedagogy recognizes that talk is never enough; it has to be linked to reciprocal learning among all participants, as well as the potential for collaborative action. As Harry Boyte explains:

> Deliberative democracy, welcome as it is, is not enough. Alone, it all too easily takes on a hortatory, idealized quality that separates out an abstract "public sphere" of communicative consensus from real world politics built upon negotiation, bargaining, messy compromise and also creative work to what was once termed, in American history, the commonwealth. (1995, para. 33)

Similarly, critics point to the seemingly apolitical nature of community engagement. This can be seen in the language and framework of service-learning, the most common form of community engagement, with its emphasis on serving "needs" and addressing community "deficiencies" (McKnight, 1995, p. 46). Many forms of community engagement also fail to recognize the nature of politics and power. Boyte contends that service routinely "neglects to teach about root causes and power relationships, fails to stress productive impact, ignores politics, and downplays the strengths and talents of those being served" (2004, p. 12).

When community engagement is a component of deliberative pedagogy, it connects—and transforms—deliberative dialogue and community engagement by attempting to create space for reciprocal conversations that are grounded in real-world experiences. Moreover, the deliberative aspects of this work (what Boyte calls "public work") can lead to "reflective learning cultures in which citizens come to understand the value of different views and in which they revisit the significance of what they create" (Boyte, 2011, p. 11).

Higher Education and Deliberative Pedagogy in the Community

Many promising efforts are taking place that infuse deliberative pedagogy into engaged learning in higher education. These efforts include a growing number of campus–community partnerships. One notable example is the Jane Addams School for Democracy in St. Paul, Minnesota, a community-based school that involves college students, young people, and immigrant community members in ongoing deliberative conversations and joint public work projects. Like other such collaborations, it "teaches that democracy happens in real time and place" (Kari & Skelton, 2007, p. 14). This approach helps participants develop civic skills such as genuinely listening in an open-minded way and recognizing the wisdom of community voices—experiences that can have a profound effect on students. One college student credits her work with the Jane Addams School for teaching her that one can't get all the answers from "reading something in a book," reflecting that "the space at Jane Addams School asks you to consider what other people are saying—to consider other voices, others' knowledge . . . as legitimate sources" (Kari & Skelton, 2007, p. 30).

Other examples of campus-based deliberative pedagogy in community settings include programs that prepare students to lead deliberative forums in community settings, multiyear efforts that allow student cohorts to master the art of on-campus deliberative dialogue while also participating in service-learning courses, and projects that help students facilitate community visioning and planning. According to London, when these kinds of community-based partnerships are done well, they serve dual purposes: they give the community the chance to come together (often for the first time) to "hammer out a set of concrete plans for the town's future," and they allow the college to "extend its reach in the community and contribute resources and expertise in a uniquely collaborative and participatory way" (2010, p. 5). Following are examples of such programs.

The University of Cape Town's Social Infrastructure Course

At the University of Cape Town, a public research university in Cape Town, South Africa, Janice McMillan has spearheaded an innovative approach to deliberative pedagogy in the community within the professional studies school. With a class of almost one hundred students, McMillan collaborates with a team of students, faculty, and community partners to enable ongoing reciprocal conversations to occur in the classroom (mostly through group activities and facilitated small-group conversations) and the community (through community exposure visits with teams of students led by community partners). The result is a space where the potentially detached, larger-scale classroom feels deliberative, while community residents are positioned as coeducators.

Jane Addams School for Democracy

Located in a neighborhood that has been called "the Ellis Island of the Midwest" on the West Side of St. Paul, the school engages students and faculty from local colleges working with new immigrants and refugees in cross-cultural learning circles several times per week. Using the mantra "We are all teachers, we are all learners," the project immerses university students in reciprocal conversations that lead to joint public work. Projects include language learning and citizenship test preparation, community gardening, youth organizing to improve schools, and interactive candidate forums (Kari & Skelton, 2007; Longo, 2007).

The Center for Public Deliberation at Colorado State University (CSU)

CSU's Center for Public Deliberation offers a year-long undergraduate course through the university's communications department on the theory and practice of deliberative democracy. Center faculty, staff, and students pride themselves on the "passionate impartiality" they bring to community issues, which Martín Carcasson, the center's director, argues is an essential but often neglected aspect of democracy. The students in the course, called "student associates," moderate community forums in Colorado using National Issues Forums (NIF) guides on topics like school funding and childcare. As facilitators in the community, students can bring a passion for the process without having an agenda with regard to the results (Carcasson, 2010).

Wake Forest University's Deliberative Democracy Project

Wake Forest University in Winston-Salem, North Carolina, has initiated a four-year project with thirty undergraduate Democracy Fellows who learn about deliberative democracy by organizing and moderating forums not only on campus but also on the road in the local community. As part of the project, the fellows organized a community deliberation on urban sprawl that involved a number of community leaders in the process, including the mayor of Winston-Salem, an executive of the chamber of commerce, and members of several neighborhood councils (Harriger & McMillan, 2007). Fellows also participated in a course, Citizen and Community, where they examined public education using an NIF issue guide, along with a service-learning project in which they partnered with a local organization to facilitate a series of study circle dialogues on public schooling (Crawford, 2008).

Hofstra University's Center for Civic Engagement

Among other work, the Center for Civic Engagement at Hofstra University in Long Island, New York, sponsored a program called "Deepening Democracy through Deliberation" to generate community-wide conversations on public issues leading up to the presidential election in 2012 (including the presidential debate hosted at Hofstra). The program organized public forums facilitated by well-trained undergraduate students in schools and public libraries on policy issues such as education and the role of the United States in the world.

Providence College's Feinstein Institute for Public Service

Providence College in Providence, Rhode Island, is experimenting with deliberative pedagogy in the community with the development of the Providence College/Smith Hill Annex. The Annex is a one-thousand-square-foot storefront that the college leases from the Smith Hill Community Development Corporation to provide a space for community and campus to come together. The Annex hosts courses open to students and community members, as well as potluck dinners, book clubs, break-dance and exercise classes, street art programs, nonprofit and community meetings, education and support groups, and more—any program or event that brings campus and community into dialogue together. The expectation is that over time the cocreation of this shared space will facilitate campus and community "getting to know one another as neighbors." Keith Morton, associate director of the college's Feinstein Institute for Public Service, concludes: "Our deep hope is that these conversations will help the people and institutions articulate and realize what it is that they find most meaningful" (Battistoni, Longo & Morton, 2014, p. 63).

Moving Forward

To grapple with an understanding of deliberative pedagogy beyond this initial survey of practices, the authors elicited the insights and knowledge of about a dozen scholars, funders, and educators with deep experience in public deliberation and civic engagement. Their responses to a set of interview questions, analyzed below, help to further unpack the concept of deliberative pedagogy and provide a roadmap for future exploration. Overall, the interviews revealed a general consensus that faculty's roles are shifting from teaching to serving as facilitators of collaborative engagement. There was also growing appreciation for the community's role in the ecology of education. In addition, the interviews surfaced some new perspectives on the connections between deliberative practices and collaborative engagement. Some general themes emerged:

- Dramatic shifts are taking place in higher education—especially with regard to the nature of knowledge creation, pedagogy, and the student experience—that make deliberative pedagogy a timely and important approach to teaching and learning.
- Integrating deliberation into community-based settings can be more effective in educating for democracy than simply including deliberation in classroom-based settings, because the former engages students in working to address real-world problems that emerge from deliberative interactions with community residents.
- Deliberation adds value to other democratic practices such as service-learning, participatory action research, and popular education. It could also be a necessary component of participatory democratic education, although some respondents believe that deliberation by itself is not sufficient—that is, it needs to be linked with other practices and approaches.
- More research is needed to understand deliberative pedagogy and its broader implications for strengthening higher education's civic mission.

These findings, explored below, have important implications for teaching and learning in higher education. Further, they raise new questions and areas for future research. Among these questions are the following: What needs to be done to understand and clarify the components and practices of deliberative pedagogy? What is the potential overlap between deliberative pedagogy and what we term elsewhere "collaborative engagement" (Longo & Gibson, 2016)? How can we elucidate the implications for a new model of teaching and learning for broader efforts to promote the civic mission of higher education?

Need for a New Pedagogy with New Faculty Roles

Dramatic shifts in the economics and demographics of colleges and universities, along with the nature of knowledge creation, are leading to a moment of transformation. This includes a change in both where and how teaching and learning takes place—a "shift from covering content to using content and using it differently," says John Saltmarsh, director of the New England Resource Center for Higher Education (NERCHE). "It's about using the experiences of students and community partners and shifting toward a more asset-based approach. The narrative structures of dialogue and deliberation are one way to do it. As soon as you move to more narrative structures and recognize that knowledge comes from all different places, it moves it beyond the university and the realization that the partners have knowledge that comes to bear." Martín Carcasson of CSU's Center for Public Deliberation describes this change as focusing on "wisdom and judgment, not just knowledge" (personal interview, 2013).

Likewise, new approaches have begun to spill into the practices of higher education institutions. Faculty members, for example, are moving from teaching content to facilitating learning, which Saltmarsh describes as a "process of collaboration with students and community to build democracy." Service-learning has become a common practice across hundreds of campuses, as have participatory research projects and other engaged pedagogies. Most relevant to our research, involving students in classroom and campus-based deliberative discussions about policy issues or social problems is also emerging as a promising way to develop critical thinking, listening, and collaboration skills.

These new approaches assume different power dynamics that require a different kind of expertise, notes Amy Lazarus, formerly the executive director of the Sustained Dialogue Institute. Employing those approaches, however, continues to be challenging because they are a radical departure from the traditional didactic education models that have dominated higher education. Persuading these same institutions to embrace a model that moves even further from the norm— such as deliberative pedagogy—will be an even greater challenge, Lazarus says, especially if it is unclear what this new approach constitutes and, most important, what its perceived value is for the institution, its faculty, and its students.

Community Matters

There is increasing awareness that colleges and universities are part of a larger ecosystem and have as much to learn from the community as the community does from them. Traditionally, higher education has tended to wall itself off from the communities in which its institutions are located. While many colleges and universities have begun to move into communities through service-learning and participatory research efforts, often "the whole premise is to learn abstractly and then go into the community," Nan Skelton, former codirector of the Center for Democracy and Citizenship at Augsburg College, argues. "That needs to be turned on its head. The biggest thing is being with people and listening. That's the first step. You have to decide that you're there and really be there. And listen to what's all around you. Listen to people talking, take in the smells, make sure you're there. And then gradually they start teaching you. It's the relationship. You've got to get into a place where you are in a relationship, where you trust yourself and them."

Auspiciously, the shift to viewing community as a collaborator—rather than a blank slate or an outsider in relation to a college or university based in that community—has led to experimentation with new forms of communication, collaboration, information sharing, and action that can be applied to higher education. Many of these initiatives are "not highly structured," Skelton notes. "They start with the human and not with the practice. People are sitting in a circle and they are paying attention to one another. There is a faith that if we sit together, we'll come to a point that it works for all of us. It's about faith in the group, not faith in a prescribed process."

When done well, deliberative pedagogy can shift the relationship between institutions and the community from partnerships—which can be fleeting or periodic—to *partnership communities*. NERCHE's John Saltmarsh, who coined this term, says that such communities require a whole new level of vision and commitment. While community partnerships can "come and go, the goal of partnership communities is to build this community over multiple decades." Likewise, John Dedrick, vice president and program director of the Kettering Foundation, believes the goal of partnerships should be "to construct interventions in which students experience the consequences of their work"—which means they need to remain embedded in the community for the long term.

Nan Skelton notes that the Jane Addams School has done this with the partnership it has built on the West Side of St. Paul, where "the focus is on the community." As noted previously, the school engages students from multiple colleges and universities in the Minneapolis/St. Paul area to work collaboratively with local immigrants on community-identified problems (Kari & Skelton, 2007). The long-term commitment involved means "overcoming the problem of time" in university structures by rethinking the limited time horizons of a university calendar. As Skelton reflects, "that's not the way communities are put together."

Several respondents pointed to one model in particular that combines deliberative practice and community-based learning: CSU's Center for Public Deliberation. The center offers a year-long course in which students study deliberative dialogue and lead community-based deliberations on community-identified issues (Carcasson, 2010). Center director Martín Carcasson believes universities have essential roles to play in providing "passionate impartiality" to exploring and finding ways to address complex community issues and problems. He adds that while this kind of work "doesn't fit the dominant university culture," it is essential for both student learning and community problem-solving (personal interview, 2013).

Is Deliberation Enough?

Peter Levine, associate dean of the Tisch College of Civic Life at Tufts University, cites three factors at the core of citizenship: deliberation, collaboration, and civic relationships (Levine, 2013). While some see these as individual concepts and practices that do not necessarily have to operate in concert with one another in a civic exercise, others believe that to achieve the longer-term goal of embedding democratic practice in communities (and in the institutions located there, such as colleges and universities), these factors need to be more than the sum of their parts. As Ira Harkavy, associate vice president and founding director of the Barbara and Edward Netter Center for Community Partnerships at the University of Pennsylvania, notes: "While deliberation is necessary for civic engagement, it is not sufficient." It is one of two essential components of what he calls "participatory democracy." In short, there must be both deliberation (a democratic process that allows people to hear one another's views) and action (a product that emerges from that process—e.g., a collective decision to take a particular course in addressing an issue).

Others question how related deliberation is to real-world problem-solving, suggesting that it can't be decoupled from community engagement if the practice is to have significant impact. At the same time, a number of public skills that are essential for community problem-solving—and democratic citizenship—are learned through participation in deliberation. As Saltmarsh says, "We want students to learn how to be able to facilitate participation in the culture of democracy. One of the tools to use is dialogue and deliberation, to get many voices into a conversation to solve problems. And we need to learn these skills by practicing them."

Still other respondents believe that while deliberation is a "good thing to do," it may not be necessary for learning about and experiencing participatory democracy. As John Gaventa, director of research at the Institute of Development Studies at the University of Sussex, points out, "If deliberative democracy practitioners emphasize the quality of the talk over the strategies of engagement by people not involved or at the table," the value added of deliberation will diminish. It's also important, he says, to ask who benefits: "Deliberative practice with students may lead to them being better cocreators of knowledge, but it won't necessarily lead to community change."

Gaventa proposes that the real value of deliberation is not only its ability to bring people together to consider others' perspectives and then take action, but also its potential for moving people to think about a complex problem completely differently as a result of the dialogue with others. In fact, he believes that this kind of thinking may be the most important element of higher education engagement work because it raises this work to a new level "by focusing on learning that encourages transformation, not just getting knowledge." Learning in this case is about changing power relations and the ways in which different actors relate to each other. "We assumed that knowledge production and civic engagement would lead to societal transformation, but we're not so sure now. They can actually reinforce the status quo," Gaventa argues. While participatory processes are important ways for people to engage in civic life, he explains, they can also lead to people "getting stuck in their own advocacy positions or beliefs or the loudest voices carrying the agenda." In contrast, deliberative processes allow people to reflect on their own position and change it after talking with and learning from others who may be different from them. "Deliberative processes," Gaventa notes, "are leading to something qualitatively different: they're trying to incite transformation by allowing people to imagine something different from what they did at the beginning of the process."

Diana Hess, dean of education at the University of Wisconsin–Madison, believes that deliberation—both learning the skills needed to do it effectively and applying those skills outside the classroom—can either be mutually exclusive or overlap with other forms of civic engagement. Through the experience of deliberation, students learn to listen to and hear all points of view and then come to a decision about what their own views are—skills that are important in and of themselves, regardless of whether they are applied in community settings.

Conclusion

Deliberative pedagogy has the potential to transcend the boundaries of the classroom. It goes beyond the traditional teacher–learner dichotomy by integrating a broader ecology of educational opportunities available to students. Deliberative pedagogy involves deliberative conversations—at the classroom, campus/institutional, and community levels—about real-world issues. It recognizes that in a networked society where information is no longer proprietary or the exclusive purview of experts and gatekeepers, the most robust forms of knowledge are cocreated by a wide range of actors. And, perhaps most importantly, it involves more than just a professor and students; it includes those in the larger community affected by an issue.

When deliberative pedagogy connects with the community in this way, it challenges our ideas not only about education but also about broader notions of democratic engagement. Without opportunities to learn about and experience all facets of the democratic process—including a wide range of deliberative, collaborative, problem-solving, and analytical/critical thinking skills—it will be difficult, if not impossible, for citizens to participate as fully and as meaningfully as required for a vibrant, healthy democracy. We believe deliberative pedagogy may provide a powerful tool for reaching that goal.

REFERENCES

Addams, J. ([1902] 2002). *Democracy and social ethics*. Chicago: University of Illinois Press.

Battistoni, R., Longo, N., & Morton, K. (2014). Co-creating mutual spaces for campuses and communities. In J. Hamerlinck & J. Plaut (Eds.), *Asset-based approaches to community engagement in higher education* (pp. 59–66). Minneapolis: Minnesota Campus Compact.

Boyte, H. C. (1995). Beyond deliberation: Citizenship as public work. Paper presented at the Political Economy of the Good Society (PEGS) conference, February, Washington, DC.

Boyte, H. C. (2004). *Everyday politics: Reconnecting citizens and public life*. Philadelphia: University of Pennsylvania Press.

Boyte, H. C. (2011). *"We the people" politics: The populist promise of deliberative public work*. Dayton, OH: Kettering Foundation Press.

Butin, D. W., & Seider, S. (2012). *The engaged campus: Certificates, minors, and majors as the new community engagement*. New York: Palgrave Macmillan.

Campus Compact. (2008). *Service statistics 2008: Highlights and trends from Campus Compact's annual membership survey.* Boston: Campus Compact.

Carcasson, M. (2010). Facilitating community democracy from campus: Centers, faculty, and students as key resources of passionate impartiality. *Higher Education Exchange*, 15–26.

Crawford, A. (2008). Notes and reflections on being a democracy fellow at Wake Forest University. In J. R. Dedrick, L. Grattan & H. Dienstfrey (Eds.), *Deliberation and the work of higher education: Innovations for the classroom, the campus, and the community* (pp. 267–88). Dayton, OH: Kettering Foundation Press.

Cremin, L. A. (1976). *Public education.* New York: Basic Books.

Dedrick, J. R., Grattan, L., & Dienstfrey, H. (Eds.). (2008). *Deliberation and the work of higher education: Innovations for the classroom, the campus, and the community.* Dayton, OH: Kettering Foundation Press.

Goodlad, J. I. (1997). *In praise of education.* New York: Teachers College Press.

Harriger, K. J., & McMillan, J. J. (2007). *Speaking of politics: Preparing college students for democratic citizenship through deliberative dialogue.* Dayton, OH: Kettering Foundation Press.

Horton, M., & Freire, P. (1990). *We make the road by walking: Conversations on education and social change.* Philadelphia: Temple University Press.

Kari, N. N., & Skelton, N. (2007). *Voices of hope: The story of the Jane Addams School for Democracy.* Dayton, OH: Kettering Foundation Press.

Levine, P. (2013). *We are the ones we have been waiting for: The promise of civic renewal in America.* Oxford: Oxford University Press.

London, S. (2010). *Doing democracy: How a network of grassroots organizations is strengthening community, building capacity, and shaping a new kind of civic education.* Dayton, OH: Kettering Foundation.

Longo, N. V. (2007). *Why community matters: Connecting education with civic life.* Albany: SUNY Press.

Longo, N. V., & Gibson, C. (2016). Collaborative engagement: The future of teaching and learning in higher education. In M. A. Post, E. Ward, N. V. Longo & J. Saltmarsh (Eds.), *Publically engaged scholars: Next generation engagement and the future of higher education* (pp. 61–75). Sterling, VA: Stylus Publishing.

Mathews, D. (2009). Ships passing in the night? *Journal of Higher Education Outreach and Engagement,* 13(3), 5–16.

Mathews, D. (2012). Foreword. In D. W. M. Barker, N. McAfee & D. W. McIvor (Eds.), *Democratizing deliberation: A political theory anthology* (pp. vii–xi). Dayton, OH: Kettering Foundation Press.

McKnight, J. (1995). *The careless society: Community and its counterfeits.* New York: Basic Books.

Nabatchi, T., Gastil, J., Leighninger, M., & Weiksner, G. M. (Eds.). (2012). *Democracy in motion: Evaluating the practice and impact of deliberative civic engagement.* Oxford: Oxford University Press.

Smith, M. (1992). The possibilities of public life: Educating in the community. In G. Allen & I. Martin (Eds.), *Education and community: The politics of practice* (pp. 105–117). New York: Cassell.

Stein, J. (2001). Youth development in context: Education in the community. In J. Stein & N. V. Longo (Eds.), *The university and the community: Renewing the relationship* (pp. 10–13). Minneapolis: Center for 4-H Youth Development, University of Minnesota.

PART 2

Classroom Practices: New Ways of Teaching and Learning

Deliberative Pedagogy as a Central Tenet: First-Year Students Develop a Course and a Community

Leila R. Brammer

After using deliberative techniques in my classes for several years, I decided to embark on an experiment to construct an entire course based in deliberative pedagogy. The course I chose was a first-term seminar with sixteen traditional-aged first-year college students. Students deliberated internally to determine key course elements, including class assignments, processes, and timelines. At the end of the course, the students led a campus deliberation. Students' responses to the deliberation, to the course as a whole, and to the idea of using deliberation to address issues and build community were universally enthusiastic. One student, whose views were representative of the class's, summarized the experience this way: "I learned that tackling issues or expanding on topics can be better dealt with [through] deliberation. Coming together and discussing your views can help open your mind to understand other people's views as well."

This experiment required a great deal of work and risk, but the outcomes in student learning and empowerment, as well as the influence on my own teaching, were remarkably positive. This chapter describes the class structure and assignments for this project, along with the challenges and opportunities that arise from utilizing deliberative pedagogy in course construction.

Deliberation as Central Course Tenet

Deliberative pedagogy grew out of a desire to develop the skills of participatory and reasoned community decision-making. As Jacobs, Cook, and Delli Carpini contend, deliberation as a practice "presents opportunities for the future expansion and rejuvenation of democracy." At the same time, they recognize that participation in deliberation takes "time, effort, and skill" (2009, pp.153-154). The skills of deliberation conform to the higher education focus called for by the Association of American Colleges and Universities in its landmark report, *A Crucible Moment: College Learning and Democracy's Future* (National Task Force on Civic Learning and Democratic Engagement, 2012). The report asserts that the mission of higher education is to "educate for democracy" and to "renew this nation's social, intellectual, and civic capital" (pp. 1–2). It further contends that deliberative skills "help refine skills in soliciting multiple viewpoints, negotiating and compromising, and organizing across differences for democratic ends" (pp. 55–56). Others have written specifically about the skills, habits, and inclinations important to (and gained through) deliberative pedagogy, as well as their importance to civic life (Alfaro, 2008; Longo, 2013; Thomas, 2010).

With this foundation and the case studies of deliberative pedagogy found in *Deliberation and the Work of Higher Education: Innovations for the Classroom, the Campus, and the Community* (Dedrick, Grattan & Dienstfrey, 2008), I began to infuse deliberation into my communication classes at Gustavus Adolphus College in Minnesota. In my courses, I have used a variety of deliberative practices, including deliberations on National Issues Forums (topics identified by the National Issues Forums Institute), course-related topics, and local issues. In addition, community-based deliberative research and advocacy are central to the foundational course in my department. Through these experiences, I have observed the influence of deliberative pedagogy on students' academic and personal growth; as a result, I have moved to incorporate additional such experiences into all my courses.

When planning a first-term seminar on deliberation and democracy, I recognized that deliberative pedagogy was a key organizing principle. If deliberation is a method by which communities reach shared and sound decisions and through which students gain skills that are central to the liberal arts, then should not a course in deliberation require students to demonstrate these skills through activities with real stakes, such as building the course and creating a community within that course? Guided by that question, I endeavored to facilitate a first-term seminar in which students were responsible for the syllabus, assignments, and course experiences.

While students practiced formal deliberation and facilitation with a few National Issues Forums, course readings, and current events, classroom deliberation largely involved decisions about the course syllabus, class assignments, and the final campus forum. Most of these deliberations took place with the class as a whole, with a few small-group experiences. Students prepared for deliberations through research or writing about the issue. At the beginning of the course, I facilitated deliberations; by the end of the semester, the class as a community had learned to self-regulate effectively. This outcome, perhaps the most impressive of the course, came as a result of students' extensive and intensive experience together.

The Course: Deliberation, Democracy, and Civility

Gustavus Adolphus College is a residential liberal arts college of 2,400 students located in southern Minnesota. Entering students at Gustavus take a first-term seminar that provides content instruction as a way to develop college skills of critical thinking, writing, oral communication, and discussion of values. These seminars, each of which enrolls sixteen students, also serve as the primary first-year student advising and orientation experience.

In fall 2011, I taught a first-term seminar in Deliberation, Democracy, and Civility. The course met twice a week in 110-minute blocks. The sixteen students were a diverse group: twelve males and four females, five students of color (a considerably higher proportion than that of the entering class as a whole, which had 11.2 percent students of color), four first- or second-generation immigrants, and three English language learners. The students represented varied socioeconomic, geographic (rural/urban), and family backgrounds, but all lived within a 150-mile radius of campus.

Deliberating about Course Elements

In order to integrate deliberation into the classroom, I constructed the class as primarily deliberative. In the first few weeks, students deliberated to create the course syllabus, having started with only a general syllabus that provided the course structure, learning outcomes, and foundational materials for the first five weeks. These materials included resources on deliberation's history, skills (e.g., facilitation), and practice (three National Issues Forums deliberations), along with sample assignments and some standard guidelines (the honor code, first-term seminar guidelines and requirements, and policies on plagiarism and student support). I made one assignment mandatory—facilitating a community deliberation on a subject of interest—but left open whether students would complete it individually, in groups, or as a whole-class project. I suggested that other assignments be structured to support this capstone assignment.

In their class-related deliberations, students wrestled with the community deliberation and the appropriate scaffolding of assignments to support it. In small-group discussions, students agreed to do the community deliberation as a whole class and began to structure related assignments (papers and speeches on the issue, facilitation practice, etc.). In the large group, they combined their ideas into a plan, which was too large to be completed in a semester. After paring down the assignments to a workload that was reasonable for one semester, we worked together through a deliberative process to construct a timeline for assignments to prepare them for the final deliberation.

Once the assignments were in place, we deliberated on point values and due dates for each assignment. Students decided how class time would be used to facilitate their discussion of course materials and their work on the community deliberation. Within two weeks, we had constructed a shared covenant for the course.

Deliberating about the Community Forum

When creating their plan for the course, students left out the process for choosing an issue for community deliberation. As first-semester students, they realized that they knew little about what issues were of interest to the campus and local community. To determine topics of interest, they decided to start the issue-selection process by having each student solicit feedback from fifteen people on campus and in the community. One group of students contacted local businesses, nonprofit organizations, and government officials and agencies to identify community issues. Another group created comment boxes asking for anonymous suggestions and placed them around the campus and local community. From the canvassing, they created a spreadsheet that organized the issues into categories and provided data for how many times the issue was raised and by whom (faculty, staff, student, community member). They sorted through the issues in small groups and decided on the top six issues. To choose from those six, they decided that the best way forward was to write about the benefits and drawbacks of using each issue.

A full-class deliberation weighing each issue narrowed the list to two: town–gown relationships and discrimination on campus. After individually writing about the benefits and drawbacks of these issues, the deliberation ended in impasse; the class voted 8–7 for town–gown relationships, with one person absent. The next class period, they decided to deliberate in small groups and then take a vote of the small groups and another vote of the whole class to see if attitudes had shifted. Some students did shift their perspectives, but an equal number shifted to the other side. The group vote was 2–2, with a fifth group unable to come to a decision. The class vote was 8–8. The group vote demonstrated that members were willing to compromise within the small groups, which resulted in much discussion about the nature of deliberation. The students considered breaking into two groups and hosting two deliberations, but they were concerned both that the process would not work and that it would represent a failure of deliberation. They decided that they would write again and rethink the issues individually in preparation for the next class period, but they remained frustrated and disillusioned.

The next class, students agreed that they were willing to compromise to move the process forward. Everyone's willingness to compromise on which issue they should choose also left the deliberation at an impasse. They wanted to flip a coin, but I explained that deliberation meant seeing the process through. After twenty minutes of again weighing the benefits and trade-offs of each issue, one student commented that the issues were not that different, in that the crux of each was how we live together in community. As he said this, students started talking at once and then worked together to craft their deliberation issue: How can we best live together in community?

The students decided that each person should research this question and return to the next class period with a list of related topics. The topics included discrimination on campus, dorm life, town–gown relations, sexual assault, the elements of strong communities, and college governance. Students wrote an issue brief on their chosen topic (five pages, with at least seven sources). They had previously determined that this piece of writing would be subject to revisions based on peer review and my feedback.

The Community Deliberation

Three weeks prior to the deliberation, a breakdown of off-campus publicity forced the students to focus the deliberation on the campus community. The students expressed frustration with the persons who had dropped the ball, but they made the best of it by agreeing that each student would ensure the attendance of five people. One week before the forum, only two students had commitments from five people, with a total projected attendance of twenty-two. They were disappointed, and some wanted to call off the forum to avoid embarrassment. Since they had agreed to complete this assignment, I insisted that they follow through with the deliberation even if no one came.

In the end, seventy-eight people—faculty, staff, students, and even a few local community members—participated in the deliberation. In pairs and individually, students in the class facilitated conversations at ten tables with six to ten participants per table. The next class period, students created a list of topics and responses they gathered from each table and developed a plan to draft a summary of the deliberation, their final class project. They also discussed their impressions of the deliberation, resultant learning about deliberation, and collective and individual abilities.

Student and Instructor Reflections on the Course and the Process

Students shared their reflections in a survey, class discussions, and a final reflection paper. In the final class period, students reflected on the class as a whole—the process, their growth, and the changes in their perspectives. Student comments crystallized around three themes: the course, deliberation as a process, and deliberation in their lives at present and in the future.

Reactions to the course focused on how students felt out of their element in the first few weeks, but at the same time, the freedom they had gave them a sense of empowerment. In terms of my role, they appreciated the guidance I provided in holding them back from making the course requirements too punishing. (They constantly wanted to make things harder for themselves and often suggested imposing what would be unreasonable requirements even for a senior-level seminar.) In the end, they felt a great deal of achievement in crafting a solid syllabus and supporting assignments. They confidently contended that I should always use their syllabus, as no other class could possibly create a better one. Many also identified the strong sense of community that resulted from the process as a benefit.

Students were equally enthusiastic about their work on the deliberation. A few statements from the survey on the deliberation point to both their empowerment and their learning.

[The deliberation] went better than I expected. I also think many did not regret coming because it was such a cool and good learning experience. It probably also made some realize that things could be discussed without having to judge and attack each other even if each has a different view.

When I occasionally looked up to see how some of the people I had invited were doing, the group looked really involved in the conversation. Laughter from some of the tables reassured me that even though things were being taken seriously, people were still enjoying themselves. Moderators were very focused, it seemed, with several groups lingering after the groups had been informed that they were free to leave.

From this event, I learned the depth at which people can think about issues and topics. I wasn't certain how deep the conversation would transcend [sic] once in smaller groups, but the group, like the entire event, greatly exceeded expectations.

It was really successful! I have talked to some people who went to the event and they are still talking about the topics that we discussed on the day we deliberated.

The constant class deliberation required a lot from students, particularly in working together. The tensions between autonomy and community needs were particularly acute in the beginning of the class. In their reflections, they discussed how they gained a sense of their place in the community and noted that everyone respected each individual's autonomy and his or her role in the class. They spoke of the class as a model for how to live together.

Although they saw the class as a model of how communities can work together, some still questioned the ability of deliberation to solve problems on a larger scale. These students stressed that the similarities among their classmates (all college students at a particular place with similar goals) shaped their ability to form a community and to work together. Nonetheless, students believed that deliberation in communities was necessary to help members understand others' perspectives and to develop increased commitment to the community. Even those with doubts thought deliberation should be a regular practice, saying it could have a positive influence on how we live together. (Interestingly, while students tended to focus on their similarities in their class reflections, they were actually not particularly similar in their beliefs, and initially they were quite opinionated and somewhat disinclined to work with others. At graduation, one student commented, "It was amazing what we accomplished together considering how difficult we all were as individuals.")

Students also reflected on how they had used deliberative techniques in other aspects of their lives over the past semester and described the changes it had brought to their relationships. From dorm councils and student organizations to other courses, students discussed how they used their deliberative skills to help groups understand different perspectives and work together. One student described using these skills to navigate a difficult relationship with his father. He noted that when he went home for Thanksgiving break, he decided that he would really listen to what his father was saying and ask questions to understand his perspective. The experience left their relationship in a better place, and the student was looking forward to the semester break, something he had previously dreaded. Other students shared similar success stories of working in a deliberative mode with friends and roommates. The mind-set and facilitation training of the deliberative process seemed to provide tools for personal as well as community relationships.

All students shared their perspectives on how they hoped to be able to use their skills in the world. An aspiring lawyer discussed how he realized that more than two sides to an issue exist and that a really successful process would bring different perspectives together in agreement. He planned on exploring the mediation aspects of law. An aspiring teacher noted a shift in how she saw her role in the classroom from that of an authority figure to that of a facilitator, guiding students to make sound decisions. A physical therapy student examined the divides in the health profession—physicians competing against physical therapists competing against alternative medicine—and wanted to be part of a process that would change the focus to the health of the patient and away from competition for health care dollars.

Facilitating and participating in this experience with first-year students deeply challenged me, both personally and professionally. The experience helped me grow as a teacher, as the successes and challenges pushed me to rethink pedagogical choices in other courses.

This experiment was a risk. Would first-year students be able to create their own class, follow through successfully, and emerge with outcomes that met course requirements? The risks made giving up control difficult. If the class failed, it would be a very public failure—on a small campus, everyone would know about it. Also, although I realized that I would have to hold on loosely to my sample assignments, when the class threw out one of them (a paper exploring deliberation), deeming it uninteresting and of little use, it was difficult not to step in to defend it.

I managed my anxiety about control through a number of tactics and strategies. In the early deliberations, I modeled ways to ensure that everyone participated and was heard. Approaches included asking individuals to contribute to the conversation, setting up small-group and pair discussions prior to class deliberations, and giving writing assignments prior to deliberations. The result was that class discussions on the readings were more robust than in any class I had ever taught. The deep relationships students built through the deliberative nature of the course were at least partially responsible for this outcome.

I used similar strategies in approaching facilitation. At first, I assigned individual students to take responsibility for facilitating for a part of each day. Later, students managed the facilitation process themselves. Students worked together organically to facilitate the class deliberations, fluidly stepping into different roles as those roles were needed. They discussed difficult ideas, explored them in depth, and made connections with previous material. They ably utilized small-group and pair discussions and writing assignments to ensure their deliberations captured each voice and moved at a pace that did not leave anyone behind.

At one point, a classmate going through a difficult situation tested their abilities and the whole experiment. After a particularly concerning outburst, I accompanied the student to support services, and for a period of days he and I worked on projects in a different room while the class met. The class diligently worked together and proudly informed me of their progress. When the student returned to class, they worked to ensure that he was included and consciously responded to moderate his anger issues during class discussions. He was able to productively participate in the classroom and in the campus deliberation.

Throughout the course, I guided students' processes to ensure that they kept on track, that they kept assignments reasonable, and that they did not miss critical points. At times, however, I felt superfluous. One day when I was away at a conference, they decided to meet over breakfast to continue their deliberations. They reported their accomplishments with pride. Certainly, I would have exercised more control if the students had made poor decisions or moved toward practices that did not reflect a solid liberal arts education, but I was fortunate to have a group of students who took the process and their education seriously. This experience led me to ask a number of questions about my role as an educator in the learning process.

Although students created their own syllabus and managed themselves remarkably well (no late assignments all semester), the workload for me was much heavier than in a traditional class. As with leading a good class discussion, preparing for a deliberation requires more work than preparing for a lecture (contrary to conventional wisdom). The deliberations required a great deal of preparation. As students researched issues and later their issue briefs, I immersed myself in content research to ensure that they fleshed out all the relevant topic areas and ideas.

Course Outcomes

Despite limitations and concerns, the course resulted in a number of impressive outcomes, both for the students and for me as an instructor.

Empowerment

I believe that students should own their education. I use contract grading and syllabus construction in senior seminars, but this course gave students much more control over class requirements, processes, and outcomes. Students felt empowered by this control. The process also empowered me to experiment with new methods and share pedagogical decisions and evaluation with the students in an open, collaborative environment. In my other courses, I am more transparent in sharing my intentions, goals, and rationale for methods and inviting feedback from students.

Sound Decisions

Frankly, the students came up with a better syllabus and assignments than I did, reinforcing the idea of deliberation as an iterative and necessary process for generating the best ideas. They also developed a better deliberation—including the issue, the questions, and the process—than I would have if it had been left to me alone.

Faculty and Student Classroom Roles

My role as a facilitator shifted my perspective further toward deliberation and discussion as transformational educational processes in much deeper ways than other classes had done. I am a facilitator in my other courses, but I have found that I have transitioned further into that role and better encourage students to take control over their own education. Giving students more responsibility and ownership of their education changes their relationship both with their academic work and with me and teaches them important skills for lifelong learning.

One cautionary note is that it was possible for me to undertake this experience because I am a tenured full professor. The risks are much greater for those who are in tenure-track or adjunct positions, which may preclude them from adopting an entirely deliberative course model. That said, the lessons and outcomes of this course are applicable to deliberative practices adopted on a smaller scale as well.

Conclusion

Deliberation resulted in student outcomes that exceeded even my high expectations. This group of first-year students developed a sense of community and supported each other in exploring deliberation and community in particularly deep ways. They also learned that the world and people are more complex than they first imagined. Two students noted:

> A community having problems is healthy. I always thought that having problems is troublesome and annoying and that having problems solved is the best way to go. In the back of my mind I did know that a community having problems is healthy, but it just never hit me hard enough to make me really realize and think about it.
>
> I learned that deliberation is impressive. It lets individuals learn so many things at once and be engaged with everyone being a winner. I read about deliberation, but being part of a deliberation is something else.

This course demonstrates that even first-semester students are capable of deliberative processes. The real consequences attached to creating the syllabus, assignments, requirements, and due dates resulted in deep and engaging deliberations, meaningful experiences, significant individual and collective accountability, and a classroom community in which students worked together. While because of scheduling I have not been able to teach first-term seminar in the past several years, I have adopted smaller portions of this experience in other courses as an individual assignment or the last section of a course and found similar patterns of growth.

The course also demonstrates that the practice of deliberation can build strong, resilient communities that are able to make shared, reasoned decisions. The skills can be taught and communities can learn to move forward together even on contentious and difficult issues. Deliberation as a pedagogical practice teaches both civic and life skills and results in deeper engagement with the course material and with students' peers, their communities, and their education in general.

REFERENCES

Alfaro, C. (2008). Reinventing teacher education: The role of deliberative pedagogy in the K–6 classroom. In J. R. Dedrick, L. Grattan & H. Dienstfrey (Eds.), *Deliberation and the work of higher education: Innovations for the classroom, the campus, and the community* (pp. 143-64). Dayton, OH: Kettering Foundation Press.

Dedrick, J. R., Grattan, L. & Dienstfrey, H. (Eds.). (2008). *Deliberation and the work of higher education: Innovations for the classroom, the campus, and the community.* Dayton, OH: Kettering Foundation Press.

Jacobs, L. R., Cook, F., & Delli Carpini, M. X. (2009). *Talking together: Public deliberation and political participation in America.* Chicago: University of Chicago Press.

Longo, N. V. (2013). Deliberative pedagogy in the community: Connecting deliberative dialogue, community engagement, and democratic education. *Journal of Public Deliberation*, 9(2), Article 16.

National Task Force on Civic Learning and Democratic Engagement. (2012). *A crucible moment: College learning and democracy's future.* Washington, DC: Association of American Colleges and Universities.

Thomas, N. L. (Ed.). (2010). *Educating for deliberative democracy.* (New Directions for Higher Education 152.) San Francisco: Jossey-Bass.

Deliberative Pedagogy in Israeli Higher Education: A Course Curriculum for Preparing a Deliberative Student Conference

Idit Manosevitch

Broadly speaking, deliberative pedagogy is an emerging field of research and practice that seeks to identify ways by which faculty members can effectively educate college students for deliberative values, norms, and behavior (Longo, 2013). To date, most of the scholarship in the field focuses on the U.S. context (e.g., Carcasson, 2010; Dedrick, Grattan & Dienstfrey, 2008; Diaz & Gilchrist, 2010; Drury, Andre, Goddard & Wentzel, 2016). This body of scholarship is informative for thinking about deliberative pedagogy and developing best practices. But democracies around the world differ in important ways because of an array of contextual factors such as cultural norms, political makeup, history, and more (Ferree, Gamson, Gerhards & Rucht, 2002). Such differences are likely to affect our thinking about deliberative pedagogy, including its goals and expected effects. Thus, exploring different contexts is necessary for developing a deep understanding of deliberative pedagogy.

Israel offers an intriguing example of such a context. Established in 1948, Israel is one of the few nations in history that has managed to sustain democracy despite deep internal divides and ongoing physical-military threats from external sources, including neighboring countries, terror organizations, and hostile distant countries. It is a deeply divided society consisting of a Jewish majority along with a large Arab minority, with a wide array of ethnic groups and varying religious affiliations within both the Jewish and Arab populations. This delicate political and security situation gives rise to controversy about core public issues. All of these factors create a challenging context for maintaining democratic values and practices in general, and in particular for fostering deliberative practices of public debate (Shamir, 1991; Pedahzur, 2002; Horowitz & Lissak, 2012).

The challenges of sustaining a strong democracy in Israel are particularly salient among those of college age. Israeli young adults (aged eighteen to twenty-four) demonstrate relatively high levels of political interest and political participation compared with their peers in other nations (Hermann, Heller, Cohen & Bublil, 2015). However, longitudinal data reveals that since the late 1990s, Jewish Israeli youth have demonstrated a strengthening of Jewish-nationalistic spirit along with a weakening of the perceived importance of Israel's democratic-liberal foundation (Yaar &

Elkalai, 2010). Thus, the Israeli student age cohort is an important target for political socialization programs designed to promote democratic norms and values. Higher education institutions are a natural place for pursuing such programs.

With this in mind, this chapter details a deliberative pedagogy curriculum designed as a means of promoting deliberative norms and values among college students in Israel. I developed this curriculum as a semester-long process that was implemented at Netanya Academic College, a private liberal arts college, during three consecutive academic years in 2012 through 2015 (Manosevitch, 2013, 2016). This curriculum offers a political socialization process for teaching public deliberation in theory and practice, thereby strengthening deliberative norms and values among young citizens. While the focus is on Israeli society, the deliberative pedagogy curriculum is not restricted to the Israeli context but may serve as an example for higher education institutions around the world.

The Israeli Culture of Political Debate

The challenges associated with pursuing deliberative ideals have been addressed by many scholars and practitioners (e.g., Ryfe, 2002, 2005). Yet it appears that Israeli culture and norms of conversation pose an additional and perhaps unique challenge for pursuing public deliberation (Blum-Kulka, Blondheim & Hacohen, 2002). Israeli speech culture has been characterized as *dugri*—a direct and often blunt speech style (Katriel, 1986). Dugri speech is not interpreted by Israelis as impolite or rude, but rather as a legitimate cultural expression that reflects the values of courage, sincerity, authenticity, and the pursuit of Israeli solidarity—all of which are important to the ethos of the *sabra*, or native-born Jewish Israeli.

However, Katriel (1999) notes that over the years, as sabra values have eroded, dugri speech has diverged into two separate branches. One branch has softened into what is known as *firgun* speech, which ascribes greater importance to interpersonal relationships and the expression of support for others' self-esteem. The other branch has stiffened into *casach* speech, or verbal aggression that impinges on the fabric of interpersonal relationships (Katriel, 1999).

These distinctions are informative when thinking about the potential of deliberative public debate in Israel. The firgun attitude and speech style lends itself to a social process of deliberation, as it aligns with the idea of inclusive, respectful, and open public discussion where listening and speaking are equally important (Gastil, 2008). In contrast, the aggressive and rough style of casach speech undermines this potential, since it reflects a dismissal of these values; and it offers no room for listening to oppositional views or appreciating and respecting others' interests and needs. Taken together, the deep political and social divides of the country and the cultural norms of casach speech pose a deep barrier for the pursuit of deliberative conversation in Israeli society, since they come in direct contradiction with the core values of mutual respect, reciprocity, and the fundamental norm of listening (Gastil, 2008; Gutmann & Thompson, 2009).

The aforementioned nature of Israeli speech causes many Israelis to perceive public debate as aggressive and noncompliant (Manosevitch, 2016), and thus impedes their ability to believe in deliberative democracy as an applicable theory. This is a major barrier for pursuing deliberative democracy in Israel, since no group of people can be expected to pursue a goal they believe to be unrealistic. Given this context, the primary goal of a deliberative pedagogy curriculum in Israel must be transforming students' attitudes about the applicability of deliberative democracy.

To achieve this end, ordinary classroom teaching is insufficient. Theoretical ideals are easily perceived as detached. In contrast, giving students personal experience in public deliberation among their own cohort seems to be an effective way to demonstrate the applicability of deliberative ideals in Israeli society. Such an experience may be transformative, serving as testimony to the feasibility of pursuing deliberative ideals even in a culture where public debate is dominated by aggressive and noncompliant discourse. Thus, in addition to the common goals guiding deliberative pedagogy—that is, enhancing students' understanding of deliberative democracy and providing students with the skills needed for pursuing public deliberation—this chapter outlines a course curriculum that may increase the prospects of pursuing deliberative practices in challenging cultures like Israel's.

The Deliberative Conference Project: A Course Curriculum

The thirteen-week curriculum process begins with laying out the theoretical foundations of deliberative democracy and continues with a process of preparing and implementing a deliberative student-led issue conference. The main challenge throughout is finding the right balance between empowering students to take ownership of the process and ensuring that the outcome is successful in adhering to the values of public deliberation and in reaching a broader audience. Following is a detailed description of each stage in the process and the specific challenges and considerations involved. The course described here is an elective senior-level communications class that meets once a week; course components described below include both in-class and out-of-class work. (See the appendix at the end of this chapter for the course outline.)

Laying the Groundwork

Preparatory work at the outset of the course includes providing students with an understanding of the theoretical foundations of deliberative democracy, and engaging them in a deliberative process as they select and study an issue for public deliberation. Following are the details.

THEORETICAL BACKGROUND

The semester begins with theoretical background in the study of deliberative democracy. Students are assigned core readings about deliberative democratic theory, and class time is devoted to learning through discussion and in-class activities. For example, analysis of a mock deliberation where several students volunteer to participate in a ten-minute deliberation about a current issue, while the rest of the students observe and take notes. In the end, the class regroups and discusses the extent to which the mock deliberation manifested normative criteria of deliberation.

ISSUE EXPLORATION AND SELECTION

Selecting the issue to be explored is the first step in students' involvement in the deliberative conference. It marks a transition point where the course turns from an ordinary elective focused on learning theoretical material to a class project that requires everyone's engagement. It is important that students take a meaningful part in selecting an issue in order to set the stage for their active engagement in subsequent stages of the process as the course proceeds. At the same time, the instructor must guide the discussions to ensure that students choose an issue that will appeal to the broader student community and be suitable for a single deliberative event.

With this in mind, the issue-selection process begins with a home assignment in which students work in pairs to prepare an issue proposal that describes their chosen issue and why they think it's suitable for the conference. They are also asked to identify the key stakeholders and explain the core differences in their issue stance. Proposals are gathered into an "Issue Proposal Booklet," which is posted on the course website for all students to read prior to the next class. Working in pairs invites an opportunity for students to experience a preliminary sense of deliberation, where they discuss various options and prepare the write-up. The proposal booklet transmits an implicit message of empowerment, since all proposals are displayed with equal prominence for the class to select from.

PREPARATION FOR DELIBERATION

The most challenging aspect of the course is preparing the issue for deliberation. This part of the process entails three tasks:

- Students need to gain sufficient knowledge and understanding of the issue so they have the skills and confidence to serve as discussion moderators at the conference.
- Students need to experience the process of preparing the issue for deliberation to deepen their understanding of what it means to think about an issue deliberatively and the challenges this process presents.
- The process must yield background materials for distribution to conference participants and serve as a baseline for deliberation.

Accomplishing these goals is challenging. Students typically lack the knowledge and experience needed to be able to translate deliberative ideals into practice. They often fail to recognize partial or biased information and language in the materials they encounter, and they have difficulty narrowing down the key points of an issue without compromising complexity and breadth. These challenges are to be expected, and in fact justify pursuing deliberative pedagogy: if students were already proficient in public deliberation, why bother? Nonetheless, because the expected outcome of the course is a public event, overcoming these hurdles to ensure preparation quality is especially important. As the instructor I must guarantee that moderators are well informed and prepared for their role in the conference and that background materials meet acceptable standards for substance and writing quality. In sum, the course framework poses the challenge of designing a meaningful deliberative process for the students in a limited time frame and at the same time ensuring a deliberative public outcome.

Keeping these challenges in mind, I designed a three-week process involving collaborative group work, division of labor among the students, and ongoing instructor feedback and guidance. In addition, it is helpful to hire a graduate-level research assistant to prepare background materials in order to avoid overwhelming students with extra assignments.

The process begins with a preliminary class discussion and brainstorming session. Students prepare by reading about the issue in news articles or official documents that they locate. I lead a class discussion in which I raise questions to help students identify various dimensions of the information—including the different stakeholders, perspectives, and interests involved—in order to reach a comprehensive understanding. The class concludes with a list of issue components that require further investigation, and student pairs are assigned to prepare a short paper about one of these issue components.

The next lesson is devoted to an in-depth class discussion based on the students' assignments. After student pairs present their work, the class discusses the information gathered and offers feedback and further scrutiny of the issue. Based on the discussion, students revise their summaries and submit them to the research assistant, who then prepares an issue document with guidance from the instructor.

The final part of this process is a class discussion of the complete issue document. All students read the draft document prior to class, and class time is used for further examination of the different dimensions of the issue.

Moving to Implementation: Conference Planning

Once students feel comfortable with the issue, the class begins preparing for the deliberative conference. At this point several processes take place simultaneously. Class time is used primarily for moderator preparation, while outside of class the students split into teams for logistical preparations and publicity.

MODERATOR TRAINING

Moderator training consists of three consecutive lessons that combine theory with practice. Students are assigned to read a guidebook for moderators of issue forums and to familiarize themselves with the role of the moderator, including the "dos and don'ts" of the job, challenges that may arise during the discussion, and strategies to address these challenges. Class time is used to discuss all of these topics and raise any additional concerns or challenges that students raise.

An important component of these lessons is a workshop dedicated to providing students with actual moderation experience. Students divide into small groups, where each student moderates a simulated discussion for ten minutes and then reflects on the experience with the other group members. This step is crucial for building students' confidence and proficiency. If possible, it is advisable to recruit experienced moderators for the practice component. This will ensure that students in the small groups have sufficient time to practice and reflect on moderating with the guidance and feedback of an experienced moderator.

MOMENTUM BUILDING

While the curriculum focuses primarily on preparations for the substance of the conference, students also engage in activities designed to publicize the event and build momentum around campus. To this end, the class divides into teams to develop an event logo, create flyers and posters to be distributed around campus, and maintain a Facebook page with updated news, information, and discussions about the issue and the upcoming conference. Students with other campus connec-tions can promote the conference in additional ways; for example, one year students in the class who worked for the college radio station used that platform to advertise the event by preparing a brief promotional spot for broadcast during the two weeks leading up to the conference.[1]

Finally, a group of students is assigned to prepare a short video that provides an overview of the issue.[2] The video is screened during the opening plenary session of the conference. Work on the video offers another useful deliberative pedagogy lesson. As I guide students through the creation of the video, I again witness the challenge that students have in translating deliberative ideals into practice—specifically, the challenge of presenting differing views without giving priority to any of them. This type of an assignment could serve as a deliberative pedagogy tool for a communications class, with students applying their editing skills while practicing the work of creating a balanced issue overview.

The Deliberative Student Conference

The conference is scheduled to take place one week before the end of the semester to allow a final week of class for reflection in order to reinforce the lessons learned throughout the course.

STRATEGIES FOR MAXIMIZING STUDENT PARTICIPATION

We take several measures to encourage maximum student participation among students across campus. First, it is important to schedule the conference at a time when most students are on campus and available. For example, our conference usually takes place from 4:00 to 8:00 pm to allow students from both the morning program and the evening degree program to participate. Second, all School of Communication classes scheduled during the time of the conference are cancelled. Finally, students can get extra credit in other courses in exchange for their participation.

CONFERENCE STRUCTURE AND ACTIVITIES

Upon arrival, participants are directed to a registration table where they are randomly assigned to discussion groups and receive nametags and conference packets with background materials. The hour-long plenary session begins with welcoming remarks, followed by short talks by guest speak-ers who present varying perspectives about the chosen issue. The plenary ends with a screening of the student-prepared video to give participants an overview of the issue.

After the plenary session, participating students break up into discussion groups moderated by students in the course. At this point, the conference is a student event in its entirety. To allow all participants to experience the moderator role and take an active part in the process, students work in pairs, with one student serving as the lead moderator and the other serving as the assistant. This structure has been well received; the option of serving as an assistant seems to liberate the less confident students from the anxiety associated with the role and at the same time empowers them to gain de facto experience in moderation. Indeed, during my three years of experience, all of the students who participated in the process have expressed satisfaction and a sense of personal fulfillment from the moderator experience.

A twenty-minute coffee break allows participants to continue their conversations in a less formal setting, thus building on the momentum generated in the discussions. Meanwhile, moderators gather to share key points and prepare for the closing plenary session. The closing plenary begins with a slideshow about the event, a recap of interesting issues raised in the groups, and a big thanks to all participants. Prior to leaving, all participants are asked to fill out a feedback questionnaire.

POSTCONFERENCE REFLECTION

In the week following the conference, students reflect on the experience by reviewing and discussing conference feedback. A final class meeting is reserved for students to share their thoughts about the experience, thus reinforcing its lessons while offering an additional opportunity for respectful discussion.

Concluding Thoughts

The deliberative pedagogy curriculum presented here is designed to affect two target audiences of students in two different types of processes. One group is a class of seniors who participate in the semester-long process. These students learn about the theory of deliberative democracy and engage in all the steps necessary for designing a deliberative conference, from selecting the issue and preparing it for deliberation to learning about and practicing the art of moderation. The other group of students affected by the curriculum is the at-large student body of the School of Communication who is invited to participate in the deliberative event. These students learn about deliberative democracy through their experience at the event, albeit without any theoretical background about deliberative democracy.

Three years of student feedback reveals that the deliberative pedagogy experience is highly appreciated by both groups of students. Notably, the group discussions were widely perceived as the most valuable component. Not only do students give the discussions high ratings, many specifically request more time for discussion in their suggestions for improvement. Thus, it appears that despite the aggressive speech that characterizes much of Israeli discourse and that might seem to undermine the feasibility of deliberative democracy in Israel (Gitai, 2010; Katriel, 1986, 1999), Israeli students appreciate the chance to participate in public discussion that manifests norms of deliberation. Perhaps the positive spirit and excitement that surround the conference are due in part to the deep contrast between this experience and students' everyday experiences with public debate.

Feedback across the three years of the program shows that for many students, particularly those participating in the semester-long process, the experience transformed their belief in the applicability of deliberative practices to their lives. To illustrate, following are a few comments written by students at the end of the course in response to the question, "Looking back at the process as a whole, what do you take from this experience; how did it contribute to you person-ally?" One student noted learning that "it is possible to conduct a conversation—not yelling and fighting—about important issues." Two other students elaborated on the same theme:

> On a personal level, the conference gave me a little hope, by seeing that there are people who are interested in sitting and talking in a serious and respectful manner about issues that are on the public

agenda. Giving an alternative [to the existing nature of public debate], even if it is preliminary, is extremely important. To me . . . this is the primary achievement [of the conference]. (Student in the 2012–13 course)

One of the most important things that I take from this conference is the idea that you can really conduct an informed and meaningful discussion (and not just in theory). It appears that sometimes the social reality in which we live cuts our wings, and stops us from dreaming and fulfilling our dreams. No doubt this conference helped strengthen the feeling of success in realizing this type of a discussion. This is a feeling that we all share, and might eventually lead to a much better society (and I say this with not a pinch of cynicism). (Student in the 2013-14 course)

All of this suggests that despite Israel's deeply conflicted political and social context—and perhaps because of it—many young Israeli students are interested in participating in structured public deliberation. This three-year experience demonstrates the potential of pursuing deliberative pedagogy in Israeli society—and, indeed, in other societies where similar conflicts exist. Many students are both receptive to attending public discussions and appreciative of public debate that is guided by deliberative norms and values.

Finally, this study demonstrates that the impact of a single elective course may extend beyond the students enrolled in the course to the school's broader student body. Thus, deliberative pedagogy may have broad reach and effects even with the limited investment required for a single course, making its implementation more feasible than it might seem. Research is needed to examine how the integration of such a curriculum into a departmental program may serve as a political socialization process that extends beyond the classroom or even campus. In time we may learn how this type of process can provide students with tools for constructive participation in public debate while helping to promote a more deliberative culture in Israeli society and beyond.

NOTES

1. See the promo spot at https://www.youtube.com/watch?v=xryoGSQ521I.
2. The 2013 clip is available on YouTube at https://www.youtube.com/watch?v=45jBObHy8yI. An English translation is available on request.

REFERENCES

Blum-Kulka, S., Blondheim, M., & Hacohen, G. (2002). Traditions of dispute: From negotiations of talmudic texts to the arena of political discourse in the media. *Journal of Pragmatics*, 34(10), 1569–94.

Carcasson, M. (2010). Facilitating democracy: Centers and institutes of public deliberation and collaborative problem solving. *New Directions for Higher Education*, no. 152, 51–57.

Dedrick J. R., Grattan, L., & Dienstfrey, H. (Eds.). (2008). *Deliberation and the work of higher education: Innovations for the classroom, the campus, and the community*. Dayton, OH: Kettering Foundation Press.

Diaz, A., & Gilchrist, S. H. (2010). Dialogue on campus: An overview of promising practices. *Journal of Public Deliberation*, 6(1), Article 9.

APPENDIX: Course Curriculum Outline for Preparing a Deliberative Student Conference

COURSE COMPONENTS	ASSIGNMENTS AND ACTIVITIES
1. Theoretical Background (weeks 1–4)	• Discussion of core theoretical literature. • Class activities designed to help students understand key concepts. For example, analysis of a mock deliberation.
2. Issue Exploration and Selection (week 5)	• Outside of class: Student pairs research a current issue and write an issue proposal describing why it would be an appropriate topic for the deliberative conference. • In class: Students present their suggested issues to the class. The class discusses all issues and selects one for the conference.
3. Preparation for Deliberation (weeks 6–8)	• Initial class discussion and brainstorming about the issue; division of issue dimensions among students. • Groups/pairs prepare draft summaries of the various issue dimensions and submit them to the instructor for feedback. • Class discussion and adjustment of draft papers. • Students submit a final version of their issue dimension. • The instructor (with the research assistant) prepares a final issue document and presents it in class, along with an outline and schedule for the discussion. • Class discussion and adjustment of outline.
4 Moderator Training (weeks 9–11)	• Students are assigned to read through the moderator guide. • In-class moderator training workshop. • Facebook group used for team preparation.
5. Momentum Building (weeks 9–12)	• Design a conference logo, flyers, and posters. • Conference promotion via classes, campus media, etc. • Prepare a video with an overview of the issue. • Maintain a virtual presence via a Facebook page.
6. Deliberative Student Conference (week 12)	• Student moderators lead discussion groups.
7. Postconference Reflection (week 13)	• Final class meeting: sharing reflections and feedback.

Drury, S. A. M., Andre, D., Goddard, S., & Wentzel, J. (2016). Assessing deliberative pedagogy: Using a learning outcomes rubric to assess tradeoffs and tensions. *Journal of Public Deliberation*, 12(1), Article 5.

Ferree, M. M., Gamson, W. A., Gerhards, J., & Rucht, D. (2002). *Shaping abortion discourse: Democracy and the public sphere in Germany and the United States*. Cambridge: Cambridge University Press.

Gastil, J. (2008). *Political communication and deliberation*. Thousand Oaks, CA: SAGE Publications.

Gitai, Y. (2010). *The Israeli discourse: Rational versus emotional argumentation*. [In Hebrew]. Haifa: Pardes.

Gutmann, A., & Thompson, D. F. (2009). *Democracy and disagreement*. Cambridge, MA: Harvard University Press.

Hermann, T., Heller, E., Cohen, C., & Bublil, D. (2015). *The Israeli democracy index, 2015*. Jerusalem: The Israel Democracy Institute.

Horowitz, D., & Lissak, M. (1989). *Trouble in utopia: The overburdened polity of Israel*. Albany: SUNY Press.

Katriel, T. (1986). *Talking straight: Dugri speech in Israeli Sabra culture*. Cambridge: Cambridge University Press.

Katriel, T. (1999). *Milot mafte'ah: Dfusei tarbut vetikshoret be'Israel* [Keywords: Patterns of culture and communication in Israel]. Haifa: Zmora-Bitan.

Longo, N. V. (2013). Deliberative pedagogy in the community: Connecting deliberative dialogue, community engagement, and democratic education. *Journal of Public Deliberation, 9*(2), Article 16.

Manosevitch, E. (2013). The medium is the message: An Israeli experience with deliberative pedagogy. *Higher Education Exchange*, 60–68.

Manosevitch, I. (2016). From skepticism to engagement: Building deliberative faith among Israeli college students. *Connections*, 16–22.

Pedahzur, A. (2002). *The Israeli response to Jewish extremism and violence: Defending democracy.* Manchester: Manchester University Press.

Ryfe, D. M. (2002). The practice of deliberative democracy: A study of 16 deliberative organizations. *Political Communication, 19*(3), 359–77.

Ryfe, D. M. (2005). Does deliberative democracy work? *Annual Review of Political Science, 8*, 49–71.

Shamir, M. (1991). Political intolerance among masses and elites in Israel: A reevaluation of the elitist theory of democracy. *Journal of Politics, 53*(4), 1018–43.

Ya'ar, E., & Alkalai, Y. (2010). Political and social attitudes of Israeli youth: Trends over time. In, H. Tsameret-Krats'er (Ed.), *All of the Above: Identity Paradoxes of Young People in Israel* (pp. 121–217). Herzliya, Israel: Friedrich-Ebert-Stiftung.

Deliberative Pedagogy in the Communication Studies Curriculum

Sara A. Mehltretter Drury and Martín Carcasson

The field of communication studies offers many courses with inherent connections to key aspects of deliberative pedagogy—including public speaking, interpersonal communication, argumentation and advocacy, and group communication—through rhetorical and social scientific methodologies. Many communication departments now also offer classes specifically developed to focus on public deliberation or communication and democracy. More saliently, the discipline encourages the development of applying reasoned judgment to contingent public problems (Carcasson, Black & Sink, 2010).

This development is at the heart of rhetoric, the subfield upon which communication studies was founded in 1914 (Keith, 2007). At its best, rhetoric is a civic art that facilitates improved community decision-making and problem-solving. Serving in this capacity, rhetorical education should push back against the worst aspects of our political culture: divisive, partisan bickering; games that serve "gotcha" politics; and a pro/con style of advocacy designed to press one's point and block openings for opponents (Hogan, 2010). Rhetorical education should not simply equip students to be good users, consumers, and critics of rhetoric but also instill in them the charge and necessary tools to take responsibility for the quality of the communication around them. This chapter outlines how current communication studies courses connect with deliberative pedagogy while advocating for stronger connections across communication curricula.

Deliberative Pedagogy and the Rhetorical Tradition

In *The Electronic Word*, Lanham discusses the "Weak Defense" and the "Strong Defense" of rhetoric. The weak defense argues that there are "two kinds of rhetoric, good and bad" (1993, p. 55). "Weak" rhetoric is the conception of rhetoric most often accepted beyond our departments and classes. In this sense, rhetoric is a tool used to influence others and thus is typically imagined as unilateral. In itself it is considered neutral, but those who use it may do so for good or ill. This is rhetoric as Aristotle defined it: "the ability, in each particular case, to see the available means of persuasion"

(2007, p. 37). It is also the primary form of rhetoric taught in basic public speaking courses, which focus on hints, tricks, rules, ideas, and methods to make one's persuasive communication more effective—that is, on teaching students how to be more successful as users, consumers, and critics of communication. It prioritizes proving one's point and winning arguments. While advocacy is an important skill in democracy, weak rhetoric stresses winning based on an initial stance rather than looking toward a contingent, adaptive, collaborative form of political discourse with the purpose of working toward solutions.

The "strong defense" is more difficult to explain, but it transcends good/bad and considers rhetoric a critical part of an ideal system of civic discourse, therefore clearly connecting with deliberative pedagogy. The strong defense defines rhetoric as a theory or system of civic discourse. It is rhetoric from the perspective of Isocrates, Cicero, and Quintilian. Lanham elaborates that the "Strong Defense argues that, since truth comes to mankind in so many diverse and disagreeing forms, we cannot base a polity upon it. We must, instead, devise some system by which we can agree on a series of contingent operating premises" (1993, p. 156). That system, we would argue, is strong rhetoric.

This strong sense of rhetoric takes on a particularly democratic epistemology and collaborative problem-solving ethos, one that focuses on the critical interactions among experts, institutional decision makers, and the public that are so necessary to democratic decision-making. Poulakos, interpreting Isocrates's view of rhetoric, offers his own strong perspective when he notes, "the art of rhetoric was called upon to address and resolve problems of division and unity, fragmentation and consolidation, diversity and cooperation" (1997, p. 1). He explains that Isocrates strove to "disassociate rhetoric from its reputation as a tool for individual self-advancement and to associate rhetoric instead with social interactions and civil exchanges among human beings" (p. 5). Farrell addresses the strong sense of rhetoric when he defines rhetoric as "the collaborative art of addressing and guiding decision and judgment—usually public judgment about matters that cannot be decided by force or expertise" (1993, p. 1). This strong sense of rhetoric focuses on a system embedded in society that attempts to deal with life's difficult questions. It respects science and the information scientific perspectives can provide while recognizing that the role of science is to inform public questions, not to answer them.

Communication studies curricula can be opportune settings to undertake deliberative pedagogy when classes focus on this stronger sense of rhetoric. Unfortunately, they often do not. In the first half of the twentieth century, communications scholars took seriously their commitment to training citizens who could speak, reason, and judge about political matters (Cohen, 1994; Keith, 2007). Two shifts have moved these courses away from the stronger sense of rhetoric. One is the overall shift toward seeing a college education as job training, which links more directly with the weaker sense of rhetoric as a tool for individual use (Eberly, 2002). The second, as captured by Keith (2007), is the move away from the liberal arts focus of the rhetorical tradition and toward a more social science focus in communication studies.

More recently, however, many rhetorical scholars have advocated for the reinvigoration of the strong sense of rhetoric in communication studies courses (Campbell, 1996; Eberly, 2002; Hogan, 2010; McDorman & Timmerman, 2008; Zarefsky, 2004) and, as Gerard Hauser argues, "reclaim [our] birthright by reasserting the centrality of rhetoric to democratic life in the twenty-first century"

(2002, p. 13). Connecting communication courses more directly with the growing deliberative democracy movement is a particularly promising way to facilitate the reinvigoration of strong rhetoric, empowering students to improve the quality of public discourse and public problem-solving in contemporary society.

Integrating Deliberative Pedagogy into the Communication Curriculum

Aspects of deliberative pedagogy can be integrated into a variety of courses in communication studies. We focus on a few commonly taught courses that hold particular promise and offer methods and resources for refocusing these courses to include deliberative skills. We begin with public speaking, which is perhaps most important because it attracts students from all majors in many of our classes and is a core curriculum course on some campuses. We then examine three additional courses that have both broad distribution and clear connections with the concepts of deliberative pedagogy: small-group communication, argumentation, and research methods. We close by detailing how newly developing elective courses focusing on the theory and practice of public deliberation can further enrich campuses and communities.

Public Speaking

Reframed through deliberative pedagogy, the public speaking classroom has the promise to become a laboratory for training twenty-first-century citizens in how to engage and improve our political culture. In the United States, public speaking is often the only general education communication class that students across the university are likely to take, so its importance in deliberative pedagogy cannot be minimized. One advantage we have in making this case is that while our primary concern is utilizing deliberative pedagogy to equip students as citizens, the perspectives and skills of a strong sense of rhetoric are clearly applicable to the marketplace as well. Increasingly, business and industry are realizing the importance of participatory decision-making and collaborative problem-solving, as well as the need for workers to be able to make judgments based on uncertain data. While the presentation skills of the weak sense of rhetoric will likely remain dominant in these settings, the higher-order skills of the strong sense of rhetoric are gaining recognition as critical to success in many arenas.

Small changes can be made to public speaking courses to better connect them to the critical ideas of strong rhetoric. For example, the course can focus on the importance of true inquiry rather than on the act of seeking out information to support a previously established point of view. Faculty can present students with the challenge of engaging the tensions between facts, values, interests, power, and policies in a diverse democracy, as well as the additional challenges brought about by the politicization and overload of information. They can expose students to the organizations involved in the deliberative democracy movement and help them understand that an alternative to purely adversarial politics exists and has a particular set of advantages and disadvantages. They can teach students to focus on discovering the underlying tensions and tough choices inherent in public issues and to develop the skills needed to help others identify and work through those choices.

Experiments with deliberative public-speaking assignments over the past several years demonstrate that deliberative pedagogy in public speaking can work on a variety of campuses. For example, at Wabash College, a small liberal arts college in the Midwest, the public speaking course includes a "Tough Choices" speech assignment in addition to the traditional informative and persuasive speaking assignments that usually make up a public speaking syllabus. In the "Tough Choices" assignment, groups of students work collaboratively to identify a public problem and three to four options for addressing that problem, modeling a deliberative framing that works to include many points of view. After presenting the problems and its options to the class as an informative speech, each group collaboratively facilitates the rest of the class in a short deliberative exercise about the topic—creating a class environment that teaches presentation skills and the capacity for public judgment present in strong rhetoric. The "Tough Choices" speech is designed to prepare students to think about their subsequent advocacy speech assignments from a perspective that moves beyond pro/con politics and toward finding common ground across differences.[1]

Another example comes from Pennsylvania State University's Rhetoric and Civic Life course, which "offers comprehensive training in written, oral, visual, and digital communication skills necessary for the twenty-first century" (Center for Democratic Deliberation, 2013). Students in this course complete traditional public speaking and composition assignments, but also engage in deliberations on relevant contemporary topics. In this course, deliberation facilitates learning of contemporary public issues, productive talk among citizens, and how to present public arguments in different settings.

Faculty seeking to develop an assignment focusing on deliberative public speaking and reasoning have the advantage of recent public speaking textbooks that include chapters on deliberation or deliberative reasoning. These resources include Abbott, McDorman, Timmerman, and Lamberton (2015) and Hogan, Andrews, Andrews, and Williams (2014).

Group Communication, Argumentation, and Research Methods

In *Democracy as Discussion*, Keith (2007) describes a trend beginning in the 1920s and 1930s, when many communication departments shifted from a focus on debate to one of small-group discussions with a focus on training students for responsible civic participation. These deliberative, process-oriented classes unfortunately did not last long; Keith notes that the teaching of democratically rooted discussion had largely disappeared from college curricula by the 1960s. The potential for such courses to reconnect with deliberative pedagogy remains, however. Small-group classes often focus on deliberative topics such as decision-making, conflict resolution, and collaboration. Textbooks such as Gastil's *Democracy in Small Groups* (2014) focus on the deliberative potential of small-group communication.

Similar to group communication, the subfield of argumentation has clear but often unrealized potential to be a hub for deliberative pedagogy. Almost every communication department has a course in argumentation and/or debate, and many host collegiate debate teams. Too often, however, debate courses—and teams for that matter—focus solely on teaching students the competitive skills of debate within a specific context. At some schools, however, instructors are refocusing these courses to include argumentation from the strong rhetoric perspective, using debate and other communication methods as critical tools to improve public discussion and complex decision-making. At Colorado State University, for example, the argumentation course has been adapted to focus on debate and deliberation as tools for public discourse. Student groups pick a "wicked problem," or difficult public issue, and after doing extensive research and performing a traditional pro/con debate, they work together to produce a discussion guide on the issue. Following the theory of deliberative inquiry (Carcasson & Sprain, 2016), the class explicitly combines public views with expert information, as students work not to support a particular perspective on the issue, but rather to give a clear presentation of the choices available to the public, the implications of those choices, and the inherent tensions among them.

Another advanced course in communication studies that can benefit from deliberative pedagogy is research methods. As faculty work on public deliberation projects, they frequently rely on multimethodological approaches to practicing and researching public deliberation (Carcasson & Sprain, 2016). Public deliberation is an ideal case study for helping undergraduate students consider the strengths and drawbacks of different avenues of inquiry and research. As a research field in communication studies, deliberation is informed by rhetorical criticism, critical methodologies and theories, and social/scientific qualitative and quantitative methodologies. For faculty seeking to include a multimethodological case study on deliberation in their course, Anderson, Kuehl, and Drury (2017) demonstrate how different aspects of a public deliberation project in Brookings, South Dakota, lend themselves to particular research questions and appropriate methodologies. Their experience also stresses the importance of democratic processes, recognizing the interplay between a collaborative research team composed of community members and academics (Kuehl, Drury & Anderson, 2017).

Working in public deliberation settings has led some faculty to adopt the term *pracademics*, suggesting a blend of practitioner and academic theories, skills, and interests. This pracademic focus could aid a research methods classroom by encouraging programs that engage students in working on real-world problems, a characteristic of high-impact learning (Fink, 2013; Kuh, 2008; Kuh et al., 2005; Pennell & Miles, 2009; Sprain & Timpson, 2012).

Classes Focused on Deliberation

As deliberative pedagogy grows in communication studies curricula, departments should consider developing an advanced elective course focusing on the theories and practices of public deliberation to enrich student learning and community-based problem-solving. This course could be structured with equal parts theory and practice, with students entering a practical laboratory of designing, facilitating, and reporting on public deliberation activities.

In the theory segments, this course can encourage students to read the growing body of scholarship on communication and public deliberation (Gastil & Black, 2008; Gastil, 2014; Kock & Villadsen, 2012; McDorman & Timmerman, 2008; Nabatchi, Gastil, Leighninger & Weiksner, 2012). Students can also learn from different real-world examples of public deliberation—for example, National Issues Forums, the Participatory Budgeting Project, and Citizens Initiative Review.[2] Faculty can incorporate a variety of activities into the practicum: early on, students may practice facilitation and reporting; later in the course, they may research and design public deliberation projects on campus and/or in the community.

A deliberation course offers many opportunities to stress the valuable skill of facilitation. Instructors can teach students how to help participants in a small-group discussion address differences head-on rather than agreeing to disagree, work through the trade-offs and tensions of public decision-making, and move toward reasoned judgment. On campus, public deliberation returns agency to undergraduate students, enabling them to frame and discuss campus, local, state, national, and international issues relevant to their lives. In the community, public deliberation teaches students about working collaboratively with diverse stakeholders. Instructors can also encourage reflection assignments that ask students to consider how engaging in collective meaning-making, deliberation, and judgment has altered their perspectives.

Our experiences in public deliberation courses on our own campuses verify the potential to teach students new ways of thinking about public issues. More than that, these courses can change students' approach to public life, including their impact on their local communities, both on and off campus. At Wabash College, students from an upper-level deliberation course have facilitated small-group deliberations on campus about issues of broad relevance, such as the quality of campus life and race in U.S. society; they have even created discipline-specific deliberations for students in other classes, such as a deliberation on genetically modified organisms for students in introductory biochemistry. At Colorado State University, the work of the Center for Public Deliberation is supported by a specialized Applied Deliberative Techniques course that teaches students deliberative facilitation skills. Students take on the role of passionate impartial facilitators, remaining committed to the process but neutral facilitators; they work on numerous local community projects, testing and refining both deliberative theory and practice (Carcasson, 2017). These opportunities for deliberation place students in leadership roles on campus and in the community, helping to name and frame relevant issues from a grassroots perspective and then work through those issues.

Conclusion

Democracy requires a high quality of communication, and we are falling significantly short. Communication scholars are particularly implicated in the issue, and we have an obligation to address it. Deliberative pedagogy offers clear opportunities to make an impact in our courses and across the entire curriculum. Many factors push our politics to be overly adversarial, but our field can work as a critical counter to such impulses. Our democracy needs a robust dose of the strong sense of rhetoric, one that fosters deliberation, as well as people dedicated to improving the quality of our public discourse rather than simply advancing their point of view. That task can begin with our public speaking courses and our communication studies professorate.

NOTES

1. David Timmerman, Todd McDorman, and Jennifer Abbott designed the "Tough Choices" speech
   assignment in 2007–8, drawing on the inspiration of the many scholars who gathered for the 2007

Brigance Colloquy on Public Speaking as a Liberal Art.

2. See https://www.nifi.org/, http://www.participatorybudgeting.org/, and http://healthydemocracy.org/ citizens-initiative-review/, respectively, for information on these initiatives.

REFERENCES

Abbott, J. Y., McDorman, T. F., Timmerman, D. M., & Lamberton, L. J. (2015). *Public speaking and democratic participation: Speech, deliberation, and analysis in the civic realm.* New York: Oxford University Press.

Anderson, J., Kuehl, R., & Drury, S. A. M. (2017). Blending qualitative, quantitative, and rhetorical methods to engage citizens in public deliberation to improve workplace breastfeeding support. *Sage Research Methods Cases.* doi:10.4135/9781473953796.

Aristotle. (2007). *On rhetoric: A theory of civil discourse.* 2nd ed. (G. Kennedy, Trans.). New York: Oxford University Press.

Campbell, J. A. (1996). Oratory, democracy, and the classroom. In R. Soder (Ed.), *Democracy, education, and the schools* (pp. 211–43). San Francisco: Jossey-Bass.

Carcasson, M. (2017). Re-engaging students in our democracy: Lessons from the CSU Center for Public Deliberation and its student associate program. In I. Marin & R. Minor (Eds.), *Beyond politics as usual: Paths for engaging college students in politics* (pp. 171–87). Dayton, OH: Kettering Foundation Press.

Carcasson, M., Black, L. W., & Sink, E. S. (2010). Communication studies and deliberative democracy: Current contributions and future possibilities. *Journal of Public Deliberation*, 6(1), Article 8.

Carcasson, M. & Sprain, L. (2016). Beyond problem solving: Reconceptualizing the work of public deliberation as deliberative inquiry. *Communication Theory*, 26(1), 41–63.

Center for Democratic Deliberation. (2013). *Rhetoric and civic life.* University Park: Pennsylvania State University.

Cohen, H. (1994). *The history of speech communication: The emergence of a discipline, 1914–1945.* Washington, DC: National Communication Association.

Eberly, R. A. (2002). Rhetoric and the anti-logos doughball: Teaching deliberating bodies the practices of participatory democracy. *Rhetoric & Public Affairs*, 5(2), 287–300.

Farrell, T. B. (1993). *Norms of rhetorical culture.* New Haven, CT: Yale University Press.

Fink, L. D. (2013). *Creating significant learning experiences: An integrated approach to designing college courses.* San Francisco: Jossey-Bass.

Gastil, J. (2014). *Democracy in small groups: Participation, decision making, and communication* (2nd ed.). State College, PA: Efficacy Press.

Gastil, J., & Black, L. W. (2008). Public deliberation as the organizing principle of political communication research. *Journal of Public Deliberation*, 4(1), Article 3.

Hauser, G. A. (2002). Rhetorical democracy and civic engagement. In G. A. Hauser & A. Grim (Eds.), *Rhetorical democracy: Discursive practices of civic engagement* (pp. 1–14). Mahwah, NJ: Lawrence Erlbaum Associates.

Hogan, J. M. (2010). Public address and the revival of American civic culture. In S. J. Parry-Giles & J. M. Hogan (Eds.), *The handbook of rhetoric and public address* (pp. 422–47). Malden, MA: Blackwell Publishing.

Hogan, J. M., Andrews, P. H., Andrews, J. R., & Williams, G. (2014). *Public speaking and civic engagement* (3rd ed.). Boston: Allyn & Bacon.

Keith, W. M. (2007). *Democracy as discussion: Civic education and the American forum movement*. Lanham, MD: Lexington Books.

Kock, C., & Villadsen, L. S. (Eds.). (2012). *Rhetorical citizenship and public deliberation*. University Park: Penn State University Press.

Kuehl, R. A., Drury, S. A. M., & Anderson, J. (2015). Civic engagement and public health issues: Community support for breastfeeding through rhetoric and health communication collaborations. *Communication Quarterly*, 63, 510–15.

Kuh, G. D. (2008). *High-impact educational practices: What they are, who has access to them, and why they matter*. Washington, DC: Association of American Colleges and Universities.

Kuh, G. D., Kinzie, J., Schuh, J. H., Whitt, E. J., & Associates. (2005). *Student success in college: Creating conditions that matter*. San Francisco: Jossey-Bass.

Lanham, R. A. (1993). *The electronic word: Democracy, technology, and the arts*. Chicago: University of Chicago Press.

McDorman, T. F., & Timmerman, D. M. (Eds.). (2008). *Rhetoric and democracy: Pedagogical and political practices*. East Lansing: Michigan State University Press.

Nabatchi, T., Gastil, J., Leighninger, M., & Weiksner, G. M. (Eds.). (2012). *Democracy in motion: Evaluating the practice and impact of deliberative civic engagement*. New York: Oxford University Press.

Pennell, M., & Miles, L. (2009). "It actually made me think": Problem-based learning in the business communications classroom. *Business Communication Quarterly*, 72, 377–94.

Poulakos, T. (1997). *Speaking for the polis: Isocrates' rhetorical education*. Columbia: University of South Carolina Press.

Sprain, L., & Timpson, W. M. (2012). Pedagogy for sustainability science: Case-based approaches for interdisciplinary instruction. *Environmental Communication*, 6(4), 532–50.

Zarefsky, D. (2004). Institutional and social goals for rhetoric. *Rhetoric Society Quarterly*, 34(3), 27–38.

Deliberative Pedagogy in Undergraduate Science Courses

Sara A. Mehltretter Drury

Today's world presents a number of problems that require collaboration between experts, government, business, and the public. These "wicked" problems—or difficult public challenges that have no single technical solution (Rittel & Webber, 1973)—are characterized by competing interests, conflicting values, scientific information that sometimes clashes with public experiences and/or desires, and a need for broad support to manage them effectively. As such, they are better addressed when multiple stakeholders are included in the process, but bringing together the experiences of scientists and citizens requires a different sort of process—namely, deliberation.

Recent evidence suggests that scientific policy deliberations aid the process of finding and implementing approaches to some of our most challenging public problems (Abelson et al., 2003; Bäckstrand, 2003; Baum, Jacobson & Goold, 2009; Dietz, 2013; Guston, 2014; Sprain & Timpson, 2012). To encourage effective public deliberation about wicked problems involving science concepts or phenomena, we need to provide scientists, government and business leaders, and citizens with better training in how to have productive conversations. Science courses offer a promising avenue for such training. This chapter examines examples of deliberation activities integrated into undergraduate biology and chemistry science courses to demonstrate the benefits of interdisciplinary deliberative pedagogy.

My academic training is in communication studies, specifically in rhetoric. Collaborating with science faculty at Wabash College, a small liberal arts college for men in the Midwestern United States, we created deliberation modules designed to encourage undergraduates with limited scientific training to apply scientific knowledge to questions in public policy. Specifically, we integrated deliberations on climate change into an introductory biology course and on energy policy into an introductory chemistry course. Our experiences suggest that student views of wicked problems and ways to approach those problems became more participatory and collaborative as a result of these deliberations. To maximize the potential of deliberation in the science curriculum, this chapter introduces deliberation activities, offers guidance for selecting a topic and implementing the deliberation activity, and reflects on opportunities for future innovation in deliberative pedagogy in the sciences.

Introducing Deliberation into Science Classrooms

Deliberation in the classroom, or deliberative learning (McDevitt & Kiousis, 2006), implements the principles of deliberative democracy in a classroom environment. This approach empha-sizes communication skills, as it requires participating in a rigorous discussion of issues—the praxis, or practice, of rhetoric—while moving toward decision-making. It encourages students to move beyond memorization and even understanding of content and prompts them to critically evaluate and engage pressing public issues for themselves, thus encouraging the development of deliberative, democratic skills (Cole, 2013; Eberly, 2000). As a classroom exercise, deliberation implements many of the "guidelines for best practice in STEM communications training" identified by Joana Silva and Karen Bultitude: it is "practical and interactive," with importance placed on an "interactive style," "discussions," and "role play" (2009, p. 11). I would add that through this role play in the classroom, deliberation connects scientific learning to the discussion of real-life problems in the community.

The deliberation activities we introduced took place in three offerings of general education courses designed for non–science majors from 2013 to 2014. To prepare students with limited science backgrounds to deliberate scientific issues, the deliberation activity was integrated into classroom lessons on related topics. In the introductory biology course, this activity took the form of a two-day (fifty-minute class) deliberation on climate change during a module on biology and human environmental impacts. In the introductory chemistry class, it consisted of a three-day (fifty-minute class) activity beginning with a one-day lecture on the chemical aspects of energy in the United States and then moving into a two-day deliberation activity.

Before each deliberation, the science faculty created interactive lectures that would expose students to scientific knowledge and findings in order to facilitate better consideration of scientific wicked problems. At the same time, I worked with student research assistants who were trained in deliberation and facilitation to prepare materials from Public Agenda, a nonprofit organization that creates deliberative framing guides for national issues.

Biology: Climate Change Deliberation

The biology deliberation activity used a framing guide from Public Agenda titled *Is It Getting Warm in Here? Clarifying the Climate Change Debate* (Bittle & Johnson, 2011). This resource guides participants through a discussion of climate change, including three approaches to addressing the issue. The framing guide first introduces the problem, reviewing relevant facts such as "How We Got Here" and "What Could Happen," with discussions of the potential effects of coastal flooding, extreme weather, droughts, and the economic and social instability that could result from climate change. It then proposes three ways of tackling the issue: reducing greenhouse gas emissions, adapting to the effects of global warming, and unleashing the power of the free market to solve the problems of climate change. These choices reflect a deliberative framing for wicked problems, offering sample actions, arguments for each approach (benefits), and arguments against each approach (trade-offs).

The Bittle & Johnson (2011) framing guide was licensed through a Creative Commons open-sourcing method, which allows the guide to be adapted for noncommercial purposes. Since the exercise included two lectures about climate change, I worked with the biology faculty members to include material in the deliberation guide with content relevant to the course lectures and to our particular state location. Thus, while we retained the basic deliberative format, including the sample actions, benefits, and trade-offs, the guide also reinforced course-specific material and sought to remind students of local examples relevant to the deliberation.

Student participants received a brief overview of the deliberative activity and a copy of the framing guide the week before the two climate change lectures. After attending the lectures, students took an online survey with questions about their views on global climate change and public problem-solving. On the day of the deliberation, trained facilitators led small groups of six to eight students through two fifty-minute deliberation sessions on the topic. Student participants then completed an online postdeliberation survey asking a series of questions about their views on global climate change and their impressions of the deliberation experience.

To encourage a higher-quality deliberation experience, I recruited trained student facilitators to lead participants through the deliberative conversations using the modified framing guide. The facilitators had completed a training workshop or taken a course in deliberation and facilitation. In both cases, their training emphasized deliberative public problem-solving, the idea of wicked (as opposed to tame) public problems, and facilitation strategies outlined in Kaner's (2007) *Facilitator's Guide to Participatory Decision-Making*, which emphasizes how to encourage a small group to examine issues from a variety of perspectives—the "groan zone" of problem-solving.

Chemistry: Energy Policy Deliberation

The chemistry deliberation also used a Public Agenda issue framing guide, this one focusing on energy policy. *A Citizen's Solution Guide: Energy* (Public Agenda, 2012) documents the contemporary constraints of energy policy in the United States and across the globe, including aspects of economics, energy security, and environmental impact. The guide also gives details about the accessibility, benefits, and concerns of using petroleum, coal, natural gas, nuclear, and renewable energy. Prior to the deliberation, a chemistry faculty member gave a fifty-minute lecture that documented how different forms of energy produce power and at what cost. Once again, students took part in pre- and postdeliberation surveys to test knowledge of chemistry and attitudes toward the topic and toward deliberative civic engagement. The deliberation itself spanned two class periods.

Aside from the topic change, there were three significant differences between the biology and chemistry deliberations. First, the chemistry class used a combination of faculty and student facilitators (all of whom received deliberation training), rather than only students. Second, we created a separate facilitator's guide for the energy deliberation that listed questions for each suggested approach to addressing the issue (Drury et al., 2016). Student facilitators worked closely with the chemistry faculty to incorporate scientific content covered in class by explicitly asking students to identify relevant scientific material and encouraging deliberation on the values, tensions, and possible actions associated with each approach. Based on the first two offerings of deliberation in biology, our goal for the chemistry deliberation was to create a facilitators' guide that would increase students' knowledge and confidence in talking about scientific issues, and therefore result in a more consistent and positive student experience. Finally, at the end of the energy deliberation, the communication faculty member led the class through a discussion of short-term and long-term public policy solutions to energy concerns.

The first difference stemmed from constraints in finding available, trained student facilitators, which necessitated using faculty facilitators. The second and third differences, however, were positive changes that helped make the deliberation process more beneficial for students. The facilitator's guide ensured that the conversations did not focus only on public policy capacities but also encouraged multistakeholder responses. Asking students to come to judgment about public policy, rather than just discuss what they felt should be done about the problem, gave the students a more significant target to deliberate toward.

Possibilities for Deliberations in Science Courses

The deliberations in biology and chemistry produced important learning opportunities for students while surfacing several challenges in the process. To understand the impact of the science deliberation activities, I used both classroom observation and surveys of student participants. This was a limited pilot study of deliberation in science courses on a single campus, and the classroom setting of the conversation meant that students had limited direct engagement with public policy and institutional change. In other words, the deliberations were unlikely to produce direct results in society. However, the activities were valuable in providing students with the skills to participate in future deliberations on wicked problems involving science issues. The results we achieved suggest future possibilities for encouraging deliberations in undergraduate science courses, as well as suggestions for implementing deliberations successfully.

First, the deliberations brought about a gain in student learning around the role of scientific knowledge in public policy discussions. Students in the deliberations were encouraged to explore scientific facts relevant to the problem and at the same time recognize that the problem has public dimensions outside of scientific expertise. In the predeliberation survey for the biology class, when asked to describe the climate change problem, students frequently pointed to specific content details, such as "over-reliance on fossil fuels, which creates a surplus of CO_2 in the earth's atmosphere." The deliberation process pushed students to consider the perspective of multiple stakeholders and to begin seeing the problem as one that uses scientific evidence but still necessitates public involvement to address the issue. Responses in postdeliberation surveys from both biology and chemistry used a large amount of inclusive language, discussing "our" problem or the importance of public involvement. When students were asked to discuss what they learned from the deliberation, many cited facts that were brought into the conversation by other students (rather than material from the guide), which represents a reinforcement of classroom teaching.

Second, as students began to see facts related to public choices about climate change and energy policy, the deliberation activities encouraged moving from the scientific-technical realm to discussion in the public sphere, which takes into account public values as well as knowledge

(Goodnight, 1982). At the close of the deliberations, students had considered and identified multiple agents as responsible for acting to address climate change or energy policy. For example, one student wrote in the postdeliberation survey that the biggest challenge was "*involving* more of the people by informing them of the facts and *making them able to help in creating a solution to the problem*" (emphasis added). In the chemistry course, when asked what the first step was in addressing energy problems and why that step was the most important, many students stressed the need for more public education, awareness, and involvement. The first step, one student wrote, was "Having individuals care about it, and making it possible for all individuals to change it. It cannot be only a wealthy person fix." While classroom deliberations about policy positions might not produce immediate political change, postsurveys from both the biology and the chemistry classes demonstrate that such deliberations can help students see scientific issues as public problems that need large-scale political involvement to promote positive change, rather than as something scientists or government will work on alone.

Furthermore, participating in the deliberation activity prompted students to consider the issue from multiple perspectives. In both courses, student participants reflected on the deliberative process, noting that their group focused on "three different options" for addressing the issue, discussed "problem solving from the various angles," encountered "different proposals out there to actually go about fixing the problem," and worked to create "a hybrid" from the three approaches in the discussion guide. Students also related the different topics they discussed; while these topics follow the framing guide's three approaches, student descriptions indicated that in leading student participants through the approaches, the facilitators helped them think about the problem from different, previously unconsidered, perspectives. Responses to the postsurvey demonstrated that students had not only explored but also understood and valued the perspectives of multiple stakeholders. For example, one student commented on the "idea of government vs. citizens" and brought up concerns about regulation and liberty, and another reported that any solution would have to involve "government intervention, business pro activism, and individual accountability."

As previously mentioned, the case study here reflects experiences at a single campus with resources for encouraging public deliberation work. The availability of trained student facilitators improved the deliberation experience, and my own experiences with the Kettering Foundation provided numerous resources for planning and implementing the deliberations. Lack of experience should not intimidate faculty wishing to undertake deliberation in science courses, as numerous resources are available for them to use and adapt to a variety of course and campus settings. Conversation guides from Public Agenda and the National Issues Forums Institute provide a coherent frame for undertaking deliberation about scientific policy issues, including guides addressing topics such as sustainability, land use, energy, climate change, biotechnology and food, and health care.[1] For those wishing to explore creating their own framing, the Kettering Foundation's (2011) *Naming and Framing Difficult Issues to Make Sound Decisions*, available online, can be a useful guide for instructors seeking to create or adapt deliberative framing guides into their curriculum. Pre- and postsurvey questions can be adapted to course and department goals while including generally applicable questions about scientific knowledge, attitudes on public capacity and engagement, and students' experiences with the deliberation.

Deliberation is a growing area of practice and scholarly interest, and a variety of resources now exist for scholars and faculty wishing to use this sort of activity in their science courses. Deliberation inserts civic inquiry directly into curriculums of study—part of what the seminal report *A Crucible Moment: College Learning and Democracy's Future* identifies as necessary for moving civic learning from the "margins to the core" of higher education (National Task Force on Civic Learning and Democratic Engagement, 2012, pp. 52–53). With deliberation's past results and future potential for teaching citizens the communication habits and practices of citizenship (Pincock, 2012), incorporating deliberations into science represents a tremendous opportunity for educators to train students to work collaboratively and come up with new approaches, now and in the future, to address scientific wicked problems facing our world.

NOTES

An earlier version of this essay and its findings was published as Sara A. Mehltretter Drury, "Deliberation as Communication Instruction: A Study of Climate Change Deliberations in an Introductory Biology Course," *Journal on Excellence in College Teaching* 26, no. 4 (2015): 51–72.

1. See http://www.publicagenda.org and https://www.nifi.org for online resources from these organizations.

REFERENCES

Abelson, J., Eyles, J., McLeod, C. B., Collins, P., McMullan, C., & Forest, P.-G. (2003). Does deliberation make a difference? Results from a citizens panel study of health goals priority setting. *Health Policy*, 66(1), 95–106.

Bäckstrand, K. (2003). Civic science for sustainability: Reframing the role of experts, policy-makers and citizens in environmental governance. *Global Environmental Politics*, 3(4), 24–41.

Baum, N. M., Jacobson, P. D., & Goold, S. D. (2009). "Listen to the people": Public deliberation about social distancing measures in a pandemic. *American Journal of Bioethics*, 9(11), 4–14.

Bittle, S., & Johnson, J. (2011). *Is it getting warm in here? Clarifying the climate change debate*. New York: Public Agenda.

Cole, H. J. (2013). Teaching, practicing, and performing deliberative democracy in the classroom. *Journal of Public Deliberation*, 9(2), Article 10.

Dietz, T. (2013). Bringing values and deliberation to science communication. *Proceedings of the National Academy of Sciences of the United States of America*, 110(3), 14081–87.

Drury, S. A. M., Stucker, K., Douglas, A., Rush, R., Novak, W. R. P., Stucker, K., & Wysocki, L. (2016). Using a deliberation of energy policy as an educational tool in a nonmajors chemistry course. *Journal of Chemical Education* 93(11), 1879–1885.

Eberly, R. A. (2000). *Citizen critics: Literary public spheres*. Urbana: University of Illinois Press.

Goodnight, G. T. (1982). The personal, technical, and public spheres of argument: A speculative inquiry into the art of deliberation. *Journal of the American Forensic Association*, 18, 214–27.

Guston, D. H. (2014). Building the capacity for public engagement with science in the United States. *Public*

Understanding of Science, 23(1), 53–59.

Kaner, S. (2007). *Facilitator's guide to participatory decision-making*. San Francisco: Jossey-Bass.

Kettering Foundation. (2011). *Naming and framing difficult issues to make sound decisions*. Dayton, OH: Kettering Foundation.

McDevitt, M., & Kiousis, S. (2006). Deliberative learning: An evaluative approach to interactive civic education. *Communication Education*, 55(3), 247–64.

National Task Force on Civic Learning and Democratic Engagement. (2012). *A crucible moment: College learning and democracy's future*. Washington, DC: Association of American Colleges and Universities.

Pincock, H. (2012). Does deliberation make better citizens? In T. Nabatchi, J. Gastil, M. Leighninger & G. M. Weiksner (Eds.), *Democracy in motion: Evaluating the practice and impact of deliberative civic engagement* (pp. 135–62). New York: Oxford University Press.

Public Agenda. (2012). *A citizen's solution guide: Energy*. New York: Public Agenda.

Rittel, H. W. J., & Webber, M. M. (1973). Dilemmas in a general theory of planning. *Policy Sciences*, 4(2), 155–69.

Silva, J., & Bultitude, K. (2009). Best practice in communications training for public engagement with science, technology, engineering and mathematics. *Journal of Science Communication*, 8(2), 1–13.

Sprain, L., & Timpson, W. M. (2012). Pedagogy for sustainability science: Case-based approaches for interdisciplinary instruction. *Environmental Communication*, 6(4), 532–50.

PART 3

Comparative, Gender, and Cross-Cultural Deliberative Pedagogy Practice

Deliberative Pedagogy's Feminist Potential: Teaching Our Students to Cultivate a More Inclusive Public Sphere

J. Cherie Strachan

A liberal arts education is intended to cultivate a capacity for reasoned deliberation, critical thinking, and good judgment. While these goals for student development have long been associated with Americans' understanding of an appropriate college education (Hartley, 2011), the task of achieving such outcomes has become increasingly difficult over the past several decades. Professors at U.S. institutions are now tasked not simply with honing these skills, but often with introducing them to students. This shift can be tracked to declining opportunities for people to engage in reasoned deliberation in the public sphere—a loss that has had dramatic consequences for the youngest generations of Americans, who are most likely to have come of age without participating in such deliberative activities. The current and upcoming classes of U.S. college students are far less likely to have experienced deliberation as an integral component of their political socialization, as the vibrant infrastructure of voluntary associations that once provided such experiences no longer exists (Putnam, 2000; Skocpol, 2003). In many ways, instructors at U.S. institutions now face the same task as our colleagues working in countries that have historically lacked a well-developed civil society: acquainting students with the basic features of deliberation and collective decision-making. As such, it has become necessary to teach our students these highly valued skills through formal civic education experiences that are explicitly designed to address the weakening of our public sphere.

As professors attempt to remedy the most recent shortcomings of our public sphere, it is important that our pedagogy not reinforce its most egregious, long-standing flaws. For many decades, patriarchal prejudices against women and members of marginalized demographic groups were used to justify restricting full and equal participation in all aspects of public life, and these prejudices still affect the ability to persuade others in deliberative settings (Benhabib, 1996; Sanders, 1997; Young, 2000). If academics intend to play a proactive role in cultivating civic leaders who will rebuild deliberative civil society, we must take care to do so in a way that avoids reintroducing these same biases back into our public sphere. While this chapter focuses on the experiences of women in Western culture, its recommendations are applicable to many other cultures as well, since patriarchal societies spread across the world thousands of years ago, and women's exclusion from the public sphere continues to cut across many current cultures and societies. Attention to these experiences in a carefully designed deliberative pedagogy provides an opportunity to bring women and other underrepresented voices into the public sphere in a way that will benefit all of society.

Insight from Deliberative Democracy Scholars

While mainstream political scientists typically assess formal, institutionalized processes (such as voting rights, electoral integrity, and majority rule) to determine the health of a democracy, deliberative democracy scholars, dismayed by the decline in opportunities for public deliberation, emphasize the role public deliberation plays in authentic, democratic governance. This definition of democracy shifts attention to the type of interactions that must take place among citizens and public officials in order to facilitate reasoned decision-making and informed judgment. These types of interactions, theorists argue, help move political participation beyond an adversarial (and likely ill-informed) process that pits citizens against one another and toward an exchange characterized by inclusiveness, mutual respect, and reason giving.

Several early theorists in this subfield of deliberative democracy attempted to identify and explain all of the essential elements of authentic deliberation required for a democratic society to claim legitimacy. While criteria vary somewhat from scholar to scholar, most would likely acknowledge that deliberation includes discursive efforts to identify solutions for shared, public problems in a process characterized by open, inclusive exchanges. Further, the participants in this process should engage in reason giving, consider one another's perspectives, and treat each other as equals (Strachan, 2016). Deliberative pedagogy builds on this work, turning to formal instruction rather than natural political socialization, to prepare students for participation in democracy's underpinning deliberative processes.

Insight from Radical Feminism

While mainstream feminism is often associated with concern for women's status within society as it currently exists, radical feminism recognizes that patriarchal cultures succeed in oppressing women because they are organized around the principles of domination and control. Hence the same rigid social hierarchies that evolved to create submissive roles for women are the root cause of all forms of oppression, including those based on race, class, ethnicity, sexual orientation, ability, and religion (Johnson, 2014). At its core, radical feminism requires overturning oppressive organizing structures that are the antithesis of deliberation. As Johnson states: "Whether we begin with race or gender or disability status or class, if we name the problem correctly, we will wind up going in the same direction" (2014, p. 244).

Biases about which types of people are most qualified to resolve public problems accompany students into the classroom. We must find a way to make deliberative pedagogy effective for all of our students, not simply for those most likely to be comfortable and well received in deliberative settings. Work in the tradition of deliberative democracy and radical feminism can be combined with that of the scholarship of teaching and learning to assess our efforts and to identify best practices for deliberative pedagogy that help to build inclusive, rather than exclusive, definitions of citizenship and community.

Patriarchy and Women's Participation in the Public Sphere

Within traditional patriarchy in America's colonial and founding era, the law of coverture eclipsed the possibility of women's unchaperoned presence, let alone participation, in the public sphere. Women had no legal identity aside from their position within a household headed by a male relative. As such, they were officially represented in all public proceedings—economic, political, civic, and religious—by a male head of household. Women were excluded from participation in the social contract that the American founders believed shaped their relationship with their newly established government—whereby men are born free with inalienable rights and must voluntarily agree to be governed—for two reasons: first, because women were deemed inherently unqualified for such participation, and second, because most thought such participation would undermine society's stability. These conclusions were based on assumptions about women's natural ability and character. Women's inability to engage in reason and their overly passionate natures justified somber male guidance, while their physical weakness necessitated male provision and protection (Kann, 1999).

Beyond their inability to meet the criteria for citizenship, women were also associated with an uncontrollable craving for all forms of self-gratification, so much so that their participation in the public sphere would result in chaos and corruption. Women who attempted to be active in public life were not only considered to be reaching beyond their limited abilities but perceived as a threat that could undermine society's fragile stability with their demands. Such unfortunate outcomes could be avoided if women were guided into their natural role as submissive helpmates within the domestic sphere, where they would focus on fulfilling the needs of their families rather than their own grasping ambitions. Indeed, patriarchy defines masculinity, in large part, as the ability to control women, with men responsible for ensuring that their wives and daughters conform to these gender-appropriate roles (Kann, 1999).

Despite the success of the first two waves of the U.S. women's movement, which relied on social protest to gain the vote in 1920 and to gain more complete access to education, the workplace, and politics in the 1960s, women's ability to participate fully in deliberation—in public life, on college campuses, and in our classrooms—is still affected by the legacies of this patriarchal system. The following sections explore some of the more damaging legacies that deliberative democratic instruction can both explore and help eliminate.

Women's Consent, Benevolent Sexism, and (Lack of) Gender Consciousness

Throughout much of American history, women's consent to playing a limited role in society has been used to justify confining women to the domestic sphere. But social constructionists are quick to point out that individuals are quite capable of embracing identities that relegate people like themselves to an inferior position in society (Berger & Luckman, 1966). The benevolent nature of many of the prescriptive stereotypes used to constrain women has made this tendency a particularly troublesome gender trap for women. The ideal "communal female" is supportive, other-oriented, and nurturing—qualities that many find difficult to argue against. More tellingly, this ideal woman serves as a resource for others' aspirations rather than pursuing her own ambitions. Even now, many people (both men and women) expect women to exemplify these idealized traits, which allows them to claim that they love and admire (appropriately behaved) women while harshly sanctioning those who reject traditional gender roles (Glick & Fiske, 2001).

To the extent that women themselves co-opt their own empowerment by internalizing such identities, it will be difficult for them to advocate for their own best interests in the public sphere (Becker & Wright, 2011). Some feminist scholars fear this pattern prevents women from even identifying, let alone voicing, their legitimate political concerns, in part because women are socialized to be more polite than men (Sapiro, 1983; Holmes, 1995; Lakoff, 1990, 1975). According to Robin Lakoff, in her seminal work on gender and politeness, "Little girls were indeed taught to talk like little ladies, in that their speech is in many ways more polite than that of boys or men, and the reason for this is that politeness involves an absence of strong statement, and women's speech is devised to prevent the expression of strong statements" (1975, p. 51). Of course, not all women modify their speech accordingly, but as benevolent sexism predicts, those who do not are often disliked and are subject to social sanction as a result.

Not only do many women avoid making strong arguments themselves, they are more prone than others to prioritize social harmony over political participation, often choosing to avoid face-to-face conflict and political disagreement within their interpersonal networks altogether (Mutz, 2006). Given that people discussing public affairs will almost inevitably disagree with one another at some point over some issues, perhaps it should not be surprising that women—and to a lesser degree, minorities—are also far less likely than white men to participate in political discourse that requires them to be persuasive. Even controlling for experiences that bolster political and social capital fails to eliminate these demographic patterns completely (Jacobs, Cook & Delli Carpini, 2009).

One final piece of evidence that many women continue to embrace the role of the communal female is their lack of group, or gender, consciousness. Unlike members of other demographic groups that have been the subject of discrimination (including the elderly as well as ethnic/racial and religious minorities), women are often far less likely to notice unfair treatment or to attribute it to their shared gender status. Hence they are less apt to mobilize in order to air these grievances in the public sphere (Gurin, 1985).

In short, one legacy of patriarchy in Western culture is that even now, women quite often do not see themselves as the type of people who should participate fully in the public sphere, especially when that participation requires them to address contested political views or to help resolve divisive issues in their communities (Polletta & Chen, 2013). Internalizing the traditional, communal feminine roles advocated by benevolent sexism further undermines women's ability to see themselves as political actors.

One approach to countering this particular remnant of patriarchy is to combine deliberative pedagogy with diversity education intended to bolster the political identities and gender consciousness of female students. These efforts might include diversity programming that focuses on the accomplishments of the two waves of the women's movement, as well as on the ways contemporary community and political issues specifically affect women and other marginalized groups. This approach can help to transform female students into political actors by developing their ability to recognize and voice concerns in a way that has heretofore been fully available only to white men of means in our society.

A second approach to this particular remnant of patriarchy is to make women as comfortable as possible in the public sphere by holding all participants to high standards of politeness and civility. Such efforts not only provide a more welcoming space for women but also will likely yield better outcomes. Studies of interpersonal communication reveal the role of politeness in facilitating exploratory talk, where people construct shared meanings as they develop ideas. Polite interactions involve soliciting others' opinions, qualifying one's claims, providing supportive feedback, acknowledging others' contributions, and avoiding confrontation. All of these conversational patterns encourage collaboration and are especially useful when assessing future undertakings. In contrast, interactions characterized by challenges, disagreements, and interruptions lead to entrenched positions, especially when these tactics are used in public. As Holmes notes, "Those attacked often respond defensively, and little progress is made in exploring the issues and ideas proposed" (1995, p. 212).

Thus, women's learned, polite communication patterns—or what some might more broadly describe as a distinct women's culture—provide a valuable resource for deliberative pedagogy (Holmes, 1995; Mutz, 2006). Many have long argued that modeling feminine interaction patterns would result in "better working relationships, better understanding of complex issues, and better decision making" (Holmes, 1995, pp. 198, 213). Indeed, recent research suggests that more inclusive processes and more empathetic policy recommendations result when women deliberate within gender-exclusive enclaves, and even when group composition substantially favors women (Karpowitz & Mendelberg, 2014). It seems feminine modes of discourse and value preferences flourish when women's participation reaches a threshold, at which point they are numerous enough to influence group norms of appropriate behavior.

We need not wait for large numbers of female participants to transform traditionally masculine public spaces, however. We can purposefully create feminized settings, as has occurred in deliberative public issue forums organized in the United States such as those organized by the National Issues Forums or AmericaSpeaks. In doing so, however, we run the risk of undermining the ability to influence political decisions as the preferences that emerge from such forums are often not perceived as political demands (Polletta & Chen, 2013). Yet it is worth noting that a similar type of socialization used to take place within American versions of civil society, where countless Americans, including both average people and, notably, ambitious political elites, learned to manage conflict in pubic settings via parliamentary procedure (Skocpol, 2003). Formal rules required turn-taking, minimized interruptions, eliminated the need to fight for the floor, and discouraged ad hominem attacks, all of which may have formally feminized public interactions (even—or perhaps especially—in male enclaves) to promote social harmony and to sustain working relationships among members of a deliberative community. Teaching our students how to perform exaggerated versions of civility and politeness may help to combat examples of aggressive, rude behavior modeled daily by media pundits and politicians, while simultaneously creating a more inviting environment for our female and minority students.

The Effects of Gendered Division of Labor on Perceptions of Likeability and Expertise

Even if women come to think of themselves as appropriate participants in deliberative decision-making and are not alienated by egregious examples of incivility in what remains of our public sphere, they face additional barriers to achieving persuasive influence in such settings. As Sanders argues:

> Some Americans are apparently less likely than others to be listened to; even when their arguments are stated according to conventions of reason, they are more likely to be disregarded. Although deliberators will always choose to disregard some arguments, when this disregard is systematically associated with the arguments made by those we know already to be systematically disadvantaged, we should at least reevaluate our assumptions about deliberation's democratic potential. (1997, p. 349)

If scholars committed to deliberative pedagogy intend to help remedy historical prejudices in the public sphere, such systemic inequality must be overcome. Empirical research on gender and social influence provides insight into the cause of the difficulties women experience achieving influence in such settings.

As noted earlier, patriarchy, until quite recently, resulted in a gendered division of labor in the United States, with women working primarily in the home and men assuming prominent roles in the workplace and in political institutions. Men have historically held more high-status positions in society than women, thus reinforcing gendered stereotypes about competency, status, and appropriate behavior. Men's assumption of leadership and efforts to influence others in deliberative settings are deemed both appropriate and laudable. Women, generally associated with low-status domestic positions, are expected to be communal and self-sacrificing rather than commanding (Carli, 2004).

These expectations pose a conundrum for women. Unlike their male counterparts, when they attempt to wield influence in a group setting, they must first work to establish their competency. Yet women who engage in displays of competence—or even who exhibit assertiveness through means such as eye contact—are less well liked and wield less influence than other women (El-lyson, Dovidio & Brown, 1992). Men and boys are particularly prone to dislike and sanction these women (although other women also often object), because such behaviors are linked to efforts to gain status or to promote narrow agendas, which violate expectations grounded in the traditional ideal of the communal female. This aversion is overcome only when women combine high levels of perceived competence with a warm, communal style of communication that focuses on helping others. In short, traditional femininity is linked to women's likability—and both trump expertise and competence as prerequisites for influencing others (Carli, 2004).

Men face far fewer hurdles in their attempts to influence others in group settings, as the success of their efforts is not predicated on displays of competence or communality. Men are already assumed to be competent and not expected to be communal. Women, on the other hand, must undertake a careful balancing act, conforming to traditional feminine norms to establish likability and proving their competency before achieving influence over others. Simply put, "as influence agents, males seem to have greater behavioral latitude than their female counterparts" (Carli, 2004, p. 144). Given the difficulty of balancing these expectations, it is possible that women avoid engaging in civic and political discourse not only because they do not think of themselves as overtly political actors, but also because it is apt to be frustrating.

Teaching students about these patterns before having them participate in deliberative discussions in class or on campus may alleviate the effects of this patriarchal legacy. When students are aware of how implicit gender biases affect their reaction to men's and women's persuasive efforts, they may be able to begin consciously checking these reactions and altering their behavior. This approach may help create more egalitarian deliberative forums, but unless such training is systematically included on college campuses across the country, women will still face gendered barriers to persuasion and influence as soon as they enter a new deliberative setting.

To address this issue, a second approach is to provide targeted training for female students to make them aware of how their contributions to deliberative decision-making will be perceived and teach them tactics to sidestep the barriers these perceptions raise. Carli (2004), for example, suggests that women purposefully combine a warm, communal communication style (to establish likability) with high levels of competence. Similar strategies, focused on effectiveness rather than eliminating biases, have been developed to help women successfully navigate workplace negotiations and leadership roles (Babcock & Laschever, 2003; Williams & Dempsey, 2014). It is important to recognize that these strategies are designed specifically to teach women how to achieve influence while appearing to conform to gender stereotypes. They may be quite useful in helping individual women, but they do little to break down—and may even help to reinforce—gendered expectations that negatively affect women in the first place.

A third approach involves taking into consideration how different features of deliberative forums will affect female students' experiences. For example, women's influence wanes when forums are framed as political discussions, because politics is still largely perceived as a masculine endeavor in American society. Women fare much better when forums are framed as community problem-solving efforts, as the community is one aspect of the public sphere where women have historically been far more active and welcome. The types of issues discussed also affect women's experiences in deliberative forums, with their influence increasing when traditional "women's issues" such as child care, education, elder care, and social welfare are on the agenda. Women are already perceived as experts on such issues, which allows them to avoid the difficult task of establishing competence. Just as important, such concerns are more readily linked to women's roles as nurturers and caregivers, making it easier to frame their preferences as part of a communal rather than a self-serving agenda (Carli, 2004). The makeup of participants may also influence women's participation in forums, as being in a numerical minority not only reduces women's status and authority but also results in more competitive and assertive communication styles that further reduce their likelihood of contributing. Finally, decision rules appear to affect women's participation, with majority rule prone to suppressing women (especially when they are in the minority) and unanimous agreement often empowering them (Karpowitz & Mendelberg, 2014).

It is one thing to know what factors make deliberative forums more comfortable spaces for women and another to act on this knowledge. Questions remain about whether structuring classroom and campus forums specifically to facilitate female students' participation is the most effective way to meet the learning objectives associated with deliberative pedagogy. If we frame deliberative forums as community rather than political events in order to facilitate our female students' participation, will they still learn to think of themselves as political actors who are obligated to participate in the public sphere? If we wish to cultivate political identities among our female students, should we prepare them for the reality they are likely to face beyond our campuses—where women will probably constitute a minority of the decision makers in the room, where unanimous agreement is rarely required, and where feminine modes of discourse are not apt to be the norm?

If we throw female students into deliberative settings that they will inevitably find frustrating, we may well diminish the likelihood that they will seek out participation in the deliberative public sphere in the future. Yet if we do not prepare them for the realities they are likely to face when we cannot manipulate decision rules and group composition, they will be in for a rather rude awakening after graduation. Given these concerns, would it would be more effective to sequence female students' experiences in deliberative forums, from the most inviting settings to the least, as a way of building their identities and skills over time? These are choices that feminist scholars and teachers must grapple with as we make choices that will affect the lessons both women and men learn as we more purposefully implement deliberative pedagogy in our classrooms and on our campuses.

Conclusion

This overview is intended to emphasize that there is no single approach to promoting a gender-neutral public sphere. It is also intended to highlight the tensions that exist among these choices. Radical feminism clearly recommends embracing the long-term goal of feminizing the public sphere so that women's culture, and the feminine modes of discourse associated with it, comes to shape norms of appropriate behavior in deliberative settings. Both empirical social science and critical feminist theory indicate the result would be more inclusive and less aggressive interactions, resulting in more empathetic, and ultimately more effective, policy recommendations. This transformation would help to dismantle the social hierarchies that prevent all marginalized people from participating in public deliberation—and would also yield reflective decision-making processes that produce the innovative solutions prized by advocates of both deliberative democracy and educational reform.

Unfortunately, creating feminized deliberative spaces appears to enervate participants' ability to influence political decisions (Polletta & Chen, 2013). Clearly, far more work must be done to encourage participants in deliberative forums to recognize the inherently political nature of their endeavors, to recognize that they are political actors, to view their collective recommendations as policy solutions, and to hold public officials accountable for implementing them. Yet this task confronts the long reach of patriarchy's influence over Western culture. Not only were U.S. women long confined to the domestic sphere, the very traits associated with femininity were used to justify the claim that women were unfit for citizenship. Hence, successfully reframing politics as a feminine endeavor (exploratory talk that produces a common good), rather than a masculine endeavor (an adversarial zero-sum game with winners and losers), will inevitably be an uphill battle and a long-term goal.

An effective short-term or interim strategy, then, may be to adopt more mainstream feminist tactics by preparing female students to wield influence in the public sphere the way that it currently exists. This approach may serve not only to empower individual women in the short-term but also to feminize deliberative institutions from the inside out. Yet this short-term strategy comes with risk. If we prepare young women to participate in masculinized institutional settings to help them wield influence now, our efforts could result in assimilating them into male culture and promoting male norms of appropriate behavior. The goal of radical feminism is not to help women succeed because they have learned to establish their own version of privilege in patriarchal social hierarchies. The goal is to help women succeed despite the differences their historic marginalization has produced, so that the sheer weight of their numbers will eventually feminize the public sphere. Yet successful women sometimes reject the goals of radical feminism because they benefit from the status quo. "Having achieved acceptance by the patriarchal system, they risk losing power, rewards, and recognition if they challenge that same system" (Johnson, 2014, p. 43). Herein lies the dilemma. If we do not teach young women how to participate effectively in current public forums, it seems unlikely that they will take part in civic, and especially in political, life at high enough rates to transform deliberative institutions and settings. Yet teaching them to participate effectively could simply reify a gender-neutral version of the hierarchical status quo, where other types of people are marginalized instead of women.

Pursuing short-term goals for women's increased participation without undermining long-term goals for a more egalitarian public sphere will require a careful balancing act as we move forward. Moreover, at these early stages in the development of deliberative pedagogy as a distinct teaching method, we cannot claim which, if any, of the approaches described throughout this chapter are best practices. As such, we should take inspiration from the turn toward empirical social science in the subfield of deliberative democracy, as well as from the scholarship of teaching and learning, to begin identifying which of these approaches, or combination of approaches, are effective, and which are unexpectedly counterproductive.

This work must be an integral part of deliberative pedagogy's development, for if we make no effort "to correct for the deliberative disempowerment of women in mixed groups, women are likely to continue to be less frequent and influential contributors" (Karpowitz & Raphael, 2014, p. 133). Given the array of options for addressing women's "deliberative disempowerment," failing to make any effort to address women's historic exclusion from deliberative decision-making is not only irresponsible, but a lost opportunity to help our students become the type of citizens who will help build a more inclusive and egalitarian public sphere for everyone.

REFERENCES

Babcock, L., & Laschever, S. (2003). *Women don't ask: Negotiations and the Gender Divide*. Princeton, NJ: Princeton University Press.

Becker, J. C., & Wright, S. C. (2011). Yet another dark side of chivalry: Benevolent sexism undermines and hostile sexism motivates collective action for social change. *Journal of Personality and Social Psychology*, 101(1), 62–77.

Benhabib, S. (Ed.). (1996). *Democracy and difference: Contesting the boundaries of the political*. Princeton, NJ: Princeton University Press.

Berger, P. L., & Luckman, T. (1966). *The social construction of reality: A treatise in the sociology of knowledge*.

New York: Doubleday.

Carli, L. L. (2004). Gender effects on social influence. In J. S. Seiter & R. H. Gass (Eds.), *Perspectives on persuasion, social influence, and compliance gaining* (pp. 133–48). San Francisco: Jossey-Bass.

Ellyson, S. L., Dovidio, J. F., & Brown, C. E. (1992). The look of power: Gender differences and similarities in visual dominance behavior. In C. L. Ridgeway (Ed.), *Gender, interaction, and inequality* (pp. 50–80). New York: Springer-Verlag.

Glick, P., & Fiske, S. T. (2001). An ambivalent alliance: Hostile and benevolent sexism as complementary justifications for gender inequality. *American Psychologist, 56*(2), 109–18.

Gurin, P. (1985). Women's gender consciousness. *Public Opinion Quarterly, 49*(2), 143–63.

Hartley, M. (2011). Idealism and compromise and the civic engagement movement. In J. Saltmarsh & M. Hartley (Eds.), *"To serve a larger purpose": Engagement for democracy and the transformation of higher education* (pp. 27–48). Philadelphia: Temple University Press.

Holmes, J. (1995). *Women, men and politeness*. New York: Longman.

Jacobs, L. R., Cook, F. L., & Delli Carpini, M. X. (2009). *Talking together: Public deliberation and political participation in America*. Chicago: University of Chicago Press.

Johnson, A. G. (2014). *The gender knot: Unraveling our patriarchal legacy* (3rd ed.). Philadelphia: Temple University Press.

Kann, M. E. (1999). *The gendering of American politics: Founding mothers, founding fathers, and political patriarchy*. Westport, CT: Praeger.

Karpowitz, C. F., & Mendelberg, T. (2014). *The silent sex: Gender, deliberation, and institutions*. Princeton, NJ: Princeton University Press.

Karpowitz, C. F., & Raphael, C. (2014). *Deliberation, democracy, and civic forums: Improving equality and publicity*. New York: Cambridge University Press.

Lakoff, R. T. (1975). *Language and woman's place*. New York: Harper & Row.

Lakoff, R. T. (1990). *Talking power: The politics of language*. New York: Basic Books.

Mutz, D. C. (2006). *Hearing the other side: Deliberative versus participatory democracy*. New York: Cambridge University Press.

Polletta, F., & Chen, P. C. B. (2013). Gender and public talk: Accounting for women's variable participation in the public sphere. *Sociological Theory, 31*(4), 291–317.

Putnam, R. D. (2000). *Bowling alone: The collapse and revival of American community*. New York: Simon & Schuster.

Sanders, L. (1997). Against deliberation. *Political Theory, 25*(3), 347–76.

Sapiro, V. (1983). *The political integration of women: Roles, socialization, and politics*. Urbana: University of Illinois Press.

Skocpol, T. (2003). *Diminished democracy: From membership to management in American civic life*. Norman: University of Oklahoma Press.

Strachan, J. C. (2016). Deliberative democracy. In S. L. Schechter (Ed.), *American governance* (pp. 13–14). New York: Macmillan Reference USA.

Williams, J. C., & Dempsey, R. (2014). *What works for women at work: Four patterns working women need to know*. New York: New York University Press.

Young, I. M. (2000). *Inclusion and democracy*. Oxford: Oxford University Press.

Russian and American Students Deliberating Online: Complementing Core Courses with Intercultural Communication Skills

Ekaterina Lukianova and Jack Musselman

This chapter describes a joint deliberation exercise in which American and Russian university students engaged in online discussions of a thorny issue with relevance across societies. But what do we mean by "deliberation exercise" in an international context, when students are not from the same country, much less members of the same campus community? In the Anglo-Saxon academic culture, particularly in the United States, deliberation is often associated with democratic politics, in part because of the influence of the deliberative democracy movement. Yet, deliberation may be said to transcend specific forms of government considered desirable or undesirable at a given point in history by any one society. In fact, as a pedagogical tool, deliberation may have a more profound impact when used to connect participants whose governments or societies have diverging ideologies. Our experience illustrated that in the global context, classroom discussions and online interactions that connect students from different countries are accessible ways to practice deliberative pedagogies.

To that end, our exercise involved students from two universities: Saint Petersburg State University, a large public university in Russia, and St. Edward's University, a small private liberal arts college in Austin, Texas. The Russian students were master's-level English and cultural studies majors, enrolled in an advanced English writing class. The Americans were bachelor's-level students, many prelaw, enrolled in a legal ethics class. In the fall of 2014, these two groups engaged in a multifaceted deliberation on the issue of corruption and various ways of approaching it in their respective countries. The deliberation process included separate in-class discussions that were shared between classes, a joint discussion in a closed online forum, and an exchange of essays.

The two instructors who led the exchange met at a Kettering Foundation meeting in Dayton, Ohio. This setting allowed us to negotiate the complexity involved in creating an in-depth dialogic exchange between classes at universities in different countries. Our partnership was designed to meet both deliberative goals and the specific needs of the classes and institutions that it connected. The broader goal of this project was to encourage cross-cultural understanding among students with diverse backgrounds and viewpoints, with an eye toward preparing students for real-world encounters that can provide thoughtful solutions to difficult social issues. The topic of corruption was chosen for its relevance to both groups of students while offering room for divergent opinions and proposed approaches. We sought to help students reflect on culturally specific dimensions of the issue, while developing skills such as information sharing and negotiating value conflicts both within and between cultures. By embedding such dialogues within existing courses, we were also able to meet the specific goals of our respective classes. The legal ethics class at St. Edward's University aimed to help students learn from moral and political perspectives about the legal profession that differed from their own. The opinion-writing class at Saint Petersburg State University aimed to inform students' writing by helping them develop sensitivity to language as a means of encoding values.

Experimental Structure for a Russian–American Online Exchange

The two groups of students engaged in a multistage discussion of the issue of corruption, where they could reflect on positions represented in their respective cultures, pose questions, and respond to each other's perspectives. Students in the dialogue did not need to do research on corruption but rather were encouraged to engage the topic from their own perspectives while noting definitions of corruption and judgments that were vague, conflicting, or provocative. Students were instructed to question each other's views and experiences rather than simply go to an authoritative source for an explanation, although the use of research and mass media texts to support their discussion was encouraged.

Stage 1: In-Class Discussion

To begin the process, Russian and American students discussed their understanding of corruption in their respective classrooms. These discussions were videotaped so they could be shared with the other class. At this stage we asked students not to think about the other country, but rather to reflect on their own experience. To set up each discussion, we supplied students with a discussion guide prepared by an international group during a seminar held at the Kettering Foundation. Students in each group received one question that was unique to each course's content, along with four common questions for all students to address:

1. How would you define corruption?
2. What is one specific example you've experienced personally or are well informed about?
3. How relevant are the examples in the Kettering guide to your own experience?
4. What is the main source of your knowledge of corruption (e.g., personal experience, mass media, education, family conversations, etc.)?

Students shared their taped discussions over the Internet. After watching the other class's dialogue, each group discussed the key themes, problem definitions, and examples provided and identified unclear, confusing, or challenging aspects of the other group's discussion.

Stage 2: Online Forum

Next, students had three weeks to sign into a private, password-protected online forum to converse with students in the other country about their perspectives. They were guided to engage in respectful and insightful conversations, with a focus on asking questions and avoiding offering judgments. All students were required to make at least three blog posts, including one question and two answers or comments. However, they were encouraged to engage in an in-depth dialogue with the other group, as well as among themselves, and instructed to do their best to respond to all the questions posted. They were also encouraged to cite sources (such as mass media stories) in their online discussions and to learn about the culturally specific dimensions of the issue in one another's posts.

Stage 3: Position Papers

In the third stage of the deliberative process, students wrote position papers on corruption drawing on personal or media examples and the taped dialogues, comparing their experiences and sharpening their definitions of corruption. One of the goals at this stage was for students to draw on their own dialogic experience and reflect on whether their examples and statements were comparable with those made by students in the other country, and whether they could agree on a more precise account of corruption that both groups might share. Each student then emailed his or her essay to a student counterpart in the other country. Students reviewed the essays and shared their feedback with the original authors. In their reviews, students were asked to address the following questions:

1. What was your first reaction to the essay (e.g., approval, rejection, etc.)?
2. Why did you have this initial reaction?
3. Do you think that after careful reading and reflection you understand the author's position? Why or why not?
4. Do you understand all the details in the writer's argument? How and why (or why not)?
5. Do you think that as an American or Russian student you can easily understand (or sympathize with) the writer's views of the problem(s) and could easily have a dialogue about them with the writer? Why or why not?

In responding to the essays, we asked students to be appreciative of their counterparts' work while not shying away from criticism in order for the authors to learn. Although the reviews were primarily regarded as individual tasks, a class was devoted to discussing students' first impressions of the essays they received. Students who were having difficulties in understanding the essay of their counterpart or didn't know how to respond were able to raise questions and receive advice.

What Worked: Trading Personal Experiences and Recognizing Diversity of Opinions

This deliberative process presented several learning opportunities for both the students and the instructors. Perhaps most important, it allowed students to engage in an international and intercultural exchange of ideas and civil disagreement without the expense of leaving their campus to study abroad. Moreover, our partnership is an example of how such exchanges can work around some of the language problems that arise during international tele-collaboration projects, where students who are learning each other's language operate at different levels of proficiency. In this case, we partnered student groups whose needs were different but complementary, which let us conduct the project in one language (English). Only one group of students, the Russians, were dealing with objectives pertaining to foreign language learning; the American students had the goal of negotiating perspectives from another culture without regard for whether participants were using English as a native or second language—a very common situation in the real world.

Creating such opportunities can extend the reach of deliberative pedagogy by exposing students to international perspectives beyond what is possible even through rigorous efforts to enroll a diverse student body. For example, even though about a third of the American students in this exercise were bilingual (mostly in Spanish) and had experience traveling in Mexico, most students in the legal ethics class indicated that they never had intercultural and international experiences like this one. Moreover, a third of the students indicated in their course evaluations that this project was the most valuable part of the course and added they wanted even more global perspectives on legal ethics in the future. For their part, although most of the Russian students had already been exposed to intercultural dialogue in their academic environments, many indicated they saw this project as less about improving their English and more about interacting with "real Americans." Very few of them had had experience of working through an issue with students from another country over a prolonged period of time.

Working through Differences

Throughout the process, there was a healthy degree of disagreement about definitions of and responses to corruption. For example, the American students discussed abuses of authority in how the U.S. military responded to sexual assault cases (which were in the news at the time), while Russian students were less inclined to see those cases as fitting the definition of corruption. In addition, American students were more likely than their Russian counterparts to think that educating children at a young age and employing civic responses such as police investigations and media exposure were viable methods of fighting corruption. Russian students tended to regard corruption as a largely moral or even spiritual phenomenon, while their American counterparts seemed to regard corruption as a civic issue and were leery of keeping children innocent by preventing them from hearing about stories of corruption.

Students in both groups demonstrated an ability to reflect on these differences and were responsive when instructors encouraged them to probe further into the experiences and values that underlie different models of social relations, as seen in this forum response by a Russian student:

> Your video led us to a heated discussion because we noticed that your perception of corruption is very different from ours. We didn't quite understand how some crimes are connected with corruption. So, to start with, could you please explain how sexual assault in the army correlates with corruption, in your point of view.

Some students were still grappling with the uncertainties and tensions even as they were writing essay reviews and filling out course evaluations:

> I thought that your paragraph devoted to corruption as a positive force for effective administration was necessary to discuss corruption and was missing from nearly all other discussions. While the theory was quickly refuted after being brought up in class, it was a necessary idea to bring up. (essay review)
>
>> It was inspiring that . . . dissatisfaction in a generic definition of corruption led her to seek a more definitive and descriptive reasoning. She acknowledged corruption is a deeper, more complex issue than initially discussed in class and that we have "missed something important." I could not agree more with this assertion. (postactivities survey)

This project was deliberative in that students became aware of the heterogeneity of views on an important issue, both between cultures and within their own culture. Given our students' reflections, it looks as if we succeeded in creating opportunities for students to experience a state of suspended judgment at various stages of the exchange. We also see evidence that students were wrestling with value tensions (for example, recognizing that some view corruption as acceptable) and inquiring into experiences or assumptions that make people from another culture categorize experiences differently.

Interacting at Multiple Levels

The depth of this deliberative exercise largely depended on its extended nature and the presence of a variety of interactions that the students experienced. For example, most students unequivocally indicated that reviewing each other's essays was the high point of the exercise and was effective in engaging them with each other. Some of them stated that the essays expressed more "thoughtful" and "sincere" opinions that those voiced in the blog entries. From the instructors' perspective, however, we would have to recognize that the students had been well primed for an in-depth discussion before receiving each other's essays. They had acquired a very good sense of the range of opinions present in both groups, read a variety of other materials that they had found to support their arguments, and reflected on a fair number of specific, often personal, examples. Indeed, some students indicated that the blog forum helped them map the range of opinions that existed in the group and for that reason found it a valuable opportunity.

Including the essay portion of the project also allowed students to negotiate a number of different linguistic and communication skills beyond, say, American students correcting Russian students' grammar and syntax (which is also useful). American students often indicated their ability to comprehend the writer's meaning, even when remarking on what they saw as strange Russian analogies (e.g., "strengthening the good apples" in describing a way to encourage good behavior). Russian students noted areas where the writing of their American counterparts was wordy or confusing. These interactions were helpful in making students more aware of the difficulties of communicating with those in other cultures, as well as their effectiveness in overcoming these difficulties. Having peer readers rather than teachers evaluate their writing was helpful in this regard. Moreover, having students from another country read their papers seemed to motivate them more than an exchange with their immediate classmates would have.

Challenges: Conflict Avoidance, Disengagement, and the Problem of Evaluation

One aspect of our exchange that merits more critical analysis is the choice of the topic and ways of moderating the discussion, both of which may have contributed to interactions that avoided strong dissent or criticism. This compounded what seemed to be a natural tendency to avoid conflict stemming from students' lack of experience in discussing difficult issues with people in another country. In addition to shying away from conflict, we believe that students were not sufficiently critical of the assumptions made in the online forum. For example, in their conversation about educating school children against corruption, students from both countries freely compared corruption to behaviors that are illegal but do not really fit the definition of corruption—such as drug and alcohol abuse—but no one questioned the analogy. We also noticed that on the blog some questions remained unanswered if they provided culturally alien framings.

It is possible that a topic more closely aligned with students' personal experience and interests would have helped overcome the hesitance to call each other's assumptions and assertions into question. Many students claimed that they did not have direct experience or strong views about corruption as a phenomenon. On the other hand, any other internationally significant topic we could have picked would no doubt have presented its own challenges. Such topics as ethnic relations or gender can be very personal; they may result in emotionally charged discussions if students feel that their identities are threatened or cause students to withdraw if they find the topic personally sensitive. Finding a topic that engages students' personal interest without being excessively threatening is important to ensuring the success of this type of project. In addition, it may help to establish a process that allows the instructors to play a more active role in prompting students to challenge each other's thinking.

Another concern was that several students withdrew from participation at various stages of the exchange. One Russian student refused to participate for an unstated reason; in addition, two of the twenty-nine American students in the legal ethics class opted out of being filmed during the dialogue and writing blog entries, although they did write the essays. Both of these students expressed concerns (despite assurances from their instructor) about these electronic forms of communication being used outside of the class in some other context. Given the sensitive nature of the recorded discussion and one or two of the blog entries, such concerns are not entirely unwarranted; it's possible again that a different topic would have alleviated some of these concerns. Students who chose not to participate were given other tasks to perform, which gave them a chance to remain connected with the project.

We think it worth noting that some of these challenges are inherent in the very aim of pursuing the deliberative ideal. Ensuring that everyone is at the table is just as much of a problem in community settings; so is the quality of the discussion, even when people representing different perspectives are in the same room. However, formal education, although a lower-stakes context in some respects, requires particular strategies for dealing with these challenges. For example, while participation in community settings is fundamentally voluntary (obstacles to participation being a separate issue), in formal education participation is likely a requirement and thus is subject to external assessment and even penalty. This factor may not necessarily motivate students to participate in an engaged way.

Perhaps the most notable challenge for the instructors was that it took considerable time and effort to arrange the content and structure of the dialogue to fit into the existing courses. Both of us had to devote class sessions to record the initial discussion and watch our counterparts' recording in class, to say nothing of setting up the blog forum and coordinating the exchange and evaluation of essays. Instructors who wish to engage in such collaborative projects should be prepared to make these commitments—although we believe they were worth the effort.

Both of the instructors made the exchange low-stakes in terms of grading. Grading criteria included the number and depth of comments on the forum, essay quality, and the reviewing activity. In terms of learning, we believed that the feedback students received from each other would be as significant as a grade, so the project didn't have a major impact on their overall course outcome. This arrangement seemed to work well: we did not see a decline in enthusiasm because of low grading stakes, and students raised no objections to the assessment criteria.

For the purpose of self-assessment as teachers, however, we were and are concerned with developing ways of evaluating these activities more precisely within our courses. Assessment of tele-collaborative exchanges presents a well-known challenge, particularly where intercultural communication skills are concerned. Often various combinations of portfolio and product-assessment approaches are used, but it is still difficult to determine the value of such a deliberative exercise in an objective way for administrative purposes. In our case, given the difficulty of evaluating opinion writing, particularly across groups and topics in different countries and cultures, we can cite only our anecdotal conclusion that students produced more coherent and thoughtful essays than they would have in a course that did not include such dialogic exercises. This definitely seemed to be the case in the Russian group, both in terms of argument structure and linguistic sophistication. More rigorous comparative research should be done to ground this conclusion more firmly.

Reliable assessment methods are of concern from a pedagogical perspective as well. While most students were responsive in assessing the written essays, some made very generic comments in their essay evaluations (and in their blog entries). Also, in our view, there was a relatively low level of self-reflection in the blog entries, where students often asked questions but did not often offer criticism or insight into ideological positions within and between groups as the questions were being answered. This was less of an issue with the essays, but perhaps more oversight by instructors (or student moderators) in the blog forum would have improved both the online dialogue and the subsequent essays.

Next Steps: Why We Want to Continue

Beyond the generic value that can be attributed to classroom deliberation, our experiment has tested a flexible format that can be used to match and satisfy the needs of classes with different overall objectives. In principle, this format offers various possibilities for ad hoc partnerships that can develop as individual teachers, programs, and classes evolve.

The combination of a video exchange, an online forum, and an exchange of essays has proved to be a fruitful format that allows students to maintain prolonged involvement with each other, exposing them to a wide variety of views as well as allowing them to engage more deeply with one or two peers. At the same time, we recognize that the model needs to be developed further to promote students' in-depth engagement with each other's views.

For ourselves, we continue to do such exchanges, involving more instructors and trying different topics. We are hoping to work out more rigorous moderating practices without becoming punitively Socratic, as well as more reliable and consistent assessment methods for this exchange format. Both of us are open to cooperation with other partners and to sharing our experiences. We do not feel the need to scale up this kind of exchange dramatically, but being part of a network of practitioners who conduct such exchanges would be valuable for all involved, allowing more varied partnerships and more possibilities for experimentation.

Tackling the "Savior" Complex: Teaching Introduction to Women's and Gender Studies through Deliberation

Ibtesam Al-Atiyat

Since the inception of women's studies programs in U.S. higher education institutions in the 1970s, introduction to women's and gender studies classes have become a space and forum wherein power relations are deconstructed, intimate and controversial issues are analyzed, and democratic values are probed. At their heart lies the promise of realizing justice, granting women and other social minorities visibility and voice, and offering students a better understanding of themselves (their identities, sexualities, and rights), their communities (power structures, diversity, cultures, privilege, and institutions), and the world around them. Given these objectives, women's studies programs are also potential sites for deliberative pedagogy.

In this essay, I draw on a multiyear experience of teaching Introduction to Women's and Gender Studies at St. Olaf College, a private liberal arts college in Minnesota. I discuss how various challenges—such as limited diversity in the classroom (students are predominantly young, white, upper- and middle-class American women who have limited familiarity with world history and cultures) and deep-seated convictions that women in the West are better off than their counterparts elsewhere—prompted me to consider a deliberation-conscious pedagogical approach.[1] This approach, as Joni Doherty describes it, "helps students better understand differing perspectives and the complexity of persistent problems that spring from ethical dilemmas" by calling on "each person to engage with others in democratic, inclusive, and respectfully discursive practices" (2012, p. 25). In other words, this deliberative teaching and learning approach recognizes knowledge as a space of contested power(s). It grants knowledge a political mission: pursuing the complex endeavor of justice and commanding that political choices be based on a deep and multifaceted understanding of controversial issues.

In implementing a deliberative teaching approach, I designed my introduction course as a semester-long "issue forum," mimicking the experiences of national forums conducted by the National Issues Forums Institute.[2] The course was designed to address two key questions: Should "we" intervene in other countries to "protect" and "save" women? Should we impose a forced assimilation to liberal gender values on groups and communities of immigrants? Readings for the course were selected to represent diverse voices that offer different perspectives on the quandary of intervention. Class activities were designed to include deliberative small- and large-group discussions, a public forum group project, and a series of deliberative individual position papers.

Designing the Course with Deliberations in Mind

I began teaching Introduction to Women's and Gender Studies in 2011. The offer to teach the course came during exciting times at St. Olaf. The women's studies program was under major revision. One of the changes to the program's curriculum was to refocus the introductory course on women's and gender studies from being U.S.-centered to including global experiences. This change is consistent with the college's mission of fostering global citizenship and intercultural understanding.

As I started planning for and designing the course, a peculiar challenge became evident. How do I, as an instructor who comes from an Arab and a Muslim background, design a globally focused course on women and gender on a U.S. campus after September 11 and teach it to students who are not just culturally Western but predominantly white, middle- and upper-middle-class Americans? Adding to this challenge, college administrators, students, and faculty too often believe that Muslim women are subject to oppression resulting from their inherently sexist Islamic culture and religion. Muslim women, according this understanding (which sometimes is expressed bluntly and other times politely held back), are passive victims in need of saving. A plethora of literature, media coverage, and scholarship affirms students' notions that Muslim women and women in developing countries are in need of saving, as Leila Abu-Lughod (2002) puts it, despite the increasing appearance of literature that challenges this view. Such claims about Muslim women too often defuse critical voices that speak against interventions both in the United States and internationally and make it easy to generate ill-informed public support for political actions in the form of war and other military interventions in predominantly Muslim countries.

This peculiar challenge informs one of the leading intended learning outcomes of my course, namely to have students realize that their racial, ethnic, and class biases are often either invisible to them or intentionally concealed by notions of politeness and political correctness. Other desired learning outcomes for the course include:

- Sparking students' interest in seeking justice and in acting as informed citizens, based on a more nuanced understanding of women's lives and the state of gender relations around the world beyond Western-centric understanding of womanhood, oppression, and gender roles.
- Utilizing a more complex framework for understanding issues that recognizes cultural differences and similarities, race and ethnic identities, and concepts such as ideology, imperialism, hegemony, colonialism, post- and neocolonialism, and globalization.
- Developing an understanding that the status of women around the globe is central to the American democratic project. This means, by becoming informed citizens, students will be able to critique decisions of invasion, war, and those of aid and assistance that are too often based on the pretenses of liberating women.

Ultimately, the greater goal of the course is to view women's status and gender relations around the world not as distant and unconnected, but as direct outcomes of national policies, political actions, and domestic decisions.

To achieve these outcomes, I have chosen readings to include a wide range of scholarly works, memoirs, creative pieces, international reports, public statements, and media reports. Readings are divided into two major sections: those that would offer support for intervening on women's behalf, and those that would argue against it. Readings that would support intervention include works by authors such as Susan Moller Okin (1999), Phyllis Chesler (2005), Azar Nafisi (2008), Malala Yousafzai (2013), and Ayaan Hirsi Ali (2006), as well as selected United Nations reports and political statements by leaders such as Hillary Clinton and George and Laura Bush. Examples of readings that would oppose intervention include the works of Leila Abu-Lughod (2002), Marnia Lazreg (1994), Leila Ahmed (1992), Hamid Dabashi (2006), and Chandra T. Mohanty (1988).

The first half of the course focuses on reading and discussing these works. Students' performance in class is measured by how critically they process the reading materials, as well as by how effectively they reflect on the readings in their discussion and writing. As part of the reading assignment, students research each author and the context from which she or he speaks. They also keep a reading journal in which they summarize key arguments and concepts and reflect on what is said in the readings and in class discussions. An unanticipated learning outcome—critical reading and discourse analysis—has emerged from this exercise as students engage in asking and answering questions about authors' lives, cultural backgrounds, and language used to frame women's issues.

During class discussions, student reflections on this exercise point to their new understanding of reading a text as an example of a specific worldview and political position. Some examples of these reflections follow:

> The texts assigned for this week were straightforward. Their arguments were very clear: women's rights are human rights. Regardless of women's religion, ethnicity or color, a woman should be entitled to equal treatment and protection from violence. Is this not the true promise of liberal democracy? Liberal democratic values should prevail and be taught to immigrants and peoples in other cultures, especially those who adhere to traditions that oppress women and justify their killing.

> I felt frustrated with the texts included in this section. They made me angry. They are based on assumptions that we (in the U.S.) are better than everybody else is, and that we have got everything right. Are we truly in a position where we could tell others how they should live their lives? Women in the U.S. are far from being treated equal, let alone are liberated!

> I see where those authors are coming from. Their arguments make sense. However, I am at this stage of the course very perplexed. I do not know what to think. We cannot simply stand still when women are killed because of their gender; but we cannot also keep invading other countries under false pretenses. There must be another way. Perhaps intervene only when we are asked to?

Students also synthesize different points of view to come up with their own suggestions:

> I agree with the premise that women need liberation worldwide, and not only in the Muslim or the developing worlds. This liberation has to come on their own terms and according to the ways they see

fit. However, in most of the cases we have covered in the class so far, the discussion has largely been about governments that oppress women. We can place some pressure on those governments to change the way they treat women: with economic sanctions.

The third quarter of the course is dedicated to whole-class deliberative forums. Over two sessions (each two hours long) students deliberate on the options for action that came from the reading and discuss the course materials. The first forum explores the issue of intervention, and the second discusses protecting women and forced assimilation. Students in the first forum deliberate on four options: (1) Yes, we should intervene in other countries to liberate and save women. (2) No, we do not stand on any higher ground to teach or force others to live our values. (3) We should intervene, but only when we are asked to. (4) We should intervene diplomatically and through imposing economic sanctions.

While deliberating, students are asked to assess each option, highlight potential blind spots, and list compromises should a certain option become policy. Students have identified a range of issues arising from the first option (military intervention), including: "The world will hate us for war," "Casualties of war are mostly women and children," and "Women's issues become a pretext to achieve political goals." For the second option (no intervention), students have noted, "We will become passive, incapable of judging evil acts," and "Women will be killed, ill-treated, and abused and we will do nothing about it." Issues with the third option (intervention on request) include the idea that "In situations where democratic representation of people is lacking, do we really know who is asking us to intervene?" A trade-off with the final option (diplomatic/economic intervention) is, "This is still an imposition of [our] values."

The second forum follows the same format. Students deliberate four options: (1) To protect women's rights, immigrants should fully assimilate to laws and the prevalent values of the host country. (2) To protect women's rights, we need to allow them to enjoy the exercise of their own cultural identity. (3) To protect women's rights, we need to criminalize and ban only certain oppressive traditions. (4) To protect women's rights, we need to rethink and restructure our values and laws to make them more representative of an increasingly diverse nation. As in the first forum, students discuss compromises and trade-offs associated with each option. Examples include: "When we allow women and groups to exercise their cultures, we create classes of citizens in relationship to the law. Immigrant women, unlike native women, will not be protected by the law; they will become second-class citizens"; and "Most immigrants do not have the right to vote, and are often subjected to laws they did not approve of or create."

I serve as the moderator for both forums. In preparing for and running the forums, I have found that no lengthy or elaborate introductions to deliberative theory are needed. With a few guidelines, students are able to get the logic behind the forum and understand its rules. Guidelines are largely based on Seyla Benhabib's features of a "valid"—that is, morally binding—deliberation. These include "1) participation in such deliberation is governed by norms of equality and symmetry; all have the same chances to initiate speech acts, to question, to interrogate, and to open debate; 2) all have the right to question the assigned topics of conversation; and 3) all have the right to initiate reflexive arguments about the very rules of the discourse procedure and the way in which they are applied or carried out" (1996, p. 70).

After each forum, students are asked to evaluate the process by reflecting verbally and in writing on their deliberation experience. In their comments, they have noted feeling uncomfortable when their long-held views about women's and gender issues are challenged (and sometimes shattered). Some of their responses follow:

> I left the forum having more questions than answers. More perplexed than comfortable. Nevertheless, happy that I do not see things in simplistic terms anymore. The discussions and forums taught me to ask more questions and learn about the complexity of a subject.
>
> My views about women in other parts of the world have changed dramatically. My views about myself and the state of women in the U.S. have changed dramatically. I learned to turn a critical eye inwards and see what comparable acts of oppression are done to women and other minorities under the promise of liberation. I want to learn more how "ideology" works in other areas of knowledge and politics.
>
> I have always thought that national politics and foreign politics are two different species. Now I realize that this is far from being true. This exercise did not only teach me what it means to be a "woman" but also what it takes to be a responsible "global" citizen.

Obviously, the forums do not yield any resolutions. The class is never close to reaching consensus at any point, but reaching consensus is not my intention. My goal is to teach students a process of making decisions by considering multiple options, listening to each other, and acknowledging biases and points of privilege.

Deliberative Writing Assignments

Although deliberations are often thought of in terms of speech, writing is another means of communicating one's values and positions. Effective writing is also a vital skill for college graduates. Deliberative writing teaches students effective exchange of views and values and transforms the writing assignment from something that is merely done for a grade to an assignment that communicates ideas by framing problems, offering solutions, and addressing different types of audiences. Because of the importance of this aspect of deliberation in my introduction course, the course has a writing general education credit attached to it.

During the first week of classes, as we cover the basic definitions, scope, and political potential of women's studies, I have students write a short (six-hundred- to eight-hundred-word) position paper describing whether they are for or against intervening to protect women's rights worldwide, including what role, if any, the United States should play in liberating women in other countries. I ask students to treat their papers as a work in progress. The first draft is due the second week of class and reflects students' prior knowledge and opinions. Students are asked to state their sources of knowledge and explain the value base from which they have taken their position. They are expected to reconsider their position in light of the readings and class discussions as the course progresses. Students revise their papers after each reading section and submit a final version after the completion of all readings and discussions. Grading criteria include the clarity with which they articulate their position, the quality of their arguments, how they use evidence (loosely defined), and their ability to accommodate and treat objectively views that differ from their own.

Students receive instructions on how to write each draft as well as on what progress they need to show from draft to draft. By the end of the semester each student has submitted four increasingly detailed drafts: the initial paper, a revised draft that includes reflections on the first set of readings (pro intervention), a third draft that reflects the second set of readings (against intervention), and a final, five-page paper after the deliberative forum. In the final paper, students are expected to support their position, reflect on changes in their views, and outline the compromises that would arise should the option they back actually come about.

The goal is for the paper to develop from a position statement into a simple policy paper. Writing clear and well-articulated policy papers is a key skill in the world of politics and should add to the value of women's studies. As we teach students and potential future activists, this form of writing is essential.

The Deliberative Forum Project

The last quarter of the class is dedicated to group projects. Groups of four to five students work to choose a gender-related issue of some concern or interest to the community of St. Olaf, research it thoroughly (through literature review, collection of statistics and other types of evidence, archival research, interviews, etc.), and lead a deliberative forum about it on campus. Although one forum may not lead to a solution for any particular problem, my intention is to teach students the skill of working with communities to address social issues by preparing for, designing, and conducting a public forum.

After they conduct their research, I give groups writing guidelines for producing a booklet that summarizes their work. The booklets have four sections. The first includes background information on the issue, gathered through accurately cited research. The background section should highlight the issue's significance to the communities on campus and explain the need for a discussion on its resolution. The second section outlines different options or proposals for resolving the problem. Each option should be laid out clearly, with well-articulated arguments in its support as well as trade-offs or compromises that the proposed solution would entail. The third section includes an issue map—a sheet that summarizes each option, along with its benefits and trade-offs. The final section includes an evaluation questionnaire that asks forum participants to reflect on their experience and explain whether and how participation in the forum changed their views.

Students select different issues of concern to the campus community. Forums have explored topics such as whether housing on campus should be gender neutral, do we need another LGBTQ organization on campus, and the benefits and costs of making Introduction to Women's and Gender Studies a general education prerequisite for all students. Students are asked to document the forum experience through videos and photographs (obtaining participants' approval beforehand).

Over the past three years, more than two hundred students, staff members, and faculty have taken part in these campus issue forums. Students use Facebook and the campus-wide e-mail as platforms to invite participation. Many also promote the forums through their classes and campus organizations. Each forum hosts fifteen to eighteen participants. Group members play different roles: they serve as moderators, participants, and rapporteurs, as well as background researchers and booklet writers. Individuals' tasks are highlighted in a two-page report the group is required to submit on completion of the forum. The report includes a discussion of the forum outcomes, a brief analysis of the evaluation questionnaire, and a one-paragraph reflection on each group member's experience during the forum. One student stated:

> The deliberative forum was by far the best thing I learned from the class (not to say that other parts weren't important). We approached a perceived problem on campus with the intent of addressing it from several different viewpoints in a forum with other members of the St. Olaf community. In this way, we learned a lot about the practical application of women's and gender studies, as well as how our school works.

Through this experience, students learned how to collect, synthesize, and articulate different views. They also learned a lot about mobilizing a community, including how diverse the interests of their fellow students are and how busy the schedules of students, staff members, and faculty can be. "It takes a great deal of effort to get people to work together," one student reflected in her final report.

Conclusions

The different deliberative exercises and activities I use in my class have enhanced students' ability to communicate clearly both verbally and in writing. Students have learned how to work with communities and how to achieve a better understanding of the complex needs of diverse social groups. Above all, students have developed new skills in working through decision-making processes that are collaborative and sensitive to others—where decisions are based not solely on personal interests and immediate needs but on what works for an entire community. Finally, students have learned that decisions made at the national level affect lives elsewhere both directly and indirectly and that, consequently, they need to take a responsible view of their role as citizens. These skills are not only important in shaping the world we live in today but also essential for training the activists, professionals, and political leaders of the future.

These results support an emerging enthusiasm among feminist scholars for embracing deliberative democracy as a form of governance that can benefit and involve marginalized groups, including women (Young, 2000; Benhabib, 1996). Despite earlier skepticism among feminists about the inability of deliberations to move beyond forms of abstraction, impartiality, and rationality all seen as masculine and Western (Young, 1990, 1997; Fraser, 1989; Mouffe, 2000), deliberations have the potential to be truly inclusive when sensitized to feminist notions of location and context. They help participants reveal biases, command a critical and deeper understanding of issues, and arrive at collective and consensual resolutions of social and ethical dilemmas through a process that includes not just reasoning and argumentation (rationality) but also working through choices (McAfee, 2004). When blended together, feminist and deliberative pedagogies appear more akin than different. Both pedagogies focus on skills of listening, ensuring that all voices are equally heard, creating a safe space for people to share their lives and concerns (in whatever way they see fit), and understanding rather than assuming.

NOTES

1. Discussions held at the Kettering Foundation within the deliberative pedagogies working group helped me think of the different exercises and activities I designed for this class. I am indebted to the advice and guidance I have received over the past three years from the group leader and members.

2. The National Issues Forums Institute defines forums as "usually small gatherings where people come together for a few hours to deliberate about important and difficult public problems (or issues) with the help of a neutral moderator and a discussion guide that presents several possible approaches to the problem." See https://www.nifi.org/en/about-nif-forums.

REFERENCES

Abu-Lughod, L. (2002). Do Muslim women really need saving? Anthropological reflections on cultural relativism and its others. *American Anthropologist*,104(3), 783–90.

Ahmed, L. (1992). *Women and gender in Islam: Historical roots of a modern debate*. New Haven, CT: Yale University Press.

Ali, A. H. (2006). *The caged virgin: An emancipation proclamation for women and Islam*. New York: Simon & Schuster.

Benhabib, S. (Ed.). (1996). *Democracy and difference: Contesting the boundaries of the political*. Princeton, NJ: Princeton University Press.

Chesler, P. (2005). *The death of feminism: What's next in the struggle for women's freedom*. New York: Palgrave Macmillan.

Dabashi, H. (2006). Native informers and the making of the American empire. *Al-Ahram Weekly*, 797, 1–7.

Doherty, J. (2012). Deliberative pedagogy: An education that matters. *Connections*, 24–27.

Fraser, N. (1989). *Unruly practices: Power, discourse, and gender in contemporary social theory*. Minneapolis: University of Minnesota Press.

Lazreg, M. (1994). *The eloquence of silence: Algerian women in question*. East Sussex: Psychology Press.

McAfee, N. (2004). Three models of democratic deliberation. *Journal of Speculative Philosophy* (Special Issue on Pragmatism and Deliberative Democracy), 18(1), 44–59.

Mohanty, C. T. (1988). Under Western eyes: Feminist scholarship and colonial discourses. *Feminist Review*, no. 30, 61–88.

Mouffe, C. (2000). *The democratic paradox*. London: Verso.

Nafisi, A. (2008). *Reading "Lolita" in Tehran: A memoir in books*. New York: Random House.

Okin, S. M. (1999). *Is multiculturalism bad for women?* Princeton, NJ: Princeton University Press.

Young, I. M. (1990). *Justice and the politics of difference*. Princeton, NJ: Princeton University Press.

Young, I. M. (1997). *Intersecting voices: Dilemmas of gender, political philosophy, and policy*. Princeton, NJ: Princeton University Press.

Young, I. M. (2000). *Inclusion and democracy*. Oxford: Oxford University Press.

Yousafzai, M. (2013). *I am Malala: The girl who stood up for education and was shot by the Taliban*. Boston: Little, Brown.

Deliberative Pedagogy for the Entire Student Body

Ferenc Hammer

In this chapter I offer a discussion of the roles deliberative student forums played in 2012–13 in the student movement in Hungary in general, and particularly in the Occupy BTK (Occupy the Humanities Faculty) events at Hungary's largest higher education institution, Eötvös Loránd University. Following a contextualizing section on contemporary Hungarian activism and the changing role of communication in political movements, I outline a set of formative functions of the forums that define the process as a powerful and unique form of pedagogy, as well as a political decision-making process.

In my discussion I draw from research, participant interviews,[1] and my own observations during some of these events to form a set of generalizable conclusions regarding the merits and limitations of institution-wide public forum processes. Deliberative forums, held at university lecture halls or elsewhere—especially when connected to student demonstrations—exemplify a genuine political learning process for young people. In this case, these forums often represented students' first political experiences, and these experiences effectively generated changes in Hungarian politics.

Recent Student Movements in Hungarian Politics

Hungary has experienced major sociopolitical changes in the 2010s. The radical transformation of the country's constitutional system, institutional politics, and basic traits of its polity executed by a center-right coalition dominated by the Fidesz party under Prime Minister Viktor Orbán has been characterized by many observers as an unlikely combination of professional democratic politics and authoritarian power maneuvers.[2] Fidesz rule has been characterized by manifestations of a majoritarian democracy, including a qualified majority in Parliament, state capture for the political and material interests of Fidesz and its supporters, and party-orchestrated intimidation of individuals or organizations critical of the regime. While in the international arena, the European Commission managed to force Fidesz to change some of its constitutional measures that conflicted with fundamental principles of the European Union, in domestic politics virtually nobody could stop

Fidesz—not the weak and dispersed parliamentary opposition, the few remaining critical media outlets, or occasional public demonstrations. That is, until early 2013, when a major education policy package was taken back by Fidesz to be reworked following a series of forums, demonstrations, and Occupy-style public events organized by university students.

During 2011 and 2012, student initiatives were organized around a few significant causes, including the perceived dismantling of Hungary's constitutional framework, issues related to poverty and social inequality, and certain education-related issues. The structure of these initiatives turned out to be truly formative in affecting subsequent events and developments within the movement. (Note that the term "movement" is slightly ambitious, as these initiatives came from a loose network of cooperating student groups with a highly fluctuating cohort of participants. The initiatives lacked any institutional anchor, such as a home base, membership, action program, or elections.)

The movement was organized under the name of HaHa, an acronym of Hallgatói Hálózat (Student Network), although some actions were identified as initiatives of the Egyetemfoglalók (Occupy University) or LÉK. Participants in these initiatives originally came from major universities in Budapest, but student groups from universities in larger cities in the countryside joined some of the actions of HaHa, and a secondary school version of the movement, KiHa (Secondary School Student Network), was established in 2013. The decentralized nature of these student initiatives, their grassroots-style democratic decision-making methods, and the open-endedness of students' tactics and strategies were basic characteristics of the movement. Most activity came from local cells at various universities, but sometimes the network launched actions on issues of national importance with the participation of network supporters and other groups. The network's main communication tools were forums and workgroup discussions, social media for communication with supporters, and a closed Loomio (a collaborative decision-making software program) platform for decision-making.

A quick glance at a few key actions of the student groups in 2011–13 may reveal the issue foci and strategic contours of the movement. When government plans leaked in May 2011 about the prospective closing of Corvinus University, Hungary's leading academic center in economics and social sciences, some of its students joined in collective action against this proposed closing and called on the government to stop engaging in education policy without professional consultation. It is noteworthy that the kick-off initiative of the network emphasized a deliberative goal, that is, proper professional and democratic consultation for political decisions. A strong emphasis on deliberation-related issues became the hallmark of the network's subsequent activities.

At the beginning, activists within the network organized rallies with speeches; as the movement progressed, its strategy become more oriented toward collaborative and media-savvy actions. One of the first one of these was an angry spoken-word group performance of students at an education policy government event in January 2012. This was followed in February by a rally that ended with an unplanned takeover of a lecture hall at the Law School of Eötvös Loránd University, where hundreds of students took part in a large debate. The network also participated in the public outcry that resulted when it was discovered that Hungary's president, Pál Schmitt, had plagiarized his doctoral thesis decades before—a scandal that led to his subsequent resignation.

The network's most influential document, titled "Six Points of HaHa," was penned and voted on at the end of 2012, following the announcement of a government education plan to introduce controversial changes in higher education.[3] The most visible of the network's actions was a series of events connected to the Occupy BTK action in February–March 2013, with a deliberative process aimed at the whole university community at its core. The student movement's most important achievement was that the government had retreated from its original plan to decrease the publicly funded university places by about 80 percent. However subsequently the government had introduced some if its intended policies in a piecemeal manner, it is fair to say that by and large the student movement had successfully protected the idea of free education at the undergraduate and graduate level.

It is worth noting that the organizing principles of this movement are in keeping with global changes in communication that favor grassroots efforts. In their influential article on political communication in the twentieth century, Blumler & Kavanagh (1999) note that despite increasing professionalism and ever higher-tech media, some older forms of political mobilization, such as street posters, rallies, and demonstrations, still play significant roles. In his analysis of the Occupy Wall Street movement, Gitlin (2012) underlines the importance of the flesh-and-blood experience, not only in organizing activity but also in establishing the movement's agenda. This approach borrows Boggs's (1977) notion that no political goal can be achieved without conceptualizing and testing it in an actual group situation. It also takes advantage of the deliberative benefits of social media, including the creation of community and nonhierarchical organization forms (Agarwal et al., 2014; Garrett, 2006; Shirky, 2008; Segerberg & Bennett, 2011).

The Student Forums

The Student Network (HaHa) and Occupy University (Egyetemfoglalók) initiatives used a particular deliberative forum format that they borrowed from student activists who had occupied the philosophy faculty (department) in Zagreb, Croatia. They learned about the Zagreb example through a documentary film and through a visit from several activists from Zagreb. The forums in Zagreb as well as in Budapest used a format based on the principles of radical democracy, including giving power directly to the people without legitimizing external structures or hierarchies.

The student forums had four key features. First was identifying the important issues at stake—that is, creating the agenda for the forum. Second was deliberation on the issues, including weighing the various choices and dilemmas attached to each. Third, each deliberative session was concluded by a majority vote, which determined the resulting action. Fourth, working groups were created to attend to the nuts and bolts and practicalities related to the task that came out of the vote. This fairly simple and logical format was key to the initiative.

Forum Features and Ethos

The most important aspect of the forums in terms of the student movement was that they provided the basic frames of time, space, and structure. Here I have to reiterate that the student movement, especially in the beginning, lacked any institutional character or anchor; it was more of a Facebook-mediated swarm-like crowd of young people than a true organization. The purposefully indefinite nature of the student gatherings preserved their spontaneity and authenticity, but this organizational form (or rather, the lack of it) presented serious drawbacks—for example, in defining what the stake was at any moment or what the crowd wanted. The instant sensational feeling of occupying a street, a lecture hall, or a bridge always contains the fear that the moment will vanish and that the collective, but somehow still aimless, effort will turn out to be futile. The forum experience brought remedies for many of these anxieties. As soon as the crowd entered into an occupied space and a voluntary impromptu moderator asked for votes on the basic issues at stake, a magical transformation occurred. The joint expression of will turned that location into a special place, sometimes into a birthplace, and the date of the voting became a reference point for the whole movement in defining its direction, aim, origin, and identity.

Another essential element of the forums' work was making agendas of all kinds, from setting broad strategies in negotiating with university leadership to arranging smaller issues, such as the proper order of issues to be discussed at the forum. The uncoordinated nature of the movement necessitated a formula that could effectively arrange the acts of the movement into a coherent process and, perhaps more important, that could establish legitimacy for the agenda.

Legitimacy is a key issue here. As could be observed from the tone of the comments at the forum, and as was highlighted by one of the student activists in an interview (Sz.T., personal interview, February 12, 2015) the driving force of the forums was the strong egalitarian ethos. This ethos was behind the choice of the radical democratic forum format, which gave all "executive powers" to the deliberating crowd and aimed to block the emergence of a vanguard or hierarchy within the movement. This firm—and frankly, sometimes slightly paranoid—disdain toward hierarchy re-sulted in some amusing scenes. For example, at one point the group of students who had become the main moderators of the deliberations agreed that when another well-known moderator spoke up as a forum participant, he or she would not be called on by name but rather identified anony-mously (e.g., as the person in the black sweater or in the third row) to avoid creating movement "celebrities" (F.B., personal interview, February 12, 2015). In order to facilitate inclusiveness in moderating, some forums of smaller importance were assigned as practice opportunities for new volunteer moderators. Mediating informational imbalances and inequalities and maintaining a plain style of talk were priorities of these forums, where comments loaded with technical jargon and clichés did not fare well.

Pedagogy was core to the student forums. When organizers sensed that the movement needed an update on certain issues, they invited experts who gave short presentations, thus making the forum a site of learning. This was an important opportunity for faculty engagement in the forum process because some faculty members, apart from participating in forums, could provide expertise on technical issues raised in the deliberations. Faculty engagement had not been an easy issue for teachers or for students. Because independence and authenticity were driving forces behind both the forums and the student movement, students tended to view any interaction with institutions of the adult world, even the university student government, with some suspicion.

Though fruitful cooperation between faculty and student forums occasionally took place, the fear of being co-opted was so strong that students often saw isolation as a safer option. This dilemma was partly resolved by the establishment in 2011 of an interuniversity group of concerned faculty members, Oktatói Hálózat (Teachers' Network), to channel faculty initiatives into an institutional form. If cooperation with faculty was a difficult task for the student movement, the relationship with opposition political parties, which had warmly welcomed the student demonstrations and taken steps to incorporate the student revolt into their agenda, was positively hostile. The student movement perceived the political establishment, including both government and opposition figures, as homogeneously responsible for the crisis in the education system. Oktatói Hálózat was an adult group to which students could relate, at least to some extent, because of their shared concerns about higher education.

In the group dynamics of the forums—which were three-, four-, or even five-hour events—certain characteristics of the process became apparent. Spontaneous silent communication with hand signs was an important norm, because participants could express their opinion instantly without waiting for their slot to say something. These gatherings had become creative sources of expression and of the ability to generate rules through establishing, presenting, and maintaining a forum ethos. In this way students defined the forums as an important site of socialization, an experience that echoes White's (1994) idea of civil society as a disciplinary agent in the relationship between state and society. An intriguing duality could be observed in this feature of the forums: while students' disdain toward hierarchy potentially jeopardized the effectiveness of the forum as an acting entity, the legitimacy produced by the lengthy dialectic that resulted built a strong foundation for the whole process.

Although the forums played numerous latent and manifest functions in the larger student movement, by far the most time was spent discussing issues that came up in the course of events. Some of these forums were closer to mass demonstrations or spectator events, with television crews and frequent chanting of sarcastic slogans aimed at government officials. Others were closer to academic roundtables with erudite reasoning in an intimate atmosphere. Forums included sessions of various styles, such as brainstorming and fact-finding discussions, agenda-setting discussions, deliberations for decision-making, and sessions for resolving practical questions of the group. As one student organizer noted, the forums also played a self-replicating role, as moderators often announced that participants should take the deliberative process back to their respective schools or communities (Sz.T., personal interview, February 12, 2015).

It is important to note that for outside observers or newcomers, these forums often appeared as slightly absurd public performances, with a bit of a chaotic character. The forums borrowed some of their rules and procedures from earlier Occupy events that took place elsewhere, such as a rule that participants must vote on everything, including the question of whether they should vote about whether voting was necessary for deciding practical questions. In addition, hand signals borrowed from the global Occupy movement let participants signal things like intention to speak, a direct response, a suggestion or comment, agreement or disagreement with the speaker, and desire for the speaker to wrap up. These signals gave everyone a chance to chime in during the proceedings. As Gergő Gy. Birtalan (2012), one of the early organizers of the movement in 2011–13, notes in an article about the Hungarian Occupy movement, the forums as decision-making mechanisms were far from majority-vote-driven; rather, they were conceived as efforts to find common ground. This feature emerged in part from the deliberate effort of forum organizers to create as consensus-based a political space as possible, but it also grew from the collective process that created a shared narrative frame for the issues as well as shared terms of conflict and compromise, thus creating strong narrative-cognitive foundations for deliberation.

Energizing the Student Movement

The contributions of the forums included more than giving the student movement time, space, processes, and actions. It may sound rather simplistic, but as one student noted, "average participants became quite excited by the sheer fact that they had been listened to by others" (Zs.H., personal interview, February 10, 2015). This helped attract students to the movement who otherwise might not have participated.

The forum experience—a spontaneous gathering of (mostly) young people, who disproportionally represent the agency of change—is no doubt an engaging spectacle and an attractive idea for many young people. The forums' ability to involve new participants came largely from the opportunity to become engaged without words—through laughter, hand gestures, the sheer bodily experience. One student activist highlighted the role of emotions in drawing her to the process, coining the term *demokráciaélmény* (democracy pleasure)—something she said she had never felt before, either at school gatherings or at public events (A.C., personal interview, February 12, 2015). This student was not alone in her feelings. Student forums managed to merge two seemingly divergent worlds: the world of politics and the world of cool. Though in political science the notion of "sexy politics" is somewhat underscrutinized, as an attentive observer and occasionally participant of rallies and demonstrations for democracy over the past five-plus years, I can attest that these street events achieve the most in terms of political aims when young people, sensing a hip factor, join the demonstration and, with their spontaneous, cheerful, and sarcastic energy, provide the event with a remarkable sense of force and vitality.

As much as forums were envisioned to make conflicts manifest and work as a political tool to reach certain ends, the forums occasionally functioned as sites of conflict resolution. One student organizer noted a case when a small forum was able to accommodate a meaningful exchange between ultra-right-wing activists and young social scientists, which would not have happened in any other context (A.C., personal interview, February 12, 2015). It was apparent in the atmosphere of the forum that while majority voting was a key instrument in decision-making, the aim of coming to a consensus was a stronger force than that of competition, a condition that precluded harsh and violent debates.

The forum machinery, with its focus on majority vote and consensus building, turned out to be an effective means of tackling hostile efforts to eliminate the forums themselves as part of the Occupy University process. At one forum, a group of soccer fans, who had played an important (if questionable) role in Hungarian politics in past years, rushed into the lecture hall with the intention of intimidating students into dissolving the forum. On another occasion, students critical of the Occupy initiative tried to take over a forum to push a vote to end the Occupy efforts. Both attempts were handled within the inclusive tone of the forum setting, the rules of which turned out to be effective in addressing such open conflicts.

Regardless of the sometimes rigid and sometimes chaotic procedures of the student forums, creativity and open-endedness came to be the defining features of the forums. In addition to sessions where students worked deliberately to brainstorm, all my interview subjects mentioned a "surprise factor" in the forums, when events could turn in unexpected directions. At one forum, for instance, hundreds of participating students decided to take a walk in downtown Budapest and ended up occupying a bridge. Another forum was halted by an announcement that helping hands were needed to carry the load of a bakery truck that had brought bread for the student activists as a sign of sympathy.

Conclusions and Recommendations

The forum experience represented the student movement's greatest strengths as well as its greatest weaknesses. Rather ironically, while a professional and academic consensus has emerged about the political significance of 2012–13 (and later 2015) student demonstrations—which were able to force the Hungarian government to retreat from certain questionable policies—many of the participants tend to remember the less successful aspects of the student movement. For the current Hungarian political leadership, it seems to be a matter of prestige not to negotiate with relevant parties or to rethink stated policies. In light of the power politics at play, it is truly remarkable that student movements could stop planned education policies twice since 2011. Nonetheless, this outcome was tempered by issues that students have taken to heart.

Interviews with student activists suggest that their slightly negative assessment stems from two features of the forum experience. As with all human congregations, the student forums had a life cycle—a structure with an optimistic beginning full of fresh input and sensation, and an increasingly cumbersome and tiring end that somehow retrospectively reflects a sense of failure for the whole process. The second problematic aspect of the forum experience is connected to certain limitations of the forum format, particularly their open-endedness and inclusiveness, which sometimes clashed with the movement's political effectiveness and efficiency in reaching specific goals. Most interviewed student activists agreed that streamlining forum procedures, particularly in defining rules, would not have jeopardized the spirit or legitimacy of the forum experience. One student expressed skepticism regarding the possibility of sticking to grassroots principles, believing that all political tools, no matter how democratic, are prone to legitimizing leadership efforts and interests (F.M., personal interview, February 11, 2015).

An assessment of the subsequent development of the movement itself and its participants shows a heterogeneous picture. Given the decentralized nature of the student initiative, it is pointless to assess what happened with its institutional framework, as even its makers thought of it as a temporary and tactical entity (Zs.H., personal interview, February 10, 2015). As for participants, one side of the movement has continued activism under different banners, while another group has chosen academia to pursue transformative goals in society. The legacy of the forums has lived on in other ways as well; there is no doubt that the 2014–15 antigovernment demonstrations inherited important lessons from the student movement, especially in tactics vis-à-vis government spin and organizational principles (Jámbor, 2014).

A few recommendations can be drawn from the student forum experiences:

- STAKE: Choose an issue that has significance in prospective participants' lives.
- EXPERIENCE: Seek organizers who have at least some experience with community action.
- BRANDING: Give a name to your event. Use this name in all subsequent communication.
- KICK-OFF: Plan your start carefully. As one activist said, "the biggest flash was when it all started" (F.M., personal interview, February 11, 2015).
- SPACE: Make the location of the meetings part of the identity of the initiative.

- FLEXIBILITY: Plan consciously to balance open-endedness with structure.
- INCLUSIVENESS: Pay attention to newcomers. Give them preference at the forum.
- DELIBERATION: Balance discussion and decision-making.
- POWER SHARING: Apart from "lawmaking," give small working groups independence.
- DOCUMENTATION: Mark the time and other details of your initiatives. Make memories. Take photos and minutes.
- NONVERBAL COMMUNICATION: Include nonverbal actions—marching, shouting, clapping, sign language—to generate energy and let participants express themselves freely.
- SCOPE: At some point invite a large group (and be prepared for surprises). Do a mass event. Experiment with the wisdom of the crowds.
- VISIBILITY: Make mass action visible for the media.
- WRAP-UP: Provide some closing at the end of the forum.
- REFLECTION: Make participants aware that this occasionally cumbersome feature of the forum is the cornerstone of legitimacy.
- LIFE CYCLE: Make participants aware that there is a life cycle for every public action.

In summary, the forums that university students organized in 2012–13 in Hungary can be assessed as a form of democratic participation and as a political tool to create a discursive community for making decisions, setting goals, and taking action. The forum as a creative space of agency gained significance because it was able to connect symbolic action with effective politics. The forum as a self-governing, inclusive, and open-ended political process played a crucial role in the democratic movements in the 2010s in Hungary. New and old ways of participation merged in these processes, often heavily mediated by social media, setting new paths for political action in contemporary public spheres.

NOTES

1. I conducted interviews with several student activists, identified in the chapter by initials to protect their identities: F.B. (born 1992), A.C. (born 1988), Zs.H. (born 1995), F.M. (born 1990), and Sz.T. (born 1991).
2. Notable critics of the Fidesz-ruled politics have included organizations like Freedom House (2015), the European Commission for Democracy through Law (2011), and Reporters Without Borders (2014), which notes that "Hungary has undergone a significant erosion of civil liberties." Other critics include Guriev and Treisman (2015, p. 3), who call Orbán's rule a case study of their "informational theory of dictatorship"; political scientist Fareed Zakaria (2014), who characterized Orbán's politics as "Putinism" following Orbán's 2014 declaration that he would build an "illiberal democracy" in Hungary; and U.S. Senator John McCain, who has called Orbán a "neo-fascist dictator" (BBC, 2014).
3. The Six Points document made these demands, summarized slightly from a HaHa Facebook post from February 11, 2013 (https://www.facebook.com/ism.global/):
   1. Enact comprehensive reform of public and higher education.
   2. Keep the limit on the number of students enrolled in a particular institution at least at the 2011 level.
   3. Stop budget cuts and reinstate denied funds.
   4. Cancel "student contracts" and do not limit movement of graduated students abroad.

5. Keep university autonomy intact.

6. Ensure that underprivileged families have a chance of enrolling their children in higher education.

REFERENCES

Agarwal, S. D., Barthel, M. L., Rost, C., Borning, A., Bennett, W. L., & Johnson, C. N. (2014). Grassroots organizing in the digital age: Considering values and technology in Tea Party and Occupy Wall Street. *Information, Communication & Society*, 17(3), 326–41.

BBC. (2014). McCain sparks US–Hungary diplomatic row over Orban. December 3. Http://www.bbc.com.

Birtalan, G. G. (2012). Alaposan bemutatnak: A diáktüntetések döntéshozatali mechanizmusai. *Magyar Narancs*, December 20.

Blumler, J. G., & Kavanagh, D. (1999). The third age of political communication: Influences and features. *Political Communication*, 16(3), 209–30.

Boggs, C., Jr. (1977). Revolutionary process, political strategy, and the dilemma of power. *Theory and Society*, 4(3), 359–93.

European Commission for Democracy Through Law. (2011). Opinion on the new constitution of Hungary, adopted by the Venice Commission at its 87th plenary session (Venice, 17–18 June 2011). Http://www.venice.coe.int/webforms/documents/CDL-AD(2011)016-E.aspx.

Freedom House. (2015). *Freedom in the world 2015—Discarding democracy: Return to the Iron Fist*. Https://freedomhouse.org/report/freedom-world/freedom-world-2015#.VOjrFovF9hB.

Garrett, R. K. (2006). Protest in an information society: A review of literature on social movements and new ICTs. *Information, Communication & Society*, 9(2), 202–24.

Gitlin, T. (2012). *Occupy nation: The roots, the spirit, and the promise of Occupy Wall Street*. New York: It Books.

Guriev, S., & Treisman, D. (2015). *How modern dictators survive: Cooptation, censorship, propaganda, and repression*. London: Centre for Economic Policy Research.

Jámbor, A. (2014). Két évvel a HaHa indulása után, a hosszú magyar őszben. *Kettosmerce.hu*. Http://kettosmerce.blog.hu/2014/12/13/ket_evvel_a_haha_indulasa_utan_a_hosszu_magyar_oszben.

Reporters Without Borders. (2014). *Biggest rises and falls in the 2014 world press freedom index*. Https://rsf.org/en/world-press-freedom-index2014.

Segerberg, A., & Bennett, W. L. (2011). Social media and the organization of collective action: Using Twitter to explore the ecologies of two climate change protests. *Communication Review*, 14(3), 197–215.

Shirky, C. (2008). *Here comes everybody: The power of organizing without organizations*. London: Penguin.

White, G. (1994). Civil society, democratization, and development (I): Clearing the analytical ground. *Democratization*, 1(2), 375–90.

Zakaria, F. (2014). The rise of Putinism. *Washington Post*, July 31.

PART 4

Deliberative Pedagogy and Institutional Change

Educating for Democracy

Scott London

A flurry of books, articles, and reports have appeared in recent years documenting how Americans have become disconnected and disengaged over the last half century. Civic participation is on the decline, membership in associations is down, and the public's penchant for "prosecuting great undertakings in common," as Alexis de Tocqueville (1958, p. 123) described it, is not what it used to be. These forces are not unique to the United States. In countries across the world, public participation is low, and many of the activities once carried out by citizens are now undertaken by professional nongovernmental organizations (NGOs) such as interest groups, watchdog organizations, and social service providers—entities that act on behalf of the public, but often without any direct public involvement.

Despite these worrisome developments—and partly in response to them—there is a growing effort across the United States, and in a number of other countries, aimed at strengthening civic engagement and reweaving the social fabric. The movement, if one can call it that, is still nascent and evolving. At its center is a burgeoning network of organizations called public policy institutes or centers for civic life. While it's a highly diversified group, these organizations share a common methodology, one aimed at tackling tough issues, discovering common purpose, and building stronger communities. The centers are founded on the proposition that democracy is more than a system of government; it's a means by which people act together in pursuit of their common goals and aspirations.

Higher Education and Centers for Civic Life

Today, there are centers operating in almost every U.S. state and in about a dozen other countries, including democracies as diverse as Russia, Brazil, and Colombia. Most are affiliated with institutions of higher learning. They combine the best of what colleges and universities provide—civics courses, leadership development, service-learning programs, community-based research—with the kinds of hands-on, collaborative problem-solving traditionally carried out by NGOs. Because they operate at the intersection of the campus and the community, their impact extends to both: they nurture and strengthen public life while at the same time enriching higher education.

Most of the centers are hybrids—part academic program and part NGO. This has freed them from some of the trappings of both traditional academic institutes and conventional community organizations. For example, they have largely sidestepped the problems of professionalization and accountability that have dogged many nonprofit organizations in recent years. Many have also maintained a certain autonomy from the academic functions of their host institutions. This independence has allowed them to develop new approaches to civic education that are innovative and in some cases groundbreaking.

These centers are pushing boundaries in a number of ways: they emphasize the importance of public work and community problem-solving (as distinct from civics instruction or service-learning) as the cornerstone of an education for democracy; they deepen and enrich scholarship by addressing its vital public dimension; they bring dialogue and deliberation into the classroom; and they foster a more democratic culture on college and university campuses. At many institutions, the centers' activities represent a promising alternative to traditional civic engagement efforts. The work is carried out in public squares, community centers, and neighborhood associations—not behind campus walls. It also goes beyond traditional outreach and service efforts by emphasizing the importance of collaborative public work where academic institutions work closely with communities in ways that can benefit and strengthen both. In the following pages, I describe several examples of these centers in the United States and abroad and offer some thoughts about what they have achieved.

New England Center for Civic Life

Rindge, New Hampshire, is a picturesque town of about six thousand people in southwestern New Hampshire. With its clapboard houses, white-steepled colonial churches, and expansive town greens, it's a prototypical New England community. But for all its history and small-town charm, Rindge faces an uncertain future. A swelling population that has increased sevenfold over the last two generations, combined with deepening divisions about whether to protect the town's historic heritage or promote commercial expansion, have stirred up a heated debate about how to go forward.

Some years ago, the New England Center for Civic Life at Franklin Pierce University brought together community leaders to tackle the issue head on. What Rindge needed, they believed, was a way for people to talk together, to explore the promises and pitfalls, and to work toward common goals. But it would take more than an old-fashioned town meeting and another community plan. As a first step, the center created a steering committee jointly led by local residents, town officials, and fellow faculty members. It then conducted a survey to evaluate where the community stood on a range of priorities for the future.

Unlike many community visioning projects, this one didn't end there. The survey was a crucial component, but while it could map people's individual preferences, it couldn't help them arrive at a common understanding of the values and aspirations of the town as a whole. To that end, the people of Rindge came together to deliberate about the pros and cons of various scenarios for the town's future. The forums were time-consuming but also deeply rewarding for many in the community. The conversations brought people together, strengthened ties between local organizations, and forged some new programs and initiatives. They also led to several key decisions, including the hiring of a new town planner, the creation of a local newspaper, and the purchase of an aquifer for the benefit of the community.

It was the first time the community had come together in such a way to voice opinions as well as hammer out a set of concrete plans for the town's future. For the center's Douglas Challenger and Joni Doherty, who led the initiative, the process was also rewarding from an academic standpoint. It got their students involved in what they describe as "problem-based service-learning" (Challenger and Doherty, 2002, p. 67). They conducted research, carried out interviews, identified the pros and cons of various actions, and led discussions in the community. The process illuminated what scientifically generated facts and expertise can and cannot do in the realm of public decision-making. It also allowed the college to extend its reach into the community to contribute resources and expertise in a uniquely collaborative and participatory way.

Virginia Tech and the Crossroads of the Blue Ridge

A few years ago, a center based at Virginia Tech began working on a similar project with the small town of Wytheville, Virginia. Sometimes referred to as the "Crossroads of the Blue Ridge," Wytheville was debating whether to divide and relocate two major highways. Over the course of three years, the center helped the community not only to resolve the highway dispute but also to develop an overarching vision for the town's future.

With the help of graduate students, the center first set about conducting interviews and research in Wytheville. It went on to spend six weeks working with local leaders to create a framework for community-wide deliberation. This was followed by a year-long series of public dialogues in which the people of Wytheville systematically examined several potential scenarios for the town's future. The process took time, but on the strength of the deliberations, the community was able to develop a long-term vision statement and move toward real action.

According to project leaders Larkin Dudley and Ricardo Morse, it was "incredible to see the evolution and broadening of the community's focus from a narrow, immediate question of road relocation to a larger question of the future of the community" (Dudley & Morse, 2008, p. 179). It was also a powerful example of what happens when people in a community change from asking what their leaders can do for them to asking what they can do for themselves, Dudley says. The shift in the discussion allowed the group to identify new lines of thinking and to imagine a new set of possibilities.

Other Centers and Initiatives

Centers like those at Franklin Pierce and Virginia Tech are emerging on campuses and in communities across the United States. At the University of Michigan, the National Forum on Higher Education for the Public Good uses deliberative dialogue to strengthen the link between community leaders and regional and state policymakers. The Center for Civic Participation at Maricopa

Community Colleges in Arizona works with leaders from Hispanic, black, Native American, and other traditionally underserved communities to make certain they have a voice in regional and state policy discussions. The Institute for Civic Discourse and Democracy at Kansas State University partners with organizations across the state on issues like immigration, land use, healthcare, and energy to ensure that new policies clearly reflect the public voice.

These activities are also being tried in other parts of the world, although typically in the form of programs, partnerships, and initiatives rather than standalone centers. At Universidad de los Andes in Bogotá, Colombia, for example, faculty in the political science department have infused dialogue and deliberation into a range of programs, from engaging low-income communities to improving relations between police officers and inner-city residents. In one of its most successful projects, the university worked with the governor's office in the state of Atlántico to improve civic education in local high schools. They began by dispensing with the traditional civics class—which the students said was dull and uninspiring—and restructuring the curriculum to give greater emphasis to dialogue, deliberation, and contact with local officials. They went on to sponsor forums where students, teachers, and community and government officials could explore possible solutions to tough issues. "People in Colombia are very impatient with how every issue is diagnosed and diagnosed," professor Gabriel Murillo-Castaño said in an interview. "They don't want to be involved unless they know that their participation will have a practical outcome." The forums with local officials gave the students a real voice.

Ultimately, the goal of these efforts is to build and strengthen communities from the ground up, although the centers approach that mission in different ways. Some strive to empower individuals by giving them the tools and frameworks to engage and make a difference, others seek to shape public policy, and still others work to build trust and reinforce social bonds. About a third of the centers pursue yet another route: they help communities take matters into their own hands and engage in public work. These organizations focus on building capacity, strengthening people's ability to identify common concerns, and engaging in real-world problem-solving.

Expanding Citizenship Education

Over the last decade or more, "civic engagement" has become a catchphrase on college and university campuses. Much is made of preparing students for responsible citizenship, developing future leaders, and inculcating civic values. But for all the talk about higher education as a public good, the academy's commitment has been mostly limited to civics instruction and service-learning. Not that students don't benefit from learning about government or from serving others, but these pedagogies too often take the place of hands-on experience tackling issues and solving problems in the community.

The centers' activities differ from conventional civics curricula or service-learning programs, which are oriented primarily at undergraduates. They also differ from traditional campus–community partnerships and collaboratives, in which institutions confer knowledge and resources on behalf of others. The work of the centers is aimed at fostering essential democratic practices and grounding them in public work carried out with and as part of the community. They bring people together, identify issues, convene deliberative conversations, promote collective action, and create spaces for social change. This is a model of citizenship education that revolves around democratic problem-solving, not simply inculcating civic values or doing good in the community.

The centers are also expanding the limits of citizenship education by pushing the boundaries of scholarship. Traditional academic research presents a difficult challenge for those working to build communities and strengthen democratic practices. What works in higher education does not necessarily work in public life. In the academy, knowledge is valued to the extent that it makes an original contribution to a given field or discipline. In the public sphere, by contrast, knowledge is valued to the extent that it advances specific public ends. The two forms of knowledge are not mutually exclusive—academic expertise can be applied toward any number of public purposes, such as developing a new vaccine or determining the effects of ozone depletion. But many of the problems of public life are not technical in nature and therefore can't be solved by expert knowledge. They are not based on conflicting information so much as conflicting values and convictions.

Through the work of the centers, scholars at many institutions are exploring new ways to deepen and enrich their disciplines by drawing on public knowledge—knowledge based on group inquiry and public deliberation. When done well, they say, it not only advances their scholarship but also serves the broader needs of the community. The centers offer an ideal laboratory for public scholarship of this sort, one that allows faculty to explore the broader civic dimensions of their research.

A further way the centers are reinventing civic education is by bringing deliberative dialogue into the classroom. "If you look at a lot of classroom activities," says Richard Dubanoski, dean of the College of Social Sciences at the University of Hawaii at Manoa, "we have an expert lecturing the students. We don't engage them in the conversation, in active learning, or in any kind of critical thinking" (London, 2001, p. 6). Participating in one-time deliberative discussions on specific issues may not transform a student's learning experience, he says, but the practice of deliberation is very powerful when it becomes part of an ongoing process of inquiry. "If students are having continual experiences from the time they come to the university until the time they leave, there is a chance they will take on the habit of deliberating" (London, 2001, p. 6).

Some centers have also partnered with academic departments to create "schools for democracy"—opportunities for students to live and work together as citizens. Larkin Dudley at Virginia Tech sees this as part of a growing movement, particularly at large research universities, aimed at developing "learning communities" where students can share ideas and work together to achieve common learning objectives. "It's an attempt to find alternative ways of creating community," she says (London, 2001, p. 7).

The true test of a college or university's civic mission is how it deals with contentious issues on campus. Many institutions are content to educate for democracy, not practice it. But some are working in partnership with centers to explore new ways to address campus-wide issues. Colleges and universities are perfect venues for deliberative problem-solving since they are communities in their own right and mirror the problems of society at large. Because they are institutions of learning, vexing social and political issues can also serve to deepen the pursuit of knowledge and the growth of understanding.

Assessing Outcomes

There is no easy way to measure the outcomes of the centers' work over the last quarter century. Even if it were possible to sum up the quantitative data—the growing ranks of institute alumni, for example, or the rate of growth of the network as a whole—the real value of the work would not be reflected in the numbers. Institute leaders routinely caution against searching for hard evidence of impact. The most powerful outcomes are the most difficult to quantify because they involve democratic norms and capacities that are intangible, says Charles Lacy, retired director of a center at the University of California, Davis. "If you can tell strong stories," he adds, "that is probably the closest you can come" (London, 2003, p. 31).

Even so, the evidence, especially when examined as a whole, constitutes more than just good stories. It suggests that the centers' efforts have contributed to the public good in a range of ways. Careful documentation—and, in a few cases, independent evaluations—have shown centers to have directly or indirectly increased voter turnout, heightened civic participation, strengthened civic capacity, deepened trust and mutual understanding, spanned social, political, and economic boundaries, reached out to traditionally underrepresented populations, brought an end to stalemates on intractable issues, influenced public attitudes, and shaped public policy. (See, for example, London, 2003; Carcasson, 2008.)

There is also some evidence—less convincingly documented but supported by interviews and secondhand reports—suggesting that some centers' programs have improved relationships between citizens and officials, enhanced decision-making, expanded the responsiveness of local institutions such as government, business, and the media, and even created new institutional arrangements.

The big question facing the centers is whether the value of their work is adequately recognized and whether they will continue to get the support they need in coming years. Many of them are tied to colleges and universities that are cutting back and shifting their priorities to other pressing demands, such as expanding enrollment, accommodating diversity, or simply making financial ends meet. But if the centers can continue to document their successes and make a compelling case for their work, both individually and as a network, they are likely to have a significant and deepening influence in the years ahead—one that can enrich our public discourse, strengthen our social fabric, and shore up our capacity to govern ourselves as democratic citizens.

NOTE

Portions of this essay were adapted from Scott London, *Doing Democracy: How a Network of Grassroots Organizations Is Strengthening Community, Building Capacity, and Shaping a New Kind of Civic Education* (Dayton, OH: Kettering Foundation, 2010).

REFERENCES

Carcasson, M. (2008). Democracy's hubs: College and university centers as platforms for deliberative practice. Unpublished report. Kettering Foundation, Dayton, OH.

Challenger, D., & Doherty, J. (2002). Living in the lap of an immense intelligence: Lessons on public scholarship from the field. *Higher Education Exchange*, pp. 54-71.

Dudley, L. and Morse, R. (2008). Learning about deliberative democracy in public affairs programs. In John R. Dedrick, Laura Grattan & Harris Dienstfrey (Eds.), *Deliberation and the Work of Higher Education* (pp. 165-90). Dayton, OH: Kettering Foundation Press.

London, S. (2001). *The civic mission of higher education: From outreach to engagement.* Dayton, OH: Kettering Foundation.

London, S. (2003). After deliberation: A field report. Unpublished report. Kettering Foundation, Dayton, OH.

Tocqueville, A. de. (1958). *Democracy in America.* Vol. 2. New York: Vintage.

Kansas State University's Institute for Civic Discourse and Democracy: Developing Civic Agency

Timothy Steffensmeier and David Procter

Kansas State University's communication studies department has a rich history of conducting political communication research. For decades, faculty in the department have studied the communication characteristics and impacts of political social movements, political speeches, and political advertising. Beginning in the 1990s and into the twenty-first century, however, several faculty members became increasingly concerned about the staggering influence of institutional political communicators—political candidates, elected political leaders, political advertisers, political marketers, and political pundits—in setting the political agenda and driving public policy. We came to believe, along with Harry Boyte (2014), that this form of political talk increased incivility, community fragmentation, and a sense of citizen alienation and powerlessness.

In response, these communication scholars—along with faculty from across departments at the university, including political science, leadership studies, engineering, geography, landscape architecture, and library sciences, as well as a rural development center—came together to address toxic political talk and develop citizen civic agency. Civic agency, as described by Boyte, refers to "self-organizing, collective citizen efforts to solve problems and create public things in open settings without tight prior scripts. A civic agency approach [to democratic participation] is built through what we call public work, based on a sense of the citizen as a co-creator of a democratic way of life" (2009, p. 1).

This group of scholars joined together to focus their efforts not on institutional political communication but rather on communication practices and competencies that citizens might learn and employ to advance their political interests and needs. Such competencies are central to civic agency. In his book *The Ecology of Democracy* (2014), David Mathews explains that civic agency is built communicatively by citizens defining problems, socially constructing knowledge, and deliberating about potential policy alternatives. Likewise, Dahlgren (2006) argues that civic competency is characterized by various communication competencies.

With this in mind, the Kansas State faculty members set out to strengthen civic agency and deliberative democracy by building community capacity for informed, engaged, civil deliberation around salient issues facing those communities. From an increased community capacity for delibera-tion, this group saw the possibility of a stronger democracy and a strengthened citizen civic agency.

This chapter describes how faculty and staff at a research university went about creating and gathering support for deliberative pedagogy. While it proceeds along the lines of a typical progress narrative—continual advancement and growth—the path forward has not been direct. In reviewing this process, the chapter outlines major developments in the effort to embed deliberative pedagogy into university practice, along with the successes and occasional setbacks this effort has encountered.

Partners and Funding

In 2004, this small group of faculty joined together to leverage their networks and academic assets to increase their research output, educate more students and citizens, and secure financial resources to sustain their work. They were interested in cultivating civic agency work in all mission areas of the university—research, teaching, and engagement. Because they saw their collective effort as emerging from a university-based faculty institute perspective, they named the group and its work the Institute for Civic Discourse and Democracy (ICDD).

ICDD's nascent efforts were aided by two significant events. As ICDD started its work, Kansas State launched an internal grant program called Targeted Excellence. The university was interested in funding campus initiatives that "had the potential to move Kansas State University forward in its quest to become a stronger, student-centered, research-oriented Land Grant institution" (Kansas State University, 2009). ICDD's small cadre of associates put together a Targeted Excellence proposal in 2005, and the institute was awarded funding for three years. Thus, ICDD went from having no financial resources to having significant funding. The Targeted Excellence funding catalyzed ICDD's work in several ways. Through the funding, the institute was able to hire a project coordinator, a database coordinator, an evaluation coordinator, and IT staff, as well as student assistants. In ad-dition, the funding allowed the group to launch the ICDD Lecture Series in Civil Discourse, which helped establish group's credibility and also helped build a national and international network of deliberative democracy scholars.[1] In addition, the funding provided significant travel support, which assisted ICDD's efforts to network with deliberative democracy scholars and organizations around the country.

In the second major development, ICDD was able to partner with the Kettering Foundation, one of the prominent organizations identified early on, whose mission meshed well with ICDD's.[2] Like ICDD, the Kettering Foundation was interested in conducting research on deliberation and democracy, as well as in training citizens in deliberative practices to build an infrastructure for civic agency. ICDD and Kettering jointly developed research collaborations and communication trainings (through moderator and facilitation workshops), with the goal of strengthening local democracy infrastructure. Thus, by 2006, ICDD had secured sufficient funding and a robust national deliberative democracy network to launch its work.

Pursuing a mission to build community capacity for informed, engaged, civil deliberation logi-cally led to discussions about the education and training of citizen leaders. ICDD saw its education work proceeding along two tracks: continuing education in facilitation training, and for-credit coursework in deliberative democracy.

Continuing Professional Education

With support from the Targeted Excellence grant and the Kettering Foundation, ICDD's Public Issues Facilitation Workshop launched in 2006. From the beginning, this workshop was about more than simply training individuals to moderate conversation. Consistent with our mission, we wanted to build citizen civic agency. Thus, we were intentional about inviting citizen leaders and policymakers to participate. Because of available funding, in the first year of the workshop we invited citizen leaders from around Kansas and told them that we would provide a scholarship for a local public policymaker to attend with them. Consequently, in the first year, our attendees included extension agents who are employed by the university and work in Kansas communities. These agents were paired with county commissioners, while nonprofit directors were paired with school board members, and chamber of commerce members were paired with city commissioners. In subsequent years, we have continued to invite and market not only to those who are interested in facilitating community conversations, but also to citizen leaders who have some capacity to affect public policy.

Our mission also guided our curriculum construction. The training has included more than facilitation skills. In addition to discussing and practicing specific moderator roles and techniques, we have highlighted the importance of community conversation and deliberation in political decision-making. We have discussed the important role citizens play in identifying "wicked" issues—important public issues that have no simple solution—and deliberating possible public policy responses to them.

ICDD has hosted the Public Issues Facilitation Workshop on the campus of Kansas State University annually since 2006. In addition, we have conducted facilitation workshops for the New Mexico State Department of Education, the International Community Development Society, the Johnson County (Kansas) Library System, the Wisconsin Institute for Public Policy and Service, and the National Council for Social Studies.

Deliberative Democracy in the Undergraduate Curriculum

In addition to these continuing education efforts aimed at developing civic agency among professionals, ICDD has built institutional support for deliberative pedagogy through a bottom-up curriculum-development process. What started as a team-taught interdisciplinary course in democracy studies has blossomed into a proposal for a new communication and leadership doctoral program rooted in community-engaged scholarship. The narrative that follows describes the various academic units, external partners, and curricula that have contributed to creating an environment where deliberative pedagogy can flourish.

Interdisciplinary Course in Democracy Studies

The initial experiment in developing a for-credit curriculum was a course on democracy studies called Dialogue on Democracy. The course was team-taught by ten faculty members from a cross section of humanities and social science disciplines, including communication studies, history, philosophy, English, political science, and library sciences. Dialogue on Democracy thus exemplified the interdisciplinary conversations we wanted to catalyze in the classroom and among faculty. The course explored the theoretical and historical foundations of the U.S. democracy, with some attention given to the skills necessary for effective citizen participation. It had four key student learning objectives:

- Understand the philosophical foundations and essential principles upon which the American democracy was founded;
- Critically examine real-life tensions among government, citizens, and private players in the enactment of contemporary democracy;
- Develop the ability to participate as a citizen through effective deliberation; and
- Analyze the prospects of democracy in the twenty-first-century global context.

This initial course was received well by students and faculty alike; so much so that it led to talks about creating a democracy studies certificate with coursework from the various disciplines represented. Moreover, there was a willingness to continue team-teaching this course. Neither aspiration came to fruition, however, in part because we could not figure how to address faculty labor issues—namely, compensation and how to count these team-teaching efforts for tenure and promotion.

Communication and Democracy

Given that ICDD's roots were in communication studies, it is no surprise that there was strong support from this department for designing a curriculum that included deliberative pedagogy. In 2006, the Interactivity Foundation (IF), a national nonprofit organization that works to engage citizens in public policy, put out a call seeking faculty from various disciplines to attend a summer workshop regarding their citizen discussion process. Upon being accepted to the workshop, faculty were expected to develop coursework that incorporated aspects of the IF public discussion framework.

When a Kansas State faculty member was selected to attend the workshop, the funding and support of IF fellows led to the creation of an undergraduate communication studies course, Communication and Democracy. Versions of this course have been taught at the university since 2008. The course examines how communication, specifically speechmaking, has shaped notions of citizenship in the United States from the time of the Declaration of Independence to the present. It explores changing notions of *citizen* and *civic leader* through a student-led facilitation process focused on the question, what does it mean to be a citizen in the U.S. democracy? The deliberative process develops an important skill set for students who seek to nourish and sustain democracies. Class objectives include the following:

- Introduce rhetorical tools to critically analyze texts;
- Explore conceptual possibilities of what it means to be a citizen and civic leader;
- Learn facilitation perspectives and techniques;

- Develop facilitation skills through group-based deliberations; and
- Create, plan, and host a public forum.

Developing students' capacity to facilitate public deliberations is a central feature of the course. Unlike the Dialogue on Democracy course, where students were learning from content experts, this class is a protopublic space (Eberly, 2000) where students can develop the critical thinking and communicative skills necessary to create public policy possibilities. In other words, the classroom is a generative space, where new content, motives, and behaviors are created to develop a heightened degree of civic agency.

Dialogue, Deliberation, and Public Engagement Certificate

The Dialogue, Deliberation, and Public Engagement (DDPE) certificate was initiated in 2004 by faculty at Fielding Graduate University (Santa Barbara, CA) and designed collaboratively with the International Institute for Sustained Dialogue, the Kettering Foundation, the Centre for Citizenship and Public Policy at the University of Western Sydney, and the Public Dialogue Consortium. The primary architect and champion for the DDPE was Barnett Pearce, a well-known scholar in communication studies at Fielding Graduate University. After Dr. Pearce passed away in 2011, Fielding decided to discontinue the curriculum. Other individuals and centers that had helped create the DDPE were interested in continuing the program, but they needed an academic home for the curriculum. They approached Kansas State because the ICDD made the certificate program a natural fit for the university.

Beginning in fall 2013, ICDD offered the DDPE through Kansas State's Global Campus as a noncredit certificate program; the first class completed the noncredit certificate program the following spring. In an effort to serve the needs of students seeking graduate degrees, the communication studies department added a DDPE for-credit graduate certificate in 2014 to provide scholarly and professional development experience for graduate students and community practitioners looking to engage the public more effectively around difficult issues. Participants in this twelve-credit-hour certificate program include city managers, mediators, extension professionals, community and organizational development specialists, conflict resolution professionals, city planners, public servants, and elected officials. The DDPE program strives to serve learning needs that are not being met in the academic market with a niche focus on developing mastery in making wise public engagement choices in our communities, organizations, and countries. To reach this audience, the DDPE is offered in a blended online and face-to-face delivery format where the cohort gathers together for two on-site meetings. The remainder of the learning occurs in a distance format.

The DDPE certificate aims to build community capacity for informed, engaged, civil deliberation around significant public issues. Students develop a range of communication skills relevant to dialogue, deliberation, and engagement, including learning how to critically diagnose situations and make distinctions among various ways of working with publics. Moreover, students engage and employ the scholarship of deliberative democracy in order to better understand themselves and the larger systems within which they live and work. The curriculum includes these sequential courses:

- COMM 790—Dialogue, Deliberation, and Public Engagement: Theoretical Foundations (4 credit hours)
- COMM 791—Dialogue, Deliberation, and Public Engagement: Process Models (3 credit hours)
- COMM 792—Dialogue, Deliberation, and Public Engagement: Core Skills and Strategies (4 credit hours)
- COMM 793—Dialogue, Deliberation, and Public Engagement: Capstone (1 credit hour)

The DDPE graduate certificate aims to develop civic agency by integrating the scholarship on public deliberation into an applied program. Unlike the proto-public classroom designed for the undergraduate students, the DDPE courses employ a scaffolding approach that culminates with planning and implementing a public deliberation. In addition, the blended online and in-person format makes it possible for participants from around the world to learn together.

Leadership Communication Doctoral Program

As we finish writing this chapter, a new PhD program rooted in deliberative pedagogy has been approved by Kansas State University and the state's Board of Regents. The PhD in Leadership Communication is an interdisciplinary doctoral program and officially launches in fall 2018. The program is a collaboration of three academic units located in distinct academic colleges: communication studies (College of Arts and Sciences), communications and agricultural education (College of Agriculture), leadership studies (College of Education), and the Institute for Civic Discourse and Democracy located within the Office of the Provost.

Faculty in these academic groups started working together because they recognized that interdisciplinary approaches to leadership and communication are needed to solve complex challenges. The doctoral program will focus on community-engaged leadership, including processes of influence, deliberation, and dialogue to make progress on the world's most difficult issues. It will integrate experiential, theoretical, and applied approaches to understanding leadership and communication. Graduates will use community-engaged scholarship to transform the academic, nonprofit, government, private, and civic spaces in which they live and work. Learning objectives for the program include the following:

- Apply communication processes of engaging publics and creating change with diverse audiences;
- Apply leadership and communication theories;
- Conduct community-engaged research; and
- Demonstrate competency in convening people and facilitating public decision-making processes.

The growing demand for individuals who have both advanced research skills and convener experience to solve complex societal problems is the impetus for this program. Our Delphi study, which engaged experts to provide input during the early idea formation stage of the proposal, indicated that this doctoral program would prepare students for jobs with NGOs, foundations, and governments that need employees who can conduct original research and engage communities and publics. In addition, the program will be helpful for students interested in leading social change and those who have a commitment to public service. Moreover, we expect some graduates to become research faculty in agricultural communications, communication studies, and leadership studies programs.

Conclusion

The institutional pedagogical structure at Kansas State University has been built through an Institute for Civic Discourse and Democracy pursuing two educational tracks: a professional, informal educational track and a formal for-credit, university-based educational track. Both educational strategies have been built from the ground up, constructed through on- and off-campus partnerships that have exploited the need and desire for greater citizen civic agency in addressing America's political environment.

In 2014—the tenth anniversary of ICDD—there was much talk about what work we ought to be doing in the next ten years. One of the most pronounced responses was that formal and informal deliberative pedagogy should be at the core of our work and identity. By engaging university students and lifelong learners in building civic agency, ICDD advances its mission of building civic capacity through deliberative pedagogy.

NOTES

1. Speakers in the Lectures on Civil Discourse Series included political theorist Benjamin Barber, Kettering Foundation president David Mathews, Jose Alfredo Miranda of Mexico's Universidad Popular Autónoma del Estado de Puebla (UPAEP), University of Wisconsin–Milwaukee professor William Keith, and former Kansas Governor John Carlin, as well as ICDD director David Procter.
2. The Kettering Foundation's work is guided by the question, "What does it take to make democracy work as it should?"

REFERENCES

Boyte, H. C. (2009). *Civic agency and cult of the expert*. Dayton, OH: Kettering Foundation.

Boyte, H. C. (2014). Deliberative democracy, public work, and civic agency. *Journal of Public Deliberation*, 10(1), Article 15.

Dahlgren, P. (2006). Doing citizenship: The cultural origins of civic agency in the public sphere. *European Journal of Cultural Studies*, 9(3), 267–86.

Eberly, R. A. (2000). *Citizen critics: Literary public spheres*. Urbana: University of Illinois Press.

Kansas State University. (2009). *Investing in excellence*. July. Http://www.k-state.edu/media/k-statement/v0131/31209targetedexcel.html.

Mathews, D. (2014). *The ecology of democracy: Finding ways to have a stronger hand in shaping our future*. Dayton, OH: Kettering Foundation.

Practical Application: A National Issues Forum at a Historically Black College

Marshalita Sims Peterson

The growing focus on civic engagement in colleges and universities across the United States reflects a commitment to tying institutional mission to citizenship and community. As such, this focus serves as a conduit for civic agency, which emphasizes the ability of groups with diverse backgrounds and views to work collaboratively to address problems. Boyte and Farr (1997) suggest that the concept of civic agency highlights the capacities required to take skillful, imaginative collective action.

Civic agency initiatives are a natural fit for minority-serving institutions such as historically black colleges and universities (HBCUs), which have an inherent civic mission. Many of these institutions are noted for developing students' commitment to leadership, civic engagement, and service. These skills can transfer to the community when students are guided in applying civic and deliberative experiences from the classroom to real-world issues. As Ryfe (2006) states, encouraging active citizenship in college students is hard work that must be done intentionally, thoughtfully, and carefully.

As institutions connect and commit to public work, they create a great opportunity to revisit course experiences that can serve as a platform for deliberative pedagogy by creating spaces for public deliberation and civic engagement. The provision of spaces within the curriculum for such activities is what framed the research presented in this chapter. In exploring curricular opportunities and pedagogical structures for civic engagement and deliberation, I sought to involve students in an experience that both probed and prompted thought regarding the impact of public voice. This chapter addresses a training process for a National Issues Forum (a forum topic and process identified by the National Issues Forums Institute) to expose students to civic engagement and prepare them to engage others. In essence, it answers this question: How can we use pedagogical processes effectively to teach students to explore, initiate, and apply public deliberation and civic engagement during their campus years and beyond? The information here is intended to invoke thought, leading to dialogue and ultimately action as it relates to public deliberation, civic engagement, and the provision of spaces for deliberative pedagogy.

How Can We Support Deliberative Pedagogy? Engaging Students in a National Issues Forum

This project included two phases. Phase 1, Train the Trainer, involved civic engagement, public deliberation, and training activities designed to prepare students both to conduct and to train others for participation in National Issues Forums. It also included reflection activities to gauge student perceptions of the training process. In phase 2, Conducting a National Issues Forum, students engaged others in a forum and explored perceptions of public involvement, collective action, and democratic change. The project took place at Spelman College, a private HBCU in Atlanta, Georgia, in the southeastern region of the United States. Spelman, a liberal arts institution with an enrollment of approximately 2,100 female students, is a recognized global leader in the education of women of African descent.

As a faculty member in Spelman's education department, I involved students in forum activities during two consecutive semesters (fall and spring) of the academic year by creating a space through curriculum programming for deliberative pedagogy. Phase 1 (fall semester) involved twenty seniors, all preservice teachers majoring in child development who were enrolled in an education research course. The education research course engaged students in an individual research project, along with involvement in the forum. The process guided students in learning the skills of public deliberation and prepared them to serve as facilitators/moderators of a National Issues Forum.

The forum process involved three components. The first incorporated a series of activities that included training in conducting public deliberations, framing national issues, preparing a forum, serving as a moderator/facilitator/recorder, and reporting forum results. The second component included integrated analysis and discussion to connect the forum with students' existing education research on topics such as deliberation approaches, civic engagement, democratic processes and practices, collective action, and implications for public policy. The third component involved conducting a National Issues Forum. The topic of the forum, identified through student research, was an issue described by the National Issues Forums Institute: "Too Many Children Left Behind: How Can We Close the Achievement Gap?"

Phase 1: Training the Trainer

The training engaged students in organizing and presenting forum materials, framing the issue, presenting approaches for addressing the issue, identifying and preparing forum roles (moderator, facilitator, recorder, and reporter), and managing logistics. Students explored three approaches for addressing the issue of the education achievement gap: raise expectations and demand accountability, close the spending gap, and address the root causes. They also prepared for their role as trainers in engaging others in the deliberation process. Training materials included the following:

- Issue Forum Book: *Too Many Children Left Behind: How Can We Close the Achievement Gap?* (National Issues Forums Institute, 2007a). The book presents the three approaches for addressing the issue, along with the advantages and disadvantages of each.

- Issue in Brief Guide (National Issues Forums Institute, 2007b). This document offers an abbreviated version of the Issue Forum Book.
- Issue Video (National Issues Forums Institute, 2007c). The video provides an introductory overview of the issue.
- Guide to Organizing and Moderating Forums (National Issues Forums Institute, 2007d). This guide offers information on moderating, facilitating, and organizing a National Issues Forum on closing the achievement gap.
- *Framing Issues for Public Deliberation* (Kettering Foundation, 2002). This publication explores processes for describing and framing issues for deliberation, presentation of options and approaches, and ways for addressing trade-offs and consequences of approaches.

Throughout the process, students had an opportunity to gain an in-depth understanding of the national issue, including trade-offs and consequences of various approaches to addressing it, as a result of their own dialogue and deliberation. In addition to delving into the forum topic and teaching students the skills and knowledge needed for deliberation, training activities focused on the practical aspects of conducting a forum, such as defining the forum's purpose, recruiting participants, selecting a site, determining the forum's format (including deliberation approaches, timeline, and process for ending the discussion), and presenting results. Students held a simulated forum to apply their training (put into practice) in advance of conducting a forum involving other students (which occurred in phase 2 of the project).

Throughout the training process, I observed students to evaluate the curricular opportunities it afforded for increasing students' knowledge and skills in addressing a public issue related to their field of study. Because student input is equally essential, I also convened student focus groups to gather information on their views of the process. Specific areas of conversation centered on student perceptions of the issue, the public forum process, their roles as moderators and facilitators, and the impact on their views of civic engagement.

Responses from students showed three recurring themes or patterns: awareness and understanding of civic engagement, the connection between research and action, and the significance of the training as it relates to national issues and public deliberation. Students indicated that the project increased their awareness of civic engagement and the opportunities available to them through campus–community activities. They also reported an increased understanding of the process of public deliberation and the need for discussion of national issues at various community levels. In addition, students noted the importance of connecting their research to current education issues—that is, of applying theory to action through civic engagement.

Finally, students indicated that the training process was effective in preparing them for taking leadership roles as forum facilitators and moderators. This included designating time for analyzing ways to frame public issues and to engage community participants in deliberating various approaches to issues. Students conveyed that they felt equipped to coordinate and moderate National Issues Forums as a result of the training process. Overall, results of phase 1 indicate that students benefited from the training process, as the experience prepared them to take on leadership roles in public deliberation through classroom-learned civic-engagement activities.

Phase 2: National Issues Forum

Phase 2 commenced the subsequent spring semester. This phase engaged students in conducting a campus-wide National Issues Forum on closing the education achievement gap and in assessing forum participants' perceptions of deliberation as a means of addressing an important public issue. In all, thirty-one students (sophomores, juniors, and seniors) across several disciplines participated in the forum. For the forum, student moderators used materials from the training process in phase 1, including the National Issues Forum Book, Issue In Brief Guide, and Issue Video. The forum was held for 2.5 hours with extended time requested by forum participants for continued dialogue and deliberation. Student moderators were actively engaged in the forum process and quite successful in demonstrating their skill in framing the issue, presentation of approaches, recording and reporting, and facilitating logistics and communication processes. The forum participants were equally engaged and expressed their interest in continued opportunities for deliberation through National Issues Forums involving the topic of the education achievement gap as well as additional issues that they identified as pubic concerns and problems.

After the forum, the thirty-one student participants completed a questionnaire focused on their perceptions of public involvement, collective action, and democratic change. Four central themes emerged: civic engagement, advocacy, deliberation through public forums, and community service. Students reported that they view civic engagement as an opportunity to participate in public issues. They also indicated that they felt a sense of obligation to be civically involved and work toward collective action and democratic practice. Students viewed their leadership role as a key aspect of involvement and engagement in the community. They noted the value of deliberation through public forums as an opportunity to discuss approaches to addressing current issues. Finally, students identified community engagement, including campus–community partnerships, as critical to addressing the root causes of issues such as the education achievement gap.

As an educator, I sought to gain insight from students about their views on how public involvement in their immediate community affects collective action and democratic change. Nearly all participants (95 percent) indicated that there is a need for greater public involvement in their community (the other 5 percent said that their community is already extremely involved in collective action and democratic change). All students indicated that they were concerned about public involvement and democratic change in their community; 85 percent indicated that they welcomed an opportunity to become more actively involved in collective action and democratic change through civic engagement on campus. Additionally, all of the students reported that the college's mission connected to issues of democracy and civic engagement, and 75 percent indicated that they felt that their opinion mattered or made a difference.

To explore their views further, I asked students which campus–community activities they valued most. Responses included activities involving community service, deliberate opportunities for community members to share their opinions, forums to address community issues such as National Issues Forums, and consistent activities such as mentoring. Students indicated that they welcomed opportunities for civic engagement through public deliberation.

Results also showed that the National Issues Forum increased participants' knowledge of the specific issue of the education achievement gap, as well as of how to address social issues in general. Students were asked about specific activities that could further their involvement as advocates for public deliberation leading to collective action, democratic change, and civic engagement. The leading responses were increased educational awareness and activism, additional opportunities for public forums, greater political engagement, and more community-service activities. They also indicated that they saw service to the community as a major component of the college experience.

Linking Civic Engagement and Public Deliberation through Curricular Experiences: Should We Continue the Conversation?

If there is an institutional commitment to civic and community engagement, then the conversation regarding engaging students in public deliberation should continue. If there is no commitment, the conversation should still continue, if only because of the learning advantages it offers students. This project provides an example of how the provision of space (curricular and pedagogical opportunities and structures) can involve and empower students. It helped students connect their research and experiences to public deliberation and civic engagement. It also helped to prepare them to assume leadership roles. Students welcomed the opportunity to embrace civic agency through public deliberation and viewed their role as essential in addressing critical issues at the local and national levels.

The results of this project align with existing literature that supports deliberative practices as engaged learning experiences (Doherty, 2008). The project also provides further support for developing civic agency through service-learning and experiential education opportunities, which are essential for engaging students in activities that address human and community needs (Jacoby, 2003). In continuing this conversation, intentionality is critical. Intentional opportunities for deliberative pedagogy promote student learning, curricular enhancements, and connecting students with community issues. National Issues Forums are a valuable tool for engaging students in public issues that affect their communities. It is important to note that although the forum topic in this case was specific to education, the process (e.g., engaging in deliberative dialogue, framing issues) is applicable across social and political issues at the local, national, and global levels.

If we agree that dialogue should continue, it is appropriate to discuss the promise of this activity as a train-the-trainer process, particularly in the context of the education curriculum. Students can use this experience to guide others (including, eventually, their own students) to engage in issues forums. The outreach aspect of the train-the-trainer process can spread practices to engage the immediate and larger communities in conversation, deliberation, action, and leadership.

A process connecting elements of issues forums with the civic mission of higher education speaks volumes regarding advancement of civic agency. Aspects of this process can serve as a navigational tool for institutional assessment and as a structure for implementing activities under designated components: civic engagement, public deliberation, and practical application. For example, civic engagement involves identifying and reviewing activities as they relate to the institution's mission, academic and civic life, and public scholarship. Public deliberation relates to intentional activities grounded in the public work of citizenship, including engaging students, faculty, and community members in dialogue, as well as active citizenship through civic agency and advocacy. Practical application involves experiences such as a train-the-trainer approach, public involvement, and deliberative practice.

Implementing a process or model requires an integrated approach as institutional leaders can address all three components (civic engagement, public deliberation, and practical application) through an ongoing process of planning, implementation, and evaluation. The utility of this approach is contingent on developing desired outcomes, progress and success indicators, and assessment processes for this work at the department, unit, and institutional levels. Ongoing evaluation should also take into account factors such as resource and time allocation and assignment of responsibility.

Classroom Deliberation as a Springboard for Community Engagement

Public deliberation and the practical application of civic engagement are essential to the intellectually and socially engaging experience of higher education. As shared by Mathews (2016), deliberation opens the door to deliberative democracy, which links to the most immediate reason for deliberating together to make decisions that will launch collective action, both for citizens with citizens and by citizens in relation to governments, schools, and other institutions. Building community connections is a central goal of a higher education collaborative for the public good (Harkavy, 2005). Engaged institutions like HBCUs seek to prepare students for lifelong learning, service, and transformative experiences. National Issues Forums as utilized at Spelman can facilitate communal experiences and serve as a springboard for advocacy, leadership, public voice, and deliberative dialogue—all of which embody practical application of classroom-based civic engagement and deliberation.

Our experiences with public deliberation as a form of civic engagement suggest ways for both HBCUs and majority institutions to advance the civic mission of higher education and the engagement of campus and community alike. To be effective, institutional mission must go beyond symbolism and rhetoric. To that end, the public work and public promise of HBCUs can serve as a model for all institutions.

In summary, the conversation regarding higher education's civic mission presents a healthy challenge for connecting the civic commitments of the academy to social realities and public issues of the community through public deliberation. The infusion of civic engagement and deliberation practices into the college curriculum serves as a primary strategy for creating sustainable experiences with civic agency. Creating spaces in the curriculum for public voice and citizenship reinforces the concepts of civic agency, collective action, and campus-community connections. A commitment to civic engagement and public deliberation provides the foundation for creating meaningful curricular and civic experiences that can stay with students through college and beyond.

NOTE

This chapter was written about the author's experience when she was a faculty member at Spelman College.

REFERENCES

Boyte, H. C., & Farr, H. (1997). The work of citizenship and the problem of service-learning. In R. Battistoni & W. Hudson (Eds.), *Practicing democracy: Concepts and models of service-learning in political science* (pp. 35–48). Washington, DC: American Association for Higher Education.

Doherty, J. (2008). Individual and community: Deliberative practices in a first-year seminar. In J. R. Dedrick, L. Grattan & H. Dienstfrey (Eds.), *Deliberation and the work of higher education: Innovations for the classroom, the campus, and the community* (pp. 59–88). Dayton, OH: Kettering Foundation Press.

Harkavy, I. (2005). *Higher education collaborative for community engagement and improvement: Faculty and researchers' perspectives in higher education collaborations for community and improvement.* Ann Arbor, MI: National Forum on Higher Education for the Public Good.

Jacoby, B. (2003). *Building partnerships for service-learning.* San Francisco: Jossey-Bass.

Kettering Foundation. (2002). *Framing issues for public deliberation.* Dayton, OH: Kettering Foundation.

Mathews, D. (2016). *Naming and framing difficult decisions to make sound decisions.* Dayton, OH: Kettering Foundation.

National Issues Forums Institute. (2007a). *Too many children left behind: How can we close the achievement gap?* (National Issues Forums Book). Dayton, OH: NIF Publications.

National Issues Forums Institute. (2007b). *Too many children left behind: How can we close the achievement gap?* (Issue in Brief). Dayton, OH: NIF Publications.

National Issues Forums Institute. (2007c). *Too many children left behind: How can we close the achievement gap?* (Issue Video). Dayton, OH: NIF Publications.

National Issues Forums Institute. (2007d). *Too many children left behind: How can we close the achievement gap?* (Guide to Organizing and Moderating Forums). Dayton, OH: NIF Publications.

Ryfe, D. M. (2006). Narrative and deliberation in small group forums. *Journal of Applied Communication Research* 34, 72–93.

PART 5

Bridging Campus and the Community

Deliberative Pedagogy and Journalism Education: Lessons from Classroom–Community Projects in Four Countries

Angela Romano

Community-based learning activities are highly valued by most universities and colleges, with common options for students being internships, practicums, and different types of service or community-engagement learning experiences. These learning activities offer opportunities for students to apply skills in real-world settings, broaden their knowledge, deepen their expertise, meet new contacts and mentors, and build a portfolio of practical work to showcase to potential employers. Classroom–community projects also increase students' exposure to "moral and civic forms of knowledge that are not academic," such as local knowledge, the wisdom of elders, spiritual perspectives, and the intelligence of a community about matters affecting it (Boyte, 2009, p. 2).

This chapter focuses on core matters of deliberative pedagogy that educators should consider if their goal is to enhance students' acquisition of these civic forms of knowledge. It presents a study of fundamental pedagogic issues addressed by university educators who have designed learning projects that engage journalism students in deliberative community projects in four countries: the United States, Australia, New Zealand, and South Africa. Vocational journalism education involves teaching students the basic knowledge and skills for detecting the places where news or human-interest stories will most commonly be found, recognizing topics of public interest, finding suitable sources of information, conducting research, analyzing the information, then creating, editing, and circulating the resultant stories. Education about deliberative journalism extends this purview by linking reporting to community engagement. This form of journalism gives greater power to citizens and communities to join the news media conversation and act as participants in collective decision-making—just as powerful individuals and organizations do—by raising topics for the public agenda, framing issues, and sharing expertise and perspectives about public problems (Romano, 2010, pp. 17–18).

Case Studies: United States, Australia, New Zealand, and South Africa

For this study, I interviewed coordinators of the U.S., New Zealand, and South African community–classroom projects about their activities and used insights from my own experiences as coordinator of the Australian project. All four projects have required students to connect deeply with their communities for the duration of at least one semester in order to identify and understand community stakeholders, leaders, and networks, then create stories based on public issues and concerns. The teaching staff who initiated and coordinated the Australian and South African projects consciously employed theories and strategies of deliberative media, public journalism, and similar philosophies. These forms of journalism contribute to public deliberation—processes by which communities identify problems or issues of public significance, frame different ways of understanding those issues, formulate potential approaches for addressing the issues, consider the pros and cons of each approach, and ultimately make decisions and/or take action (Romano, 2010). The U.S. and New Zealand projects embody the main elements of deliberative journalism, but the project coordinators did not draw overtly from such philosophies. Instead, deliberative opportunities arose organically from the coordinators' commitment to service-style learning.

In the ongoing U.S. project, final-year journalism students at Temple University in Philadelphia are required to produce multimedia stories about one of the city's neighborhoods or another prescribed news beat, such as city hall, education, or housing. The students must spend extensive amounts of time visiting their neighborhood or organizations associated with their beat, attending meetings, speaking with formal and informal leaders, and listening to community members. From that process, students create stories that contain text, still images, and audio-visual content for the university's news and feature site, Philadelphia Neighborhoods. In keeping with public journalism traditions, these stories regularly profile individuals and organizations that are trying to overcome problems or make a difference in their communities. In the process, students learn and report about neighborhood issues and approaches for addressing them. Student reporters and the overall site have won multiple awards for student journalism (Philadelphia Neighborhoods, 2015).

The Australian project invited final-year students from the Queensland University of Technology in Brisbane to create stories for three deliberative radio programs about the nation's response to incoming asylum seekers and refugees. Over a five-month period, twelve students engaged in listening and research. They spoke with asylum seekers and refugees, academics, lobbyists, activists, nongovernment support groups, the region's residents, and other stakeholders to identify their presumptions, direct experiences, expectations, and concerns about asylum seekers and their arrival to Australia. The resulting *New Horizons, New Homes* documentary-style programs won a national Media Peace Award for Best Radio, ahead of finalists from the country's biggest news broadcaster, the Australian Broadcasting Corporation (United Nations Association of Australia, 2015).

In the ongoing New Zealand project, graduate journalism students from the University of Canterbury in Christchurch collaborate in storytelling with grassroots community residents. Students are assigned to work with a particular community group, whose members help the students identify individuals with whom they cowrite stories. The project commenced in 2013 with an aim of "community enrichment and engagement" through stories about Canterbury residents' recovery following the devastating earthquakes of 2011 (Ross, 2013). Because different groups partner with the journalism program each year, different themes are addressed each time the project proceeds. Since 2013, for example, students have learned and reported about infrastructure redevelopment and issues affecting community-based sports organizations.

In South Africa, students from Rhodes University in Grahamstown create hyperlocal journalism projects with, for, and about economically marginalized local communities. Various projects have run since 2003, with most stemming from the Journalism, Development and Democracy–Critical Media Production (JDD–CMP) course that began in 2006. Each year, final-year students in JDD–CMP construct content with a specific focus on community problems. Some students have maintained traditional journalism practices and media formats, such as newspaper stories in standard news style with quotes from official sources. Other students have used a range of communication styles and media formats to report on and address issues as facilitators, collaborators, and activists. Projects have included multilingual pamphlets, a deliberative community forum, a mockumentary, an advocative video narrowcasted to local businesspeople, and video documentaries coproduced with schoolchildren.

Learning to Listen

The starting point for deliberative journalism is learning the art of "public listening," or listening to ordinary community members to identify public perspectives, priorities, issues, agendas, and trends (Romano, 2010, p. 18). This type of listening has been a core component of learning activities in all four journalism education projects.

The prioritization of listening is a prominent feature of the New Zealand project. Once students are assigned to work with a community group, they have months to network with that group, find one person to write about, then engage in extended conversations before jointly determining the theme for the story they will cocreate. Project coordinator Tara Ross says that learning activities focus on the process of working with community sources to gather and report information rather than on the slickness of the outcomes (personal communication, 2015).

The U.S. and Australian project coordinators emphasize listening across a broad cross-section of the community rather than concentrating intently on one individual or group. Philadelphia Neighborhoods convener George Miller directs his students to find activists and community leaders to "learn about the neighborhoods from their perspective" (personal communication, 2015). For the *New Horizons, New Homes* project in Australia, the other instructors and I led students in conducting focus groups and vox populi conversations with more than one hundred of the region's residents. We also modeled deliberative processes for sharing and analyzing the results of these conversations by facilitating a workshop that used the issue-framing strategies outlined by Belcher and colleagues (2002). Staff and students reviewed the input from the community, then pinpointed the themes, frameworks, values, and priorities being expressed. The issue-framing process established the agenda for the project's three documentary-style radio programs and determined the topics for the individual stories that made up those programs.

The coordinators of these four projects employ a range of pedagogic approaches to cultivate students' competencies in "listening across difference"—listening to people from different ethnic communities, religions, political affiliations, economic classes, or other social backgrounds in a respectful, systematic, and productive way (Dreher, 2009; Young, 1996). Learning activities have included readings, class discussions, workshops, and reflective assessments that examine communication protocols and the social, political, ethical, and emotional dimensions of talking with different types of community members. The discussions and assessments have provided students with opportunities to exchange ideas and cultivate personalized understandings about how the specific personalities, cultures, and contexts of their local communities affect the nature of public listening.

Out of the four projects, the South African project had the most intense emphasis on listening across difference. This focus stems from the nation's enormous ethnic and cultural diversity, as well as the extreme economic disparity between Rhodes University students and residents of the municipalities that surround the campus. A key theory taught by staff has been "proper distance" (Silverstone, 2007), a system that requires students to acknowledge how their personal preconceptions, social backgrounds, and subjectivities shape their responses to other people. Theories of proper distance also mandate that media practitioners accept "the obligation to open their space to the stranger" and allow "the bodies and voices" of minority, disadvantaged, and marginalized people to be "seen and heard on their own terms" (Silverstone, 2007, p. 137).

Learning about Community Dynamics

To contribute effectively to deliberation, students and professionals need to accompany listening skills with a strong grasp of community dynamics. They must learn how to locate the key institutions and spaces where people meet to talk about or act on problems. They need to distinguish a range of stakeholders, formal leaders, and informal leaders in communities. They should develop rich pictures of the connections that link different places, groups, leaders, and stakeholders, while also seeing the ruptures or gaps that may divide them. Such knowledge about community dynamics enhances the student's (or, for that matter, the professional's) ability to find personalities with significant ideas to share and to interpret whether those personalities' perspectives are typical or atypical of dominant trends within community life. The four projects used a variety of techniques to boost student knowledge of community dynamics.

The Australian and South African projects have relied on civic mapping to teach students how to find places, organizations, leaders, and networks within communities. Using approaches pioneered by Harwood and McCrehan (2000), students learn how to identify different layers—or spaces—that form the pulse points of civic life. Traditional journalism education is designed to give students a strong sense of the location, purpose, stakeholders, and unspoken rules of the official and quasi-official layers of government, business, nongovernment, and community organizations (Harwood & McCrehan, 2000). In these deliberative learning projects, civic mapping extends such knowledge by providing tactics for finding and tapping into productive third places for civic life where people gather to talk and do things together, such as shopping malls, hair dressers, and child-care centers (Harwood & McCrehan, 2000).

Civic mapping also facilitates student discovery of different types of leaders. Traditional journalism education focuses on journalists' relationships with official leaders of governments, businesses, unions, and other major organizations; civic leaders of faith-based, nonprofit, community, and interest groups; and experts with high-level professional knowledge. Civic mapping recognizes the role and capacities of these leaders but additionally opens a window into two rarely acknowledged types of civic leaders that exist in all communities. First are the "connectors," who interact, spread ideas, and build relationships with many people, organizations, and groups. Second are the "catalysts," who encourage others to become involved in civic life; community members routinely seek out these leaders for information, guidance, or help (Harwood & McCrehan, 2000).

A second pedagogic approach employed in some deliberative-learning projects has been to establish partnerships with community organizations. In New Zealand, students have connected with groups as diverse as church, gay-rights, retirement-support, and community-advocacy organizations. In South Africa, libraries, local high schools, and a children's shelter have been partners. At a cognitive level, members of partner organizations assist the educational process by sharing insights built over years or decades about different personalities and groups in the communities, including their histories, their politics, their cultures, and their connections. The partners reveal which buildings and community spaces are hubs for civic talk and action. At a practical level, partners often help with introductions or organize entry to places that are not immediately accessible to outsiders.

The South African and U.S. projects exemplify a strategy of progressive scaffolding of student learning throughout the degree program, with learning approaches encompassing competencies for understanding and working with local communities as well as discipline-specific proficiency in journalism research and writing. In their first year, Rhodes University students commence civic mapping of their campus. After several months, they progress to exploring the culturally diverse, economically disadvantaged municipal wards beyond the campus gates. Temple University students undertake a theoretical class in their first semester about ethical and other issues pertinent to covering neighborhoods. In their first production class, students complete two reporting exercises on campus, then move to reporting on Philadelphia's neighborhoods. By the time students commence their sustained experiential projects in their final year, they have developed templates for navigating their cities' spaces, organizations, and personalities.

Instructions and formal requirements, often linked to assessment, are another way to create impetus for students to probe different civic layers and to network with different types of leaders. In the U.S. project, for example, students are instructed to conduct a neighborhood overview and to name at least twelve people—not politicians—who can assist them on their beat. This discourages students from taking a superficial approach by listing easily identifiable official leaders and instead compels them to penetrate the community's layers if they are to fulfill course requirements.

Conclusions

Deliberative pedagogy immerses faculty and students in "collaborative engagement," in which communities are "reciprocal partners and co-educators" (Longo, 2013, pp. 2, 14). In the four learning projects described in this chapter, community members can be considered partners and coeducators, given their importance in informing how students identify, frame, and analyze public issues. In return, the students create or cocreate journalistic stories about underreported issues, experiences, and activities in communities that affect civic life. In doing so, students learn important skills that will serve them as engaged and informed professionals.

Underpinning these connections has been pedagogy that prioritizes public listening and strategies for respectful, productive exchanges with diverse community members. Teachers use approaches such as civic mapping, partnerships with community organizations, progressive scaffolding of community encounters, and targeted instruction and assessment to introduce students to significant community spaces, organizations, and stakeholders, and to illuminate the links between them. Such pedagogic approaches are fundamental not just for teachers of journalism but for all educators who seek to boost the power of community members to formulate views on public affairs, participate in deliberation and collective decision making, and improve public life.

NOTE

Some of the research presented in this chapter is also discussed in Angela Romano, "Teaching about Deliberative Politics: Case Studies of Classroom–Community Learning Projects in Four Nations," *Asia Pacific Media Educator*, 25, no. 2 (2015): 208–21.

REFERENCES

Belcher, E., Kingston, R. J., Knighton, B., McKenzie, R., Thomas, M., & Arnone, E. (2002). *Framing issues for public deliberation: A curriculum guide for workshops*. Dayton, OH: Kettering Foundation.

Boyte, H. C. (2009). *Civic agency and the cult of the expert*. Dayton, OH: Kettering Foundation.

Dreher, T. (2009). Listening across difference: Media and multiculturalism beyond the politics of voice. *Continuum*, 23(4), 445–58.

Harwood, R. C., & McCrehan, J. (2000). *Tapping civic life: How to report first, and best, what's happening in your community* (2nd ed.). Washington, DC: Harwood Institute for Public Innovation and Pew Center for Civic Journalism.

Longo, N. V. (2013). Deliberative pedagogy in the community: Connecting deliberative dialogue, community engagement, and democratic education. *Journal of Public Deliberation*, 9(2), Article 16.

Philadelphia Neighborhoods. (2015). Awards. Http://philadelphianeighborhoods.com/awards/.

Romano, A. (2010). American public journalism versus other international media models. In A. Romano (Ed.), *International journalism and democracy: Civic engagement models from around the world* (pp. 16–32). New York: Routledge.

Ross, T. (2013). Co-creating the news: An experiment in teaching and doing community journalism. Paper presented at the Journalism Education Association of New Zealand Conference, November 28–29, Auckland University of Technology.

Silverstone, R. (2007). *Media and morality: On the rise of the mediapolis*. Cambridge: Polity.

United Nations Association of Australia. (2015). *UNAA Media Peace Awards winners and finalists*. Http://unaavictoria.org.au/media-peace-awards/winners-finalists/past-winners-and-finalists/.

Young, I. M. (1996). Communication and the other: Beyond deliberative democracy. In S. Benhabib (Ed.), *Democracy and difference: Contesting the boundaries of the political* (pp. 120–35). Princeton, NJ: Princeton University Press.

I Understand that Infrastructure Affects People's Lives: Deliberative Pedagogy and Community-Engaged Learning in a South African Engineering Curriculum

Janice McMillan

A student ended his final learning review essay on the Social Infrastructures: Engaging with Communities for Change (SI) course I teach in the engineering department at the University of Cape Town (UCT), South Africa, as follows:

> Linking social infrastructure to civil engineering has been rewarding in the sense that I understand that infrastructure affects people's lives, and taking a moment to critically think as a citizen, you hold these lives in high regard.

Creating deliberate spaces for deep and engaged learning is a challenging but critical task if higher education is to play a role in graduating socially conscious professionals who can act as caring and empathetic citizens. This approach is particularly relevant to higher education in South Africa, which is increasingly influenced by both global pressures and national priorities (Thomson, Smith-Tolken, Naidoo & Bringle, 2008). More than twenty years into our postapartheid history, issues of citizenship, democracy, and infrastructural service delivery are constantly on the agenda and in profound need of scrutiny and transformation.

A number of authors have commented on the need for more civic-minded graduates in order to help build our fledgling democracy. Renowned local scholar Yusuf Waghid (2005; 2009) argues that attributes such as "compassion, criticality, and a sense of responsibility" are necessary to enable people to contribute toward what he calls "civic reconciliation and transformation" (in Leibowitz et al., 2012, p. xi). In examining students' experiences in an international development course, Kassam asks: "What pedagogical framework assists in transforming students who know about the major challenges of the twenty-first century to those who know how to respond to such challenges in a particular socio-cultural and ecological context?" (2010, p. 205).

This question, together with an intentional approach to pedagogy designed to facilitate engaged learning through shared discussion and decision-making, is at the heart of deliberative pedagogy. Longo argues that an increasing number of programs in higher education are "breaking new ground in bridging pedagogical divides by being more intentional about connecting deliberative dialogue with education in the community" (2013, p. 1). He calls this "deliberative pedagogy in the community" (p. 1), a collaborative approach to teaching and learning that brings together deliberative dialogue, community engagement, and democratic education. In particular, "students are stepping outside the classroom and connecting theory with real-world community problem solving" (p. 2).

This chapter explores this approach via a case study of a course I teach in Engineering and the Built Environment (EBE) at UCT. The SI course is taught each winter term to a class of approximately one hundred students.[1] It serves as a humanities elective for engineering students and is also open to students across campus. The course demonstrates the possibilities for deliberative pedagogy in a large classroom setting of professional students in the Global South, as well as the challenges of this practice.

The Broader Sociopolitical and Institutional Context

To understand the significance of this course to the students and the community, it is helpful to examine the context in which it was created and continues to evolve. The global context in which we work and learn is becoming increasingly unequal and unpredictable, and universities are being asked to play a more active role in building more civic-minded global citizens who can deal with these complex challenges.

The course also reflects issues that are specific to UCT and its surrounding communities. UCT has just over twenty-six thousand registered students, 65 percent of whom are undergraduates. Racially the campus is diverse, with approximately 50 percent of the student body consisting of black students. However, this ratio is not yet reflective of the South African population as a whole; in addition, as UCT is a Research 1 university, the vast majority of both black and white students are middle or upper-middle class. In terms of the broader institutional profile, the current UCT Strategic Plan places an emphasis on the notion of social responsiveness in teaching, research, and community-service activities. This approach encompasses the multiple ways in which faculty and students are engaging with UCT's broader social context.

Recently, UCT has been under enormous pressure from a student-driven transformation movement called "Rhodes Must Fall" (RMF) to talk about issues of colonialism, racism, and institutional change on campus. Students demanded that statues of colonialists on campus—and in particular, one of Cecil John Rhodes—be removed, and they were successful.[2] A group of largely "black"[3] students have held heated discussions and protest marches on campus to highlight their alienation from UCT as a colonial institution and the need for fundamental change. The RMF movement has called for UCT's commitment to transformation in terms of staff demographics but also in terms of curriculum and pedagogy. Protesting students have been supported by a number of black staff who have formed "#Transform UCT" as an allied group. The RMF movement has called for the "decolonization" of the curriculum as part of the broader call for institutional transformation and an end to "epistemic violence."[4] People interested in issues of epistemic violence ask questions about what the university is teaching and researching, how they are doing it, and why they are doing it in the particular way that they are. Furthermore, Pillay (2015) argues that "because the university is a place of authoritative knowledge, certified knowledge, it is at the heart of epistemic violence. It is where authorized and legitimate knowledge is cultivated, preserved and protected." For Pillay, such knowledge is not inclusive in that it does not include the diversity of knowledge forms that students and staff bring to the university.

However, the means to address these complex challenges—that is, the strategies, processes, and programs that would reflect real efforts to decolonize the curriculum—are by no means clear. Transformation is thought by many to be about introducing more African content into the curriculum. While this is essential, it's not enough. Transformation also has to be about building new models of teaching and learning that position educators and learners in new relationships—to each other, to knowledge, and to the world beyond the university. (See Garuba, 2015, and Morreira, 2015, for more on this issue.) When this happens, "faculty and students co-create . . . shared spaces for dialogue and collaborative action in the community and rethinking long-held power dynamics between the campus and the community" (Longo, 2013, p. 2). This is what happens, I believe, in my SI course each year.

As part of the engineering curriculum, EBE students must demonstrate multidisciplinary work and understand the impact of their decisions on the personal, social, and cultural values and requirements of those they affect and interact with—including at least one humanities elective as part of their degree.[5] These factors led to the development of the SI course that ran for the first time in 2013, with thirty-three students. (The rapid expansion of the class since that time is one marker of its success.) The course was developed via a partnership between EBE and the Centre for Higher Education Development and has some of its roots in UCT's Global Citizenship Program, which I helped found in 2010.

The Social Infrastructures Course: Engaging with Community for Change

The SI course is deliberately framed to interrogate and engage the nexus between the technical and social domains of learning and knowledge, something that is increasingly important in understanding the design of curriculum and pedagogy in professional degree programs. The term *social infrastructures* recognizes that urban development is a sociotechnical process, giving rise to particular relationships between households and communities and between materials and technologies, shaped by the institutional and political context. While the course is tailored to the needs of all undergraduate students in EBE, the hope is to attract students from other departments to allow a fully interdisciplinary experience for the students involved.[6] Since its inception in 2013, 174 students have taken the course, with the last two years being fully subscribed (at 60 and 91 students, respectively). Only three of these students have come from nonengineering disciplines.

The pedagogic approach in the course combines classroom-based learning and reflection with community-engaged, experiential learning through learning exposure visits. The course is conducted in two parts. Part 1 introduces students to some of the key concepts and processes of learning and engagement that might assist us in understanding how to think about engagement with off-campus constituencies. These include concepts of community, the problem of "single story" or one-sided perspectives and paradigms of engagement, and the process of community engagement itself. The focus is therefore on learning about engagement and about the self (as student, professional, and citizen) in the engagement process. I teach all the sessions in this part of the course.

Part 2 is designed around a series of key challenges facing cities and communities. It is less about in-depth theoretical or content knowledge linked to the issues and more about how the particular issue is reflected in social infrastructures. Taught by faculty leaders in their fields, themes include infrastructure and social change; urban food security; cities and climate change; water, sanitation, and service delivery; and sustainable urban development.

The course runs for a two-hour class-based session daily during the four-week winter term block, and students each go on two of eight field visits to community organizations. The field visits are usually about five to six hours in length. In the class-based sessions, students work in their assigned color-coded groups each with a student facilitator. There is a question posed to the groups that links with the readings and major theme of the day; for example, the topic of "community" might be introduced via questions such as "What/who is community? What communities are you a part of? What facilitates you feeling included/excluded from community? How do community, race, and politics intersect, if at all?" Or citizenship: "What does 'citizenship' mean? How does the context in which citizenship is being discussed shape it's meaning? Is citizenship about having the right to vote or is it also about inclusion and rights?" The students are usually asked to draw on their own ideas about these concepts first in the groups, and then they can draw on the prescribed readings that may critique or support their own views. The role of the student facilitators in the groups is to encourage participation, to link aspects of the conversation to the readings, and sometimes to present a summary of their group's discussions to the whole class at the end. The key issue is the need to build an environment of trust and safety in the groups for students to share their stories.

The field-based visits are aimed at helping students understand the complexity of the issues in many underresourced, marginalized communities. The community members are positioned as educators for the day and organize the visit for the class, based on the issues they feel are important for students, as future engineers, to understand. This might be, for example, water and sanitation, housing, or lack of transport. The students are taken to visit relevant community members who are the leaders in the community. At the end of the visits, the students need to pull together their learning from the visit, and the community is then invited to the student presentations where the students talk about a particular issue—for example, urbanization, water, and sanitation—and how engaging with the community on this issue helped them to understand the complexity of the experiences of the community. The end result (at least in 2015) is an infographic that is then given to the community organization that in turn they can use for funding purposes or education work within their communities.

Essential Course Elements: Learning through Engagement and Cocreation

Barnett and Coate argue that curricula for new kinds of learning and engagement also entail pedagogies for engagement. A curriculum for engagement, in particular, "can only be brought off consistently, can only engage the students . . . if engagement is present in the pedagogical relationship" (2005, p. 128). I believe that teaching in this context requires that educators engage with the past, and with how the past has shaped one's complex identity. The kind of perspective transformation that we aim to achieve in this program for both students and educators requires generating an awareness of "how and why our presuppositions have come to constrain the way we perceive, understand and feel about our world" (Mezirow, 1990, p. 14). We cannot do this without interrogating the context in which learning occurs, how we are all positioned, and what has shaped prior learning.

In order to create the space for engaged learning that takes this context into account, I give particular attention to five aspects of my pedagogical practice that support or contribute to its deliberative nature:

- Creating space for an immersion experience,
- Structuring classes to optimize engagement,
- Rethinking assessment practices,
- Working with student facilitators as collaborators, and
- Building reciprocal partnerships with community members as educators.

Creating Space for an Immersion Experience

One of the challenges we had in the first year of the course was that it was slotted in between other core classes (e.g., math, chemistry). Students therefore did not have the time needed to immerse themselves fully in the issues. We also had to have our field visits on Saturdays, not really suitable for either students or community partners.

Running the course in the winter term (June–July) as we have done the past two years has enabled us to provide a more intensive experience, as students can take only one course during this term. This means that their time is more flexible, which makes it easier for them to work in the community. The winter term was originally set up for two reasons: to help students make up courses they had failed during the regular semester, and to experiment with new kinds of pedagogy given its nontraditional timetable. From the perspective of the SI course, this has definitely been worth it and creates a very deliberate space for learning and teaching, and for innovation and flexibility.

Optimizing Engagement

The SI course has at its core the idea of engagement, both in terms of community engagement and in terms of engagement in learning. Engagement needs to be understood as a relational concept: it indicates a connection between the student and the act of learning. In particular, it is important to extend "collective space" to students "such that they are prompted to engage with each other . . . epistemological space, practical space, and ontological space may all be enhanced through collective engagement among the students, for through collective engagement students gain educational power" (Barnett & Coate 2005, p. 149).

One of the main ways of doing this is the use of learning groups. Students are allocated to a group at the beginning of the course and remain in that group for the duration. In 2015, we had four groups of about twenty-five students each. Each student facilitator is each responsible for one group, which means learning the names of the students, talking to them about how they are faring in the course, building relationships with them, and assisting them with understanding course content. This is a key strategy that many students comment on in their evaluations. The field visits to communities are organized as group visits to allow additional time for building relationships.

Another way I enhance engagement is to make a deliberate attempt to draw on students' existing knowledge about the issues. Many of the small-group class discussions start in this way. This also provides an opportunity for students who live in the communities we visit to be knowledgeable in new ways in the classroom. This is very important for creating agency in the learning process.

Rethinking Assessment

Class-based assignments are of four kinds: two reflection papers written up as blogs to share with their classmates; a group presentation on an issue from part 2 of the course, linked to their learning about community engagement; a conceptual paper in which they need to clarify their understanding of the concept of "social infrastructures"; and a learning review paper in which they need to reflect back on their learning over the duration of the course. The assignments are designed to enable students to articulate three voices/identities that I argue are simultaneously present in the classroom and that are discussed explicitly: a student voice (the conceptual paper); an emerging professional voice (the presentation); and a citizen voice (the reflective blogs and learning review essay).

Having to think of themselves in terms of these different intersecting identities helps to dislodge the more traditional focus on the single identity of engineer. In particular, while students identify as engineers in their presentations, their conclusions reflect a more socially conscious and aware engineering voice. These assessment practices are, I believe, a core element of the deliberative nature of the pedagogical approach I bring to the course.

Working with Student Facilitators as Collaborators

Engaging students as collaborators in their own learning is a vital component of the practice developed in my course. The deliberate effort to bring student facilitators into both classroom practice and the design of the sessions is key to providing them with a sense of agency. All of them have commented on their sense of ownership over the learning process.

Before the course begins, we hold two training sessions on curriculum and pedagogy and the course itself. During the course, I meet regularly with facilitators as a group to think about and plan class sessions. These meetings are particularly important in part 1 of the course, during which we build the overall course framework. This sense of collaboration in their learning not only gives students more confidence in their ability to facilitate class sessions, it also instills a sense of responsibility and leadership in the course. This is important both in itself and as a transformation issue in terms of bringing more young black scholars into academia. (Three of the four student facilitators in 2015 were black students; all had either completed the SI course or participated in the Global Citizenship Program in previous years.)

Building Reciprocal Partnerships

Because the course focuses on the relationship between communities and infrastructure, the site visits are designed as learning exposure visits to help students understand the complex relationships between people, communities, and infrastructure. Given this, the communities in each case are positioned as educators during the visits. We do not think of this work as service projects but rather as learning and engagement opportunities for students and community partners alike.

In the first two years of the course, all students went together to three site visits. These visits involved very different projects and communities, but all of them focused on an aspect of social infrastructure. All were communities with which I have long-standing relationships. In 2015, however, I decided to take a different approach and work with a nongovernmental organization (NGO) with its own existing partnerships. The particular NGO we worked with is the Development Action Group (DAG), a highly respected organization working with underresourced communities and community organizations in the urban sector.[7] DAG is a political organization in the sense that they constantly challenge the City of Cape Town in aspects of urban infrastructure, hence the relevance of linking with my course. Their current project working with communities and engaging with the city is called "Re-imagining Cape Town," and they see the link with our course as an important aspect of this in that by engaging our engineering students, they are working to create more social awareness in future professionals. In all, the course included eight site visits, five of which were brokered by the NGO partner and three of which were in areas the course had used previously. Each of the four groups of students visited two very different community projects; this meant that groups at each site were no bigger than twenty-five students, which helped in establishing meaningful relationships.

Conclusion: Ways Forward in Linking Deliberative Pedagogy and Transformation

The success of the course over the past three years offers evidence of the power of engagement and deliberation, which is illustrated in the voices of students. For example, one student stated in the final paper for the course:

> We interrogated the concepts of community, citizenship, and even bilateral knowledge exchanges between the community and engineer. What I had expected to be a short community project course, progressed as an intriguing discussions course, intellectually thought-provoking and [a] morally educating experience.

The themes that consistently emerge from student evaluations include the importance of several key factors:

- Understanding perspectives, including providing a space for students to explore how their perspectives shape the way they view, interpret, and understand the world.
- Realizing that knowledge exists in many places other than the university—in particular, exploring the knowledge that resides in marginalized communities.
- Recognizing the problem of "the single story"—how partial truths seen through a narrow lens can distort our views and lead to stereotyping.
- Building community ownership and participation in development by realizing that artifacts are not in themselves enough for positive development; as one of our community partners puts it, "people support what they help to create" (Don Shay, Violence through Urban Upgrading (VPUU) project, 2015).

Students in the 2015 course were particularly active in articulating their experiences with the course. A delegation actually approached the dean to request that she make the course compulsory. While this was not possible, the dean spoke of the course's success in transforming learning and students' experiences at a panel discussion on transformation in the curriculum.

We cannot rest on our laurels, however. Transformation is critical, and we need engaged students as leaders and active citizens.[8] I believe, therefore, that we need to ask ourselves some serious questions if we wish to take forward an agenda of deliberate pedagogy linked to transformation:

- How do we find more spaces for immersed learning when curriculum space is broken up into lecture slots within departments and schools?
- How do we use pedagogical approaches that prioritize engagement, especially when such approaches might mean reexamining power relations in the classroom?
- How can we design assessment tasks that look both ways: toward the content that needs to be covered, but also toward the larger context (beyond the university) in which the learning is taking place?
- In the context of busy schedules and demanding timetables, how do we find time to mentor student facilitators as collaborators—both before and during our courses?
- How do we ensure reciprocal partnerships, where we value our community partners as coeducators of our students, particularly in contexts where inequality is both pervasive and acute?

All of this requires intentionality, commitment, and a belief in alternative paradigms of teaching, learning, and engagement. But this is not sufficient. Accomplishing these goals requires more than individual staff in individual classrooms on isolated journeys. It requires whole institutions committing to the process of change and asking different questions about the relationship between the university and its broader context. Perhaps most crucially, it requires us as educators to be willing to step back from preconceived ideas of academic work and, where appropriate, acknowledge our own complicity in the decisions that shape the learning of our students. In other words, it requires a change from within, and from my context in the Global South, this means challenging the structures in which decisions are made that reinforce the education of technically excellent but socially and politically dislocated student-citizens.

NOTES

1. Winter term refers to a short, four-week course.
2. Under apartheid, UCT students and staff were often involved in protests and engagements with the state. The postapartheid RMF movement and related protests are indicative of how challenging institutional transformation processes can be.
3. I use this term broadly to encompass all students who identify as black, be they African, mixed race, or Indian.
4. See http://africasacountry.com/2015/06/decolonizing-the-university/ for a fuller explanation of the concept.
5. While it is beyond the scope of this chapter to discuss details of the degree structure in South Africa, it is important to note that we inherited the British system's emphasis on learning through the disciplines. This means that there is little if any opportunity to develop broad general education courses.
6. See Kabo, Day, & Baillie (2009) for an interesting discussion on a similar course.
7. See http://www.dag.org.za for more information.
8. As evidence of this need, the RMF movement is gaining momentum on campuses across South Africa, including Rhodes University, the University of Kwazulu-Natal, and Stellenbosch University (as well as Oxford University in England).

REFERENCES

Barnett, R., & Coate, K. (2005). *Engaging the curriculum in higher education*. Maidenhead: Society for Research into Higher Education and Open University Press.

Garuba, H. (2015). Towards an African curriculum: Notes for a seminar. Unpublished work, University of Cape Town.

Kabo, J., Day, R. J. F., & Baillie, C. (2009). Engineering and social justice: How to help students cross the threshold. *Practice and Evidence of Scholarship of Teaching and Learning in Higher Education*, 4(2), 126–46.

Kassam, K.-A. (2010). Practical wisdom and ethical awareness through student experiences of development. *Development in Practice*, 20(2), 205–18.

Leibowitz, B., Swartz, L., Bozalek, V., Carolissen, R., Nicholls, L., & Rohleder, P. (Eds.). (2012). *Community, self and identity: Educating South African university students for citizenship*. Cape Town: Human Sciences Research Council Press.

Longo, N. V. (2013). Deliberative pedagogy in the community: Connecting deliberative dialogue, community engagement, and democratic education. *Journal of Public Deliberation*, 9(2), Article 16.

Mezirow, J. (1990). *Fostering critical reflection in adulthood: A guide to transformative and emancipatory learning*. San Francisco: Jossey-Bass.

Morreira, S. (2015). Steps towards decolonial higher education in Southern Africa? Epistemic disobedience in the humanities. *Journal of Asian and African Studies*, March 31, 1–15.

Pillay, S. (2015). Decolonizing the university. Talk given at Azania House, University of Cape Town, April. Http://africasacountry.com/2015/06/decolonizing-the-university/.

Thomson, A. M., Smith-Tolken, A., Naidoo, T., & Bringle, R. (2008). Service learning and community engagement: A cross-cultural perspective. Presentation at the Eighth International Conference for the International Society for Third Sector Research, July 9-12, University of Barcelona, Spain.

Waghid, Y. (2005). On the possibility of cultivating justice through teaching and learning: An argument for civic reconciliation in South Africa. *Policy Futures in Higher Education*, 3(2), 132-40.

Waghid, Y. (2009). Cosmopolitanism and education: Learning to talk back. *South African Journal of Higher Education*, 23(1), 5-7.

Transporting Communication: Community College Students Facilitate Deliberation in Their Own Communities

Rebecca M. Townsend

eliberation is an atypical classroom activity. Students who engage with others in the process of deliberation take a leap. They are not sure of the outcome, and they are often too new to the process to trust it. And in many college classes, students do not know one another enough to trust each other. If they take that leap, however, they can go places that they would never expect.

That is what happened in my classes during the 2010–11 academic year and in subsequent years in which I have taught Public Speaking and Group Communication at Manchester Community College (MCC) in Manchester, Connecticut. In these courses, I often use deliberative pedagogy and democratic engagement by introducing student-led community discussions through the Partnership for Inclusive, Cost-Effective Public Participation (PICEP2), a project model that was initially funded by the Federal Transit Administration (FTA) in 2009; these funds helped to catalyze my ability to engage students in deliberative pedagogy in later semesters. While I have focused my use of deliberation with community college students and communities on the public issue of transportation planning, this model may be adapted for any kind of democratic engagement where public voice is required or would help policymakers improve their decision-making.

Deliberative Pedagogy in the Community College Setting

Community colleges are prevalent, with more than one thousand institutions in the United States. These colleges serve mostly students from local communities, including a higher proportion of first-generation, minority, older, and low-income students than their four-year counterparts. Nearly half of all U.S. undergraduates, or 12.4 million students, study at a community college; of these, 36 percent are the first in their families to go to college. Some 21 percent are Hispanic, and 14 percent are black—57 percent and 52 percent, respectively, of all students in these groups who attend an undergraduate institution (American Association of Community Colleges, 2015). Yet outside of research on institutional outcomes (like that performed by Columbia's Center for Community

College Research, e.g. Hodara & Rodríguez, 2013; Belfield & Jenkins, 2014; Crosta & Kopko, 2014), these colleges have received relatively little scholarly attention for the strong roles they play in their communities. In particular, little attention has been paid to the curricular and pedagogical innovations occurring within those institutions.

As Traver and Katz (2014) note, most research on service-learning is from the perspective of non–community college settings. These settings feature students who, as Butin states, are pre-dominantly "white, sheltered, middle-class, single, without children, unindebted, and between the ages of 18–24" (2010, p. 31). There is very little understanding of what it means to be a community college student conducting this kind of learning, and almost none focused on deliberative projects. Neither service nor deliberation ought to be reserved for the elite or presumed to fix a broken people. Rather, we should take advantage of the pedagogical richness of working with diverse students to help them recognize their common stake in their neighborhoods through practices that encourage collaboration, trust, and respect.

Deliberative pedagogy—with its ability to help students think through advantages, trade-offs, and consequences of possible actions—helps to build civic capacity, something that all communities need. The positive outcomes that civic engagement offers students and communities (Chan, Ou & Reynolds, 2014) ought not to be relegated to those who can afford the most expensive education.

The MCC Model

The PICEP2 is an amalgam of a research method and deliberative pedagogy, in which students use deliberative discussion as one method of researching community needs with regard to transporta-tion. Elsewhere (Townsend, 2014), I have described it as participatory action research because of the conjoint investigation of an issue that was of concern to community members.

Students work in small teams to connect with a community group—ideally one to which a team member belongs, based on the insight that people are best suited to solve their own problems through deliberative pedagogy. Students and community members generate opinions and ideas about the community's transportation needs, after which teams conduct on-site deliberative discussions with the group about possible approaches for meeting those needs. In addition to taking field notes on the discussions, students conduct surveys to add to their research. After compiling their results, they prepare a presentation for an end-of-semester symposium with invited community-group members, local transportation planners, transportation providers, and government officials and policymakers. Through this work, students gather and analyze data and engage in public problem-solving using deliberative methods.

The Big Picture: Philosophy and Goals

This work is based on a set of attitudes and goals for scholarly work and the relationship between those goals and the community. These attitudes can be summed up with the notion that scholarly work can be shared; that is, it can be cocreated by students, community members, and faculty members. Scholarly work is ultimately about understanding the world better and leaving it stron-ger than one found it. To understand a community situation fully requires that faculty members bring disciplinary knowledge and practices to bear on a community concern with the help of that community.

Faculty engaged in this kind of deliberative pedagogy believe that academic work should increase community capacity. They value and respect community members, regarding them as sources of local knowledge and expertise. We do this work because we want students who are of a community to realize that their connection to that community is a source of strength and that through scholarship with the community, they can increase their own conceptual power and communicative skills. This work also requires faculty to be curious, patient, and capable of recognizing the dignity of local people, no matter their situation. We should not believe we hold all the answers or are superheroes ready to save the day.

My goals for this project were modest. I hoped students would gain skills in a new way. I hoped they would be able to lead discussions with their fellow community members and that those community members, knowing and trusting the students, would feel comfortable participating. These goals were exceeded in every way.

A Closer View: Course Establishment and Structure

MCC is one of twelve community colleges in Connecticut. With seven thousand students and forty majors, it is one of the largest community colleges in the system. Some 40 percent of credit students at MCC are from underrepresented racial and ethnic groups.

My development of the deliberative course at MCC began when a fellow volunteer on a town board (Stephen Gazillo, a transportation planner who served as a member of the Transportation Research Board's Public Involvement Committee) asked if I knew of ways to hear from community members whom planners had found difficult to reach. In a 2009 study, "Public Involvement on Transit Studies: State of the Practice," his committee identified key barriers to public involvement, three of which this project directly addresses: difficulty engaging youth, low-income, and minority populations; lack of public interest in transportation planning; and the financial cost of public involvement. Gazillo mentioned the FTA grant and agreed to write a letter of support, provide pro bono consulting, and connect me with the Capitol Region Council of Governments (CRCOG), the regional planning agency.

After participating in a seminar led by Martín Carcasson, John Gastil, and William Keith at the National Communication Association convention that helped me see the potential of student-conducted deliberative forums, I queried the National Coalition for Dialogue and Deliberation to see who in my region was conducting deliberative discussions. Shelby Brown, a facilitator who was, coincidentally, about to begin her year as a Minority Fellow at MCC became a valued consultant. I also solicited and received assistance from other departments and individuals, including Martin Hart, an accounting professor at MCC who advised me on the budget preparation; Tim Woods, a sociologist at MCC who helped create a questionnaire; and David Elvin, a public participation consultant who agreed to serve as the evaluator. The strength of the team and the uniqueness of the approach helped the project win funding. Matthew Robinson, a graduate student in public administration at the University of Connecticut (who was also an MCC graduate), served as project coordinator.

Together, this team conducted an opening discussion with forty-seven community members, transportation planners, transit providers, local legislators, and organizations that required services for people with disabilities to determine what community members felt were the most compelling aspects of transportation planning to study. Discussion at that event concluded with the need to study multiple modes of transportation in order to allow the community group to determine its own most important areas of focus. In the subsequent two semesters, students in a Group Communication course, together with the faculty and consultant team, composed a discussion guide that was developed along the lines of the ethnography of communication as a theoretical framework (Hymes, 1964). Since this project would involve research as well as public engagement, we obtained Institutional Review Board approval for the human subjects work.

The process we established has carried on since, on an as-needed basis according to community or CRCOG need. Working in teams based on geographic proximity, students in Public Speaking and Group Communication courses brainstorm to determine which groups within their social networks might be open to a thirty- to sixty-minute discussion. These groups may be church, sports, social, service, or other community groups. Students contact the groups, describe the planned deliberation, and obtain permission to hold it. They then go to each community group's regular meeting time and place to conduct a discussion and administer the survey. Students make an audio recording of the deliberation and take ethnographic field notes. Following the event, the project coordinator enters data from the surveys and a transcription company transcribes the recordings. Students then present their findings at a symposium at the end of the semester, either as a poster presentation or as a speech. The symposia have drawn a wide range of participants, including community members, transit providers, planners, elected officials, and representatives from government agencies.

The deliberative discussions themselves involve participants sharing stories about transportation to and from school and/or work and about the benefits and drawbacks of different modes of transportation (e.g., bus, train, bicycle, walking). They discuss their expectations for and experiences with the various transportation modes. One group, clients at a homeless shelter, noted how their dependency on public transportation affected their ability to find work. One noted, "I saw an ad; it fit me perfect for a job but it's not on a bus line." Later in that same deliberation, while discussing who should be able to get free bus passes, one advocated for the mentally ill, another for senior citizens, and another for people who use wheelchairs. Others chimed in to offer support or qualifications. A different participant noted:

> I didn't say free passes because then, you know, the bus company has to make some money. . . . They're subsidized by the State of Connecticut but they still have to make money. If they start giving it out, everything free, somebody's going to have to pay for it. In the long run, somebody's going to have to pay for it.

Participants in the deliberations are able to take positions, explore issues, and identify drawbacks to proposals. They deliberate about a wide range of relevant topics, including convenience, cost, environment, speed, trust, cleanliness, independence, dependability, timing, safety, respect, bus route and transportation mode availability, comfort, bicycles, children and strollers, involvement and efficacy, and having a voice and feeling valued. The deliberative discussions shed a great deal of light on what the participants value in transportation and in the social world more broadly. Participants are also able to reflect on their reasons for not contacting anyone about their needs.

Opportunities and Challenges

Several unexpected results have emerged from this course, including both a few challenges and many opportunities. The most unexpected challenge occurred on campus, when the student government, which had agreed to participate in an early deliberation, did a rapid about-face, refusing in dramatic fashion. Undaunted, the student group that was to work with the student government found another group to work with instead.

The success of the deliberations, which reached hundreds of people who were able to share their opinions, led to the expectation that this project would occur yearly. This proved to be a challenge, since audio recordings would not be able to be transcribed in future semesters without project funding. It was adapted for a specific project at the planning agency's request, and it was further adapted in other states. In all, twenty-nine groups, varying from church members to fantasy soccer leagues, homeless shelters to senior center belly dancing classes, contributed their ideas in the deliberations about transportation needs and preferences. The surveys in the first year netted 108 respondents, 59 percent of whom were nonwhite, 53 percent of whom take a bus regularly, and only 8 percent of whom had ever previously attended a public meeting.

Students have reported positive outcomes on their own learning and community connections. One student who delivered a speech at a public forum received a public engagement internship from a transit provider who attended the forum. Another student reflected, "This class was a rarity, it was both fun and it was a great learning environment. I feel as if the roles inspired a lot of creativity, which isn't something that happens a lot in school nowadays." A young African American student from a large city, who had worked with a group of youth and youth services providers, wrote, "I am also grateful for the privilege of being their voice on improving the fairness, convenience, and safety of public transportation because many of them are non-participants of meetings like this." A middle-aged white student from a suburb, who had worked with employees at a rural dentist's office, added, "Our discussion proves that people have good ideas and would be willing to get involved but do not know how." Though from different backgrounds, both of these students recognized the common need that people have to share their ideas, weigh options, and make recommendations to policymakers and planners. These students did this work initially for class credit, but their reflections show that they were proud of what they were able to help others achieve.

Engagement with the campus was another major benefit. Students who participated in these classes were more than twice as likely to earn a degree or certificate than their peers who attended different Public Speaking classes: 12 percent vs. 5 percent (Townsend, 2014). One Latino student who had not been very active or prepared leading up to the symposium came to me the next semester to talk about the discussion he had facilitated with a group of young men in a mentoring program for African American and Latino students. He told the story of a student in a wheelchair who spoke up during the deliberation to note frustration with the lack of bus shelters and the problem that causes him on rainy days. My former student, having been moved by this story, created a proposal for the college to build a shelter, which the college has committed to building. This student went on to become student government president and to intern in the state governor's office.

Other results continue to accrue. The FTA brought me to Washington, DC, to showcase this work as an example of innovative public engagement. The project took first runner-up in its category in the International Association of Public Participation's Core Values Award program. Based on the FTA nomination, the White House awarded me the "Champion of Change for Transportation Innovation" award. A civil and environmental engineering faculty member at the University of Connecticut, who had guest lectured at MCC through the PICEP2, helped establish a partnership through which the two institutions collaborated on a grant project involving deliberation and pedestrian safety.

Conclusion

Though the ability to share the ideas and opinions of people who often remain unheard has been a major success, the most transformative aspect of this project is its ability to inculcate in community college students a sense of achievement. Too often community college students are dismissed as low quality. Too often colleagues at four-year colleges and universities, if they think about community college students at all, perceive their work as less rigorous because exclusivity is seen as a mark of excellence. Too often the students themselves are perceived as the beneficiaries of others' service rather than as benefactors. Many students adopt others' perceptions about them. This project helps combat those perceptions by placing students in leadership roles within their own communities.

One student's reflection on his work during the semester demonstrates how students benefit from this new kind of role:

> We all were placed in a role where we taught each other and learned from each other. This made the learning experience a million times better. . . . I think the most important part was we the students were almost like teachers in a way. We had to gather the information by ourselves to have a meeting based around the information we gathered and we needed to attend meetings out of class to get the informa- tion. This is a lot of responsibility that you don't receive in other classes. I think this was the key to the amazing learning environment that we had. We felt that what we did mattered and that what we were doing in and out of class not only mattered to our grades but it mattered to the community.
>
> What we did in class was going to make a positive effect on something more than us and that was honestly a really great feeling. I felt like this was more than school for once. . . . Going into it I was a little nervous thinking how the hell am I going to do this, I don't know anything about transportation, but that wasn't the case at all and I was delighted with the end results. . . . I just can't express how awesome it was to actually have [an] impact on something for a change. I don't think people give students enough credit for what we are capable of.

Students who participate in this program are treated as experts in their own social networks. As students in deliberatively focused communication courses, they learn about audience analysis and coming up with things to say. They learn about organization of messages and various ways to structure communication for specific purposes, how to be informative and persuasive, and how to listen to others' content and relational messages. They apply their classroom knowledge to their community life in a way that they had not planned. They learn about the connections the public physical infrastructure has with the public sphere infrastructure and offer means of building bridges for both.

The opportunity to expand the kinds of work done by students leading deliberative sessions to other topics is a broad one. From this experience, I have seen how a deliberative civic engagement process embedded in community college courses can help members of a community derive the benefits of deliberation. It can also help government agencies (which are bound by law to engage the public but are often wary of the costs of doing so) receive important information. Through trusted members of their own community, in safe spaces where they are used to gathering, members of the public whose voices are often unheard—including minorities, youth, and people with low incomes—are able to share their stories, examine options, and offer opinions. The knowledge that their opinions are not just going to stay in the room but will be shared with officials who can make a difference offers participants a chance to be bold. Supporting that boldness provides students with lessons they never anticipated learning.

REFERENCES

American Association of Community Colleges. (2015). *Fast facts from our fact sheet*. Hhttp://www.aacc. nche.edu/AboutCC/Documents/FactSheet2015.pdf.

Belfield, C., & Jenkins, D. (2014). Community college economics for policymakers: The one big fact and the one big myth. January. CCRC Working Paper No. 67. Http://ccrc.tc.columbia.edu.

Butin, D. W. (2010). *Service-learning in theory and practice: The future of community engagement in higher education*. New York: Palgrave Macmillan.

Chan, W. Y., Ou, S.-R., & Reynolds, A. J. (2014). Adolescent civic engagement and adult outcomes: An examination among urban racial minorities. *Journal of Youth and Adolescence*, 43(11), 1829–43.

Crosta, P. M., & Kopko, E. M. (2014). Should community college students earn an associate degree before transferring to a four-year institution? (CCRC Working Paper No. 70). New York: Community College Research Center.

Hodara, M., & Rodríguez, O. (2013). Tracking student progression through the core curriculum. (CCRC Analytics Brief.) New York: Columbia University, Teachers College, Community College Research Center.

Hymes, D. (1964). Introduction: Toward ethnographies of communication. *American Anthropologist*, 66(6), 1–34.

Townsend, R. M. (2014). Mapping routes to our roots: Student civic engagement in transportation planning. In A. E. Traver & Z. P. Katz (Eds.), *Service-learning at the American community college: Theoretical and empirical perspectives* (pp. 225–41). New York: Palgrave Macmillan.

Traver, A. E., & Katz, Z. P. (Eds.). (2014). *Service-learning at the American community college: Theoretical and empirical perspectives*. New York: Palgrave Macmillan.

PART 6

Assessing Deliberative Pedagogy

The Value of Longitudinal Assessment: The Impact of the Democracy Fellows Program over Time

Katy J. Harriger, Jill J. McMillan, Christy M. Buchanan, and Stephanie Gusler

Deliberative pedagogy is being explored and implemented in many settings across the United States and around the world. Those of us who do this work do it because we have come to believe, through a combination of normative concerns and hands-on experience, that these approaches help prepare young people for lives in a pluralistic democracy. We do not need to be persuaded that learning to deliberate has a powerful and positive impact and that programs that use deliberative pedagogy are worthy of resources and replication. But it is clear that we live in a larger political and economic environment that is more skeptical and that requires systematic assessment to make the case for supporting deliberative work.

Why Assessment Matters

Perhaps because assessment has become ubiquitous at all levels of the educational system, many higher education professionals regard it with skepticism, seeing it as possibly no more than a bureaucratic hoop-jumping exercise. But there are some important reasons to assess the impact of deliberative pedagogies that go beyond the fact that we operate in an environment where assessment is expected or required. Assessment taken seriously and done well can help build support for deliberative pedagogies by demonstrating impact and encouraging more educators to adopt these methods. If our ultimate goal is to better prepare citizens for lives in a pluralistic democracy, assessment that helps us tell the story of what works can make a substantial contribution to that long-term goal.

Concern about the Democratic Deficit

Attention on how to better educate students for their future roles as democratic citizens has increased significantly in the last decade. Several years ago the Association of American Colleges and Universities (AAC&U) released a call to action, authored by the National Task Force on Civic

Learning and Democratic Engagement, stressing the importance of higher education's role in preparing students for civic life. The report cites a 2009 survey of 2,400 college students in which only a third of respondents felt that "their civic awareness had expanded in college, that the campus had helped them learn the skills needed to effectively change society for the better, or that their commitment to improve society had grown" (2012, p. 41). The report chronicles many ways in which colleges and universities are responding to the call for civic learning, including using dialogue and deliberation as a means of teaching students citizenship skills and dispositions. In addition to the 2007 study by Harriger and McMillan, the report notes research on the impact of intergroup dialogue projects (Association for the Study of Higher Education, 2006; Gurin, Nagda & Sorensen, 2011) and concludes that the research thus far suggests deliberative dialogue is a high-impact methodology for preparing students to take on their civic roles (National Task Force on Civic Learning and Democratic Engagement, 2012, pp. 56–57).

The impact of deliberation on attitudes and behavior has been studied now in multiple contexts, including not just the classroom and higher education (Dedrick, Grattan & Dienstfrey, 2008) but also in communities and across the world (Niemeyer, 2011; Nabatchi, 2010a, 2010b; Nabatchi, Gastil, Leighninger & Weiksner, 2012). The degree to which interest has grown in this approach as a way of addressing the "democratic deficit" (Nabatchi, 2010a) is reflected in the fact that the 2004 *Annual Review of Political Science* included an extensive essay on the research into deliberation (Delli Carpini, Cook & Jacobs, 2004); two additional essays in 2008 addressed using empirical methods to study the impact of deliberation on participants (Thompson, 2008; Mutz, 2008).

The Need for Longitudinal Research

An additional indicator of the importance of civic education practices is the attention being paid to the need to assess what we do and don't know about what works to create "long-lasting habits of civic engagement" (Hollander & Burack, 2009, p. 1). The Spencer Foundation, which focuses its philanthropic efforts on supporting educational research, brought together a group of civic engagement scholars and practitioners in 2008 to discuss the state of the field. The group was asked to think about what we already know and what we still need to learn in order to establish a research agenda going forward. The conclusions most applicable to this discussion included (1) the need to identify "the academic and co-curricular elements that most impact student civic engagement and *long term commitment* to civic engagement" (emphasis added), and (2) "the need for longitudinal approaches and data" (Hollander & Burack, 2009, pp. 6–8). Further, Peter Levine, of Tufts University, Tisch College of Citizenship and Public Affairs, notes that "the application of deliberative democracy to youth civic engagement has not been thoroughly explored" but that the research shows promise (2011, p. 17).

Beyond our own 2007 study, reviews of the impact in the educational context suggest that the experience of deliberating has a positive impact on developing civic skills (Hess, 2009). In addition, because of the Spencer Foundation's role in providing significant philanthropic support for educational innovation, the organization's findings suggest that being able to provide longitudinal data on impact will be important in foundation funding decisions going forward.

The Assessment Environment and Its Implications for Resource Allocation

We recognize that the current assessment climate in higher education may be the least inspirational reason for assessing deliberative pedagogies; nonetheless, as pragmatists, we believe it is important to think about the broader political context within which higher education institutions are operating. If we want programs and courses utilizing deliberative pedagogies to be supported and to become institutionalized, we need to take advantage of the assessment climate in order to show impact. There is little reason to believe that regulators' and funders' enthusiasm for assessment and accountability will subside any time soon.

In a 2015 report written for the Council for Higher Education Accreditation, Jamil Salmi notes that while the economic downturn in 2008–13 led to cuts in higher education budgets in forty-eight out of the fifty U.S. states, "governments have not lightened their demands on [higher education] institutions. If anything, it seems that the role of government has become more intrusive in recent years and the accountability requirements have grown significantly" (2015, pp. 3–4). States are increasingly tying funding decisions to performance. According to Salmi, since 2010 the number of states using a performance-based funding approach has increased from seven to thirty-three.

In the current environment, the role of higher education in developing democratic citizens seems to have taken a back seat to getting students a job when they graduate. The Spellings Commission report on the future of higher education gives passing notice to the historic democratic role of colleges and universities, saying that "much of our nation's inventiveness has been centered in colleges and universities, as has our commitment to a kind of democracy that only an educated and informed citizenry make possible" (U.S. Department of Education, 2006, p. xii). The report notes, however, that the new environment for higher education is "becoming tougher, more competitive, less forgiving of wasted resources and squandered opportunities. In tomorrow's world a nation's wealth will derive from its capacity to educate, attract, and retain citizens who are able to work smarter and learn faster" (p. xii). A major recommendation of the report is to increase accountability for learning outcomes. While the U.S. Department of Education under the Obama administration demonstrated more openness to the democratic purposes of education (National Task Force on Civic Learning and Democratic Engagement, 2012), it continued the pressure on keeping costs down and on implementing accountability measures.

Whether one thinks higher education's primary mission is to prepare students for citizenship or for the workforce (or both), the common ground for action appears to be the development of critical thinking skills. The AAC&U report identifies such skills as a key characteristic of ideal democratic citizens (National Task Force on Civic Learning and Democratic Engagement, 2012, p. 4), and the Spellings Commission report notes that the ability to engage in critical thinking is a key skill that current employers find deficient in their employees (U.S. Department of Education, 2006, p. 3). In this context, the opportunity for demonstrating the value of deliberative pedagogies probably centers on the impact of these pedagogies on the development of critical thinking skills.

Assessment of the Democracy Fellows Program (2001–5)

Given the importance of assessment for all of the reasons listed above, the editors of this volume thought that our experience in assessing a program at our university might be helpful to others engaged in the work of deliberative pedagogy. What follows is a summary of how we approached longitudinal assessment of our Democracy Fellows program and what we found in that assessment. For a much more detailed description of the program and its outcomes, we encourage you to read *Speaking of Politics* (Harriger & McMillan, 2007).

The Democracy Fellows program at Wake Forest University in Winston-Salem, North Carolina, began in the summer of 2001 when we recruited thirty entering freshmen. We selected these students from a pool who applied to the program through a process that included several essay questions about their conceptions of citizenship and their forms of civic engagement. During the first semester of the program, students enrolled in a first-year seminar that focused on the theory and practice of deliberation. They ended the year by choosing a campus issue to frame for a campus deliberation. In their sophomore year students wrote an issue guide and organized a campus deliberation. In their junior year they researched an issue, wrote an issue guide, and organized a deliberation in the community. During their senior year students helped moderate several campus and community events. We assessed the impact of these various interventions throughout the four years.

Quasi-Experimental Design with Yearly Assessments

The first decision we made in designing our assessment was that in order to isolate the impact of the deliberative experiences, we needed a control group of students who were also going through four years of college at the same institution. Political socialization literature makes clear that the very experience of higher education has an impact on political and civic engagement (Flanagan & Levine, 2010; Steckenrider & Cutler, 1989; Schlozman, Verba & Brady, 2012). If we studied only the group in the Democracy Fellows program, it would be difficult to say which outcomes resulted from the program and which were simply the product of four years of schooling at a liberal arts college.

We did two things that were important for being able to make claims about the impact of deliberation. First, we made careful decisions about which applicants we would choose for the program. We got a list of key demographics of the entering class from the admissions office and used that to make the fellows group demographically representative in terms of gender, race, and residence. We also used the application essays to choose a diverse group of students in terms of their notions of citizenship and their high school activities, turning down a number of enthusiastic student government presidents in favor of students who listed their most satisfying high school activities as band, French club, or cheerleading.

Second, once school began, we asked the registrar's office to provide us with a random sample of the entering class (leaving out the fellows), from which we selected a control group, again using the demographics provided by admissions. We picked a larger sample than thirty since we knew some students we contacted would not participate out of lack of either interest or time. One thing we could not match was area of academic interest since our students do not declare majors until the end of their sophomore year and frequently change their minds about what they want to study in the early years of college. We assume that some selection bias existed since the Democracy Fellows were students who chose to apply for the program. However, it should be noted that the control group had a similar choice in deciding to participate in the assessment and thus had a similar bias in terms of having at least some interest in public affairs. Invitations to both groups described the study as focusing on young people's attitudes about civic engagement.

Finally, as part of the study design, we committed to doing yearly assessments of each group. This was important because it allowed us to study of the impact of particular kinds of interventions. Had we done only entry and exit interviews, it would have been harder to know what students had learned specifically in the classroom, in the campus deliberation, and in the community deliberation. Yearly assessments allowed us to evaluate the impact of different deliberative interventions in different contexts (Harriger & McMillan, 2008).

Mixed Methods: Interview, Focus Groups, and Surveys

We assessed the impact of our program using multiple methods. While most of the data we gathered were qualitative, we did gather some survey data that allowed us to track activities over time and to compare both of our groups to the entire class from which they were drawn.

Obviously, we wanted to gather the most data from the Democracy Fellows. Consequently, we taped individual entry and exit interviews with each fellow, using the same questions for both interviews so that we could assess change. The senior exit interviews had some additional questions to assess fellows' thinking about their deliberative experiences. After the interviews were transcribed, we used content analysis as a way of assessing themes in the interview data.

In each of the four years of the study, we met the class (control) cohort in focus groups consisting of six to eight participants. We asked them the same questions we asked the Democracy Fellows, except for reflections on deliberative experiences. In the second and third years, rather than more interviews, we did focus groups with the Democracy Fellows as well. After the campus deliberation in the second year, we also held focus groups with students who had participated in the event to assess the impact of a single deliberative experience on students who had not attended the first-year seminar or had any responsibility for organizing the deliberation. With all of the focus groups, we had the discussions transcribed and used content analysis to compare themes across the groups.

Finally, we gathered two kinds of survey data that helped us to make the comparisons. First, in each of the four years, we had the Democracy Fellows and the class cohort fill out a short survey of their activities to find out whether the two groups differed in terms of their levels of civic and political engagement. Second, we had our Office of Institutional Research add three questions to the exit survey that goes to all graduating seniors, asking them the degree to which they thought their education had prepared them for civic and political engagement and the extent to which they felt they had a voice in campus life and decision-making. We included an additional filter question that allowed us to isolate the Democracy Fellows and the class cohort from the rest of the class. While nowhere nearly as in-depth as the interview and focus group transcripts, the senior exit survey allowed a quantitative assessment of the fellows compared with their peers. Ideally, mixed-method approaches are complementary and provide important and different insights into the data. This proved to be the case with our approach, as the quantitative data confirmed findings in the qualitative data.

Our Findings

This longitudinal mixed-method approach to assessing the impact of the Democracy Fellows program provided us with extensive data to conclude that learning to deliberate was a powerful pedagogy for developing democratic dispositions and engaged citizens. A more extensive explanation of the findings is available in the book by Harriger and McMillan (2007), but a brief summary here can demonstrate the benefit of these assessment approaches.

By the end of the four years, the Democracy Fellows differed from the class cohort in a number of important ways. They were more politically engaged, defined the responsibilities of citizenship in more active and communal ways (emphasizing working with others to solve problems rather than working to promote one's self-interest), analyzed and critiqued the political process in more sophisticated and nuanced language, and demonstrated a stronger sense of political efficacy in both their language and their actions. In addition, we found that the fellows were using the deliberative skills they had learned in all manner of ways that would not traditionally be recognized as political. They talked about using these skills in classroom discussions, in their social organizations, with their roommates, and in their family life. We also found that even students who had had only a single deliberative experience, attending the campus deliberation, could recognize and appreciate the ways in which deliberative talk was different from their other experiences of political talk. We concluded that deliberative pedagogies can reach and have an impact on students through many venues, whether in the classroom, in campus life, or in the community. What we couldn't know at the conclusion of that study was whether the differences we saw as students graduated would endure in the face of their encounters with the real world.

Alumni Assessment (2014–15)

With the tenth anniversary of the Democracy Fellows' college graduation arriving in 2015, we began a follow-up alumni study in 2014. We wanted to know whether the results we found in 2005 had endured. Were the Democracy Fellows still different from their class peers in how they thought, talked, and engaged in politics and civic life? Were they still putting to use the deliberative skills they had learned a decade ago? If not, why not? Was there something about their experiences in the real world, as they transitioned to the responsibilities of adulthood, that counteracted the positive outcomes they demonstrated at graduation?

More broadly, we were interested in how all of our study group, fellows and class cohort alike, were experiencing their political lives. Their four years of college and their first decade out of college had been framed by significant national and international events, beginning with the September 11 terrorist attack in 2001 and going through two wars, a historic election in which young people played a significant role in electing the country's first African American president, and the deepest economic recession since the Great Depression. Our alumni had seen years of both trouble and hope, and we felt that there was value in assessing whether these events had affected their views about politics and citizenship.

Study Design and Instruments

We studied two groups of alumni from our university. The treatment group was the Democracy Fellows who had participated in our original four-year program. With the help of the alumni office and social media, we were able to locate twenty of the thirty students from this group. The control group consisted of alumni from the same class (2001–5) who were not exposed to the program. This group was randomly selected from a list obtained from the alumni office. From the list, we matched the control group's characteristics to those of the Democracy Fellows in terms of race and ethnicity, gender, and major in college. Research on selecting control groups in quasi-experimental designs such as ours suggests that such a matching process can help to strengthen the ability to conclude that differences between the control and treatment groups were caused by the treatment rather than other differences (Ho, Imai, King & Stuart, 2007).

Deciding that we again wanted both qualitative and quantitative data, we constructed an online survey as well as an open-ended questionnaire for phone or WebEx interviews that would be transcribed. Our subjects now lived all over the country, which meant face-to-face data gathering was out of the question, but we did manage to do most of the interviews using WebEx, which allowed the interviewer and interviewee to see each other while they talked. To avoid the possibility that the Democracy Fellows would feel obligated to make positive responses to Harriger and McMillan (the faculty members who had run the fellows program), those interviews were conducted by two individuals on the research team who had had no association with the fellows or with the original project.

In constructing our interview and survey instruments, we started with the findings from the 2001–5 study and connected those findings to the particular interview and survey questions we used during that study. Then we adapted those questions and added new ones based on a review of the literature of the best ways to measure political and civic engagement and attitudes about the political system—in particular, questions that have been tested with this age group (Flanagan, Syvertsen & Stout, 2007; Bobek, Zaff, Li & Lerner, 2009; Lopez et al., 2006; Delli Carpini & Keeter, 1996). In addition, we made changes in language to reflect the fact that the subjects were no longer enrolled at the university.

We took some additional steps to ensure that our subjects would have anonymity and that when conducting our analysis of the data we would not be aware of whether the interviews or surveys came from Democracy Fellows or the class cohort. All names and direct identifiers were removed from transcripts to protect participants' confidentiality. All identifiers, including the numbers, were removed from transcripts for coding so that coders did not know whether the answers they were coding were from the fellows or the class cohort.

Methods of Analysis

We employed three different approaches to analyzing the data: integrative complexity scoring (ICS), quantitative analysis of survey data, and content analysis of the interview transcripts.

INTEGRATIVE COMPLEXITY SCORING

We chose ICS as an assessment approach because we wanted to know whether the differences we saw in 2005 between the two groups in terms of their critical thinking about politics were still present. ICS measures the existence of two cognitive components: differentiation and integration. Differentiation entails the ability of the research subject to identify different dimensions of an issue and to recognize that there is more than one way to see an issue. Integration involves the ability to identify the relationships or interactions between those dimensions and to recognize tensions and trade-offs. The highest IC scores are earned by those who can imagine novel solutions to complex problems through the integration of the multiple dimensions of an issue.

The parallels between what is valued in ICS and the focus in the deliberative process on considering multiple perspectives, evaluating values, tensions, and trade-offs, and looking for common ground for action made ICS an ideal methodology for assessing the long-term impact of exposure to deliberation on the Democracy Fellows. Research on cognitive complexity has demonstrated that experiences that challenge people's worldview, or that create dissonance between their beliefs and new information that they are exposed to, can lead them to make more cognitively complex judgments as a way of resolving the tension. This is particularly true when they are being held accountable by audiences that hold both points of view (Tadmor & Tetlock, 2006; Tetlock, 1986, 1992). Education and other significant life events can also have an impact on the complexity of one's thinking about issues (Suedfeld & Bluck, 1993; Neuman, 1981). This research suggests that college students exposed to extensive opportunities to deliberate might have higher IC scores than those who do not.

Another advantage of ICS in the assessment realm is that it provides a direct measure of student outcomes rather than the more easily gained indirect measures such as self-reporting surveys. Students can tell you that they became better critical thinkers in surveys or interviews, but ICS can provide independent verification as to whether that is indeed true. ICS can be done on written work such as essays or on transcribed oral communication of the sort we had in the interview transcripts.

QUANTITATIVE ANALYSIS OF SURVEY DATA

We constructed an online survey using primarily existing scales (Bobeck, Zaff, Li & Lerner, 2009; Flanagan, Syvertsen & Stout, 2007; Harvard University Institute of Politics, 2013) to measure the following constructs:

- Involvement in traditional venues of political action vs. service activities
- Active vs. passive citizenship
- Views of the political process and one's role in it
- Sense of political efficacy, power, and voice
- Communal vs. individualistic political language, outlook, and motivation

- Views of and attitudes toward deliberation and applying deliberative knowledge
- Political ideology
- Impact of higher education on citizenship
- Demographics

CONTENT ANALYSIS

Beyond the question of integrative complexity, we wanted to know the ways that Democracy Fellows might differ from their class cohort in terms of how they talk about politics, citizenship, and democracy and in terms of their participation in related activities. Given the amount of qualitative data amassed through the interview process, we decided that we could analyze the content of the interviews more systematically and efficiently by using some of the new software available for content analysis. Software of this sort assists in the systematic identification of themes in the interviews, but we learned that it does not reduce the amount of critical thinking researchers need to do. We spent many hours developing codes that we could use to get meaningful and reliable results before we were able to use the software to analyze the transcripts.

Some Results of the Alumni Study

Detailed reports of the results of our alumni study have been published elsewhere (see Harriger, McMillan, Buchanan & Gusler, 2015, 2016). Here, it is enough to say that ten years after college, significant differences along a number of dimensions continue to surface between the Democracy Fellows and their class cohorts. Our assessment has produced strong evidence that the extensive exposure the fellows had to deliberative pedagogy both inside and outside the classroom continues to influence them and their civic engagement into their young adult years. For example, the fellows are more politically engaged. They also have a more complex understanding of how the political system operates and what it would take to make it more effective. In addition, they continue to use in their daily lives the deliberative skills they learned in college and believe to a greater degree than their peers that their college education prepared them for political and civic engagement.

Conclusions and Questions for Further Research

Two movements are afoot in higher education that appear, at first glance, to be on a collision course. The 2006 U.S. Department of Education report and the 2012 AAC&U report discussed earlier in this chapter exemplify these two movements. One emphasizes the importance of assessing learning outcomes as a means of holding institutions of higher education accountable for preparing a new generation for the workplace. The other emphasizes the democratic mission of higher education in preparing citizens for life in a pluralistic democracy. In true deliberative fashion, this chapter suggests that we need not think of these developments in zero-sum terms. Advocates of deliberative pedagogies can use the techniques of assessment to demonstrate the power and long-term impact of these pedagogies. The benefit of our longitudinal assessments is that we can say with confidence that deliberative pedagogy, above and beyond any impact of higher education itself, develops skills of critical thinking and patterns of behavior that enhance the civic and economic goals of higher education.

We are not suggesting that one must do all of the assessments we did in order to make the case for deliberative pedagogies. We tell the whole story here only to show that gathering longitudinal data is both possible and productive as a means of assessing the impact of deliberative pedagogies. We also think that a combination of qualitative and quantitative data provides the richest assessment and allows us to claim with a greater degree of certainty that deliberation develops the kind of skills needed both in our democracy and in the workplace.

Our research shows that sustained exposure to deliberative practice and a combination of classroom and experiential learning made a difference. Yet important questions about these pedagogies remain to be explored. How much intervention is enough for these outcomes to endure? Do our results reflect only the cumulative impact of a four-year program or could similar results be obtained with fewer and/or shorter interventions? How important was the first-year seminar to the outcomes we observed in comparison to the hands-on experiences of organizing deliberations on campus and in the community? These are important questions that further assessment can and should help us answer.

REFERENCES

Association for the Study of Higher Education. (2006). Research on outcomes and processes of inter-group dialogue. *Higher Education Report* 32(4), 59–73.

Bobek, D., Zaff, J., Li, Y., & Lerner, R. M. (2009). Cognitive, emotional, and behavioral components of civic action: Towards an integrated measure of civic engagement. *Journal of Applied Developmental Psychology*, 30(5), 615–27.

Dedrick, J. R., Grattan, L. & Dienstfrey, H. (Eds.) (2008). *Deliberation and the work of higher education: Innovations for the classroom, the campus, and the community.* Dayton, OH: Kettering Foundation Press.

Delli Carpini, M. X., & Keeter, S. (1996). *What Americans know about politics and why it matters.* New Haven, CT: Yale University Press.

Flanagan, C. A., Syvertsen, A. K. & Stout, M. D. (2007). Civic measurement models: Tapping adolescents' civic engagement. CIRCLE Working Paper #55. Http://www.civicyouth.org.

Gurin, P., Nagda, B. A., & Sorensen, N. (2011). Intergroup Dialogue: Education for a broad conception of civic engagement. *Liberal Education*, 97(2), 46–51.

Harriger, K. J., & McMillan, J. J. (2007). *Speaking of Politics: Preparing college students for democratic citizenship through deliberative dialogue.* Dayton, OH: Kettering Foundation Press.

Harriger, K. J., & McMillan, J. J. (2008). Contexts for deliberation: Experimenting with democracy in the classroom, on campus, and in the community. In J. R. Dedrick, L. Grattan & H. Dienstfrey (Eds.), *Deliberation and the work of higher education: Innovations for the classroom, the campus, and the community* (pp. 235–66). Dayton, OH: Kettering Foundation Press.

Harriger, K. J., McMillan, J. J., Buchanan, C. M., & Gusler, S. (2015). The long-term impact of learning to deliberate. *Diversity & Democracy*, 18(4), 27–28.

Harriger, K. J., McMillan, J. J., Buchanan, C. M., & Gusler, S. (2016). *The long term-impact of learning to deliberate: A follow-up study of Democracy Fellows and a class cohort.* Dayton, OH: Kettering Foundation Press.

Harvard University Institute of Politics. (2013). Survey of young Americans' attitudes towards politics and public service: 24th edition. December 4. Http://www.iop.harvard.edu.

Hess, D. E. (2009). *Controversy in the classroom: The democratic power of discussion.* New York: Routledge.

Ho, D. E., Imai, K., King, G., & Stuart, E. A. (2007). Matching as nonparametric preprocessing for reducing model dependence in parametric causal inference. *Political Analysis,* 15(3), 199–236.

Hollander, E., & Burack, C. (2009). *How young people develop long-lasting habits of civic engagement: A conversation on building a research agenda.* Http://www.compact.org.

Levine, P. (2011). What do we know about civic engagement? *Liberal Education,* 97(2), 12–19.

Lopez, M. H., Levine, P., Both, D., Kiesa, A., Kirby, E., & Marcelo, K. (2006). *The 2006 civic and political health of the nation: A detailed look at how youth participate in politics and communities.* CIRCLE report. Http:civicyouth.org.

Mutz, D. C. (2008). Is deliberative democracy a falsifiable theory? *Annual Review of Political Science,* 11, 521–38.

Nabatchi, T. (2010a). Addressing the citizenship and democratic deficits: The potential of deliberative democracy for public administration. *American Review of Public Administration,* 40(4), 376–99.

Nabatchi, T. (2010b). Deliberative democracy and citizenship: In search of the efficacy effect. *Journal of Public Deliberation,* 6(2), Article 8.

Nabatchi, T., Gastil, J., Leighninger, M., & Weiksner, G. M. (Eds.) (2012). *Democracy in motion: Evaluating the practice and impact of deliberative civic engagement.* New York: Oxford University Press.

National Task Force on Civic Learning and Democratic Engagement. (2012). *A crucible moment: College learning and democracy's future.* Washington, DC: Association of American Colleges and Universities.

Neuman, W. R. (1981). Differentiation and integration: Two dimensions of political thinking. *American Journal of Sociology,* 86, 1236–68.

Niemeyer, S. (2011). The emancipatory effect of deliberation: Empirical lessons from mini-publics. *Politics & Society,* 39(1), 103–40.

Salmi, J. (2015). *Is Big Brother watching you? The evolving role of the state in regulating and conducting quality assurance.* Washington, DC: Council for Higher Education Accreditation.

Schlozman, K. L., Verba, S., & Brady, H. E. (2012). *The unheavenly chorus: Unequal political voice and the broken promise of American democracy.* Princeton, NJ: Princeton University Press.

Steckenrider, J. S., & Cutler, N. E. (1989). Aging and adult political socialization: The importance of roles and role transitions. In R. S. Sigel (Ed.), *Political learning in adulthood: A sourcebook of theory and research* (pp. 56–88). Chicago: University of Chicago Press.

Suedfeld, P., & Bluck, S. (1993). Changes in integrative complexity accompanying significant life events: Historical evidence. *Journal of Personality and Social Psychology,* 64(1), 124–30.

Tadmor, C. T., & Tetlock, P. E. (2006). Biculturalism: A model of the effects of second-culture exposure on acculturation and integrative complexity. *Journal of Cross-Cultural Psychology,* 37(2), 173–90.

Tetlock, P. E. (1986). A value pluralism model of ideological reasoning. *Journal of Personality and Social Psychology,* 50(4), 819–27.

Tetlock, P. E. (1992). The impact of accountability on judgment and choice: Toward a social contingency model. *Advances in Experimental Social Psychology,* 25, 331–76.

Thompson, D. F. (2008). Deliberative democratic theory and empirical political science. *Annual Review of Political Science*, 11, 497–520.

U.S. Department of Education. (2006). *A test of leadership: Charting the future of U.S. higher education.* Washington, DC: U.S. Department of Education.

Assessment through a Deliberative Pedagogy Learning Outcomes Rubric

Sara A. Mehltretter Drury, Leila R. Brammer, and Joni Doherty

Several years ago, the Association of American Colleges and Universities (AAC&U) released *A Crucible Moment: College Learning & Democracy's Future* (National Task Force on Civic Learning and Democratic Engagement, 2012), an influential report calling on higher education institutions to educate for democracy. The report identifies key student learning outcomes in knowledge, skills, values, and collective action needed to realize this goal, including "deliberation and bridge building across differences" (p. 4). According to the AAC&U, deliberation is a critical and necessary skill if we are to "renew this nation's social, intellectual, and civic capital" (p. 2). Deliberative practices are ones that "help refine skills in soliciting multiple viewpoints, negotiating and compromising, and organizing across differences for democratic ends" (p. 56).

Grounded in the scholarship of deliberation, this chapter offers a rubric-based methodology for assessing deliberative learning in the classroom. The rubric is intended to advance the effective learning of deliberative democratic practices through the integration of a variety of deliberation activities. Unlike discussion, which is used to develop a better understanding of complex course material, deliberation involves developing the skills and commitment necessary for "dealing with morally grounded disagreements and facing up to difficult tradeoffs" (Mathews, 2014, p. 77), with the aim of moving toward shared and well-considered judgments. Deliberative pedagogy therefore teaches the value of "working to make a difference in the civic life of our communities and developing the combination of knowledge, skills, values, and motivation to make that difference" (Nabatchi, 2012, p. 7).

Alfaro defines deliberative pedagogy as teaching strategies designed to introduce students to "a diversity of perspectives in explaining and understanding events and experiences"; such strategies encourage students to develop the habits of weighing the trade-offs of every choice, keeping an open mind, being willing to "stand in someone else's shoes," believing in the opportunity to create change, and working with others "to make decisions for the common good" (2008, p. 147). Longo defines deliberative pedagogy as the integration of "deliberative decision making with teaching and learning," in contrast to deliberative politics, which integrates decision-making with public action

(2013, p. 2). Longo contends that *"where* and *how* learning takes place is as important as *what* is learned" (p. 5) and that deliberative pedagogical practices should therefore connect classroom and campus-oriented activities with community-based engagement.

Although many teach deliberative theory and skills or practice deliberation in civic and educational settings, assessments of deliberation focus primarily on the public arena. In other words, most scholarly accounts have examined public deliberation for political efficacy and civic capacity; little attention has been paid to deliberation as pedagogy. In light of the increasing emphasis on deliberation as a means of teaching necessary skills for citizens, we need effective ways of assessing what students learn about deliberation, including identifiable learning outcomes. Measures have been developed to assess pedagogy and learning outcomes in the broader area of civic engagement (Finley, 2011; Rhodes, 2010). This rubric does the same for deliberative pedagogy.

Identifying learning outcomes and avenues for meaningful assessment is crucial for teachers and students alike. Instructors will find the rubric useful for assessing specific student learning outcomes for classroom-based pedagogies. It will also be helpful for those who seek to integrate teaching and learning with public action. To illustrate how the rubric can be used, we suggest several potential applications of this model using examples drawn from some of the practice chapters in this volume.

Deliberation in the Classroom

Calls for the practice of democratic deliberation in higher education have produced case studies and research on using deliberative techniques in the classroom. The Kettering Foundation's edited volume *Deliberation and the Work of Higher Education* offers eleven case studies of how deliberation can function in the campus setting (Dedrick, Grattan & Dientsfrey, 2008). In separate essays, D'Innocenzo (2008) and Ingham (2008) argue for the use of deliberation as a means of introducing and understanding multiculturalism. In the same volume, Doherty (2008), Farland (2008), Cooper (2008), and Harriger and McMillan (2008) offer perspectives on how deliberation can be used to engage students in ways that integrate subject and civic learning. Other essays consider the role of deliberation in preprofessional and professional higher education and in the broader campus community (Dudley & Morse, 2008; Walters, 2008). *Educating for Deliberative Democracy*, edited by Nancy L. Thomas (2010), argues for the inclusion of deliberation as part of the civic mission of colleges and universities. These accounts, along with the previously mentioned AAC&U report (National Task Force on Civic Learning and Democratic Engagement, 2012), clearly demonstrate the value of deliberation as a core component of civic education.

In *Talking Together: Public Deliberation and Political Participation in America*, Jacobs, Cook, and Delli Carpini argue that deliberation can benefit American politics not as an idealistic "salvation of democracy," but rather as a practice that "presents opportunities for the future expansion and rejuvenation of democracy" (2009, p. 153). Many of the characteristics of deliberation align with more general goals of higher education, including developing students' abilities to synthesize information, understand tensions and trade-offs, provide reasons for their conclusions, and work collaboratively. The future of democracy, at least in some measure, depends on how students learn how to become citizens—that is, people who see themselves as part of a community, engage with others to make judgments about what should be done for the common good, and work to make those things happen. Being introduced to and trained in the skills of democratic deliberation is a critical part of that development. In this context *citizen* is not defined in the legalistic sense, but rather is someone who has a sense of responsibility to others, sees themselves as part of a community, engages with others to make judgments about what should be done for the common good, and is willing to work to make those things happen.

Deliberation Assessment

Challenges in studying group deliberation include interdependence of data, group size, and difficulties in interpreting discursive outcomes. Black, Burkhalter, Gastil, and Stromer-Galley note that public deliberation researchers have "drawn on diverse literature to create research designs aimed at empirically capturing aspects of deliberation" and that assessments of deliberation may focus on the individual, the group, and/or units of discourse, depending on the research questions. Most studies analyze group outcomes or units of discourse, often using "close, systematic attention to communication that occurs during the deliberative discussion" (2011, p. 326). Accordingly, scholars studying these aspects of public deliberation use a variety of direct measures, including discussion analysis, microanalytic approaches (such as content analysis and the discourse quality index) that investigate elements of deliberation in the face of unfixed or loosely fixed meaning, macroanalytic approaches that examine the deliberation as a total unit, participant assessments, and case study integration (Black, Burkhalter, Gastil & Stromer-Galley, 2011). For example, Stromer-Galley (2007) has articulated six elements to code in determining whether a discourse is a deliberation: reasoned opinion expression, sourcing, disagreement, equality, topic, and engagement. In their working paper for the Kettering Foundation, Kadlec, Sprain, and Carcasson utilize Stromer-Galley's analysis techniques to examine sourcing and framing of public issues in their deliberation experiment, emphasizing that qualitative methods allow for reflections on the quality of deliberations from "a range of different theoretical orientations and backgrounds, including rhetoric, argumentation, social interaction, cultural anthropology, and democratic theory" (2012, p. 9).

As noted earlier, many public deliberation studies focus on outcomes, such as whether a deliberation was effective in solving a problem or encouraged political participation beyond the initial event. These studies focus on elements and outcomes of deliberation rather than on how participating in deliberation influences student learning. Developing learning outcomes and assessment methods for deliberative pedagogy provides an opportunity to build on previous research in evaluating deliberation in the public arena but with a focus on how individual students learn knowledge, skills, and applications that better prepare them to participate in public life in the twenty-first century.

The Importance of Assessing Classroom Deliberation

An examination of the *Chronicle of Higher Education* and the education columns in the *New York Times* reveals the emphasis education places on testing and assessment. In part this emphasis is motivated by an effort "to show citizens and consumers that institutions are improving and are worthy of the public's trust" (Johnson, Rochkind & DuPont, 2011, p. 6). In a survey of chief academic officers, the National Institute for Learning Outcomes Assessment notes that "over the past decade [1999–2009], regional and specialized creditors have gradually shifted from encouraging to requiring member institutions to assess and provide evidence of student performance and how these results are being used to improve outcomes" (Kuh & Ikenberry, 2009, p. 6). In this climate, for deliberation to be successfully implemented in higher education curricula, faculty and staff practitioners must identify learning outcomes and develop assessment tools for classroom deliberations.

As part of the release and promotion of the Liberal Education and America's Promise initiative and its Essential Learning Outcomes, the AAC&U initiated the development of sixteen Valid Assessment of Learning in Undergraduate Education (VALUE) rubrics to support the assessment of these outcomes (Association of American Colleges & Universities, n.d.). These rubrics are intended to be used by both teachers and learners to enhance understanding of the skills required for success in each learning outcome, to increase student learning, and to assist with meeting institutional, state, and national assessment requirements. Similarly, to adopt and successfully utilize deliberative pedagogy practices requires establishing learning outcomes and a way to assess the progress of individual students. Developing these teaching and learning tools will also help faculty, programs, and institutions meet internal and external requirements for student learning assessment.

Deliberative Pedagogy Learning Outcomes Rubric

To formulate a list of outcomes for our Deliberative Pedagogy Learning Outcomes (DPLO) rubric, we utilized a process similar to the one used by the AAC&U in developing the VALUE rubrics. Through a collaborative process of reviewing the literature, reflecting on our teaching experiences with students, assignments, and outcomes, and consulting with others who use deliberative teaching practices, we identified, defined, and benchmarked seven specific learning outcomes of deliberative pedagogy: collaboration, reason giving, synthesis of ideas and information, understanding of trade-offs and tensions, reflection, awareness of relationships, and empathy (see Table 1).[1]

The DPLO rubric provides a basis for instruction, learning, and assessment of deliberative practices. Because deliberative pedagogy has progressive learning outcomes rather than a single objective, we created four levels for each of the seven outcomes: entry level, benchmark, milestone, and capstone. These levels are guidelines for understanding the progression and deepening of student learning. Although each learning outcome has an entry-level category that reflects a lack of awareness of that outcome, it should be noted that not all new students begin at this level. Some students may have previous experiences or inclinations that place them at a more advanced level. The capstone level, which is essentially a definition of what is being tracked, indicates that the student has acquired the capacity for using that particular skill and understands the reasons for doing so.

As a student comes to a fuller understanding of deliberation and public problem-solving, he or she may progress through different levels of the rubric. Progress is not inevitable, however; students may not further their skills in every element during a semester. In class, students will demonstrate their level of development for each outcome through their comments and participation in deliberative activities and processes. In addition, their postdeliberation reflections, whether written or oral, may showcase a particular learning outcome.

Table 1. Deliberative Pedagogy Learning Outcomes (DPLO) Rubric

LEARNING OUTCOMES	ENTRY LEVEL: SELF-AFFIRMING	LEVEL ONE: BENCHMARK ABSORBING	LEVEL TWO: MILESTONE PROCESSING	LEVEL THREE: CAPSTONE DELIBERATING
Collaboration	Prioritizes one's self-interest and opinions.	Begins to engage in political discourse, comparing one's own self-interested position to others' self-interested positions.	Recognizes that in a democracy, perspectives may differ; demonstrates tolerance.	Understands civic responsibility and demonstrates a commitment to work with others to come to shared decisions.
Reason Giving	Affirms one's own opinions or positions without offering evidence.	Recognizes the importance and use of evidence to support positions.	Evaluates the strengths and weaknesses of different types of evidence.	Uses complex reasoning to balance different types of evidence in own and others' arguments.
Synthesis of Ideas and Information	Uses ideas and positions that affirm one's own position.	Primarily uses summary and paraphrase to consider other positions.	Critically analyzes positions in light of individual, community, and global realities.	Analyzes and crystallizes a variety of positions to draw out conclusions for the community good.
Understanding of Trade-Offs and Tensions	Seeks solutions that do not recognize the tradeoffs or tensions in a position.	Recognizes that there are trade-offs and tensions in public decisions but may minimize those associated with one's own position.	Identifies various things that are valued for a given issue; weighs trade-offs and tensions for different groups in the community.	Prioritizes values in tension by articulating the trade-offs and benefits of choices, and identifying preferred choices for the community.
Reflection	Maintains position without engaging other perspectives.	Pauses in decision-making; uses active listening skills to better understand other positions.	Reconsiders or modifies a position in light of new information or perspectives.	Recognizes information as situational and contingent; applies new insights to create innovative options for addressing a problem.
Awareness of Relationships	Focuses on self without engaging others in the community.	Tends to prioritize self in relation to the community.	Acknowledges and recognizes diverse opinions in the community.	Considers the complexity of community relationships.
Empathy	Others' lived experiences and perspectives are not or rarely considered.	Acknowledges that others have different lived experiences and perspectives.	Willing to listen to and shows interest in others' lived experiences and perspectives.	Understands different perspectives and demonstrates willingness to work through differences or disagreements.

Applications for the DPLO Rubric

The DPLO rubric serves several purposes in setting the stage for learning as well as demonstrating outcomes:

1. *Establishing learning expectations.* Particularly for innovative pedagogical practices, the DPLO rubric can help teachers and students understand the components of effective deliberation and

the reasons for using deliberative practices. Sharing the rubric with students makes expectations transparent and clear. This is especially important in deliberative course activities that do not have a tangible artifact associated with them.

2. *Familiarizing students with new skills and premises.* The rubric allows teachers to assess each student's development during the course using mutually shared criteria. This is especially helpful for students as they move from discussion or debate to deliberation, which requires a different set of skills and is based on a different set of premises about how we come to well-considered judgments and take action for the common good.

3. *Allowing multiple forms of assessment.* Instructors can use the rubric to assess students or to guide self-assessment or peer assessment. This can help teachers target specific areas of instruction to support deliberative processes, such as activities that can assist students in learning to weigh trade-offs or to highlight the importance of empathy. Also, the rubric can be applied to assignments that ask students to demonstrate deliberative capacity and skills in writing or research.

4. *Promoting reflection.* The rubric provides an important collaborative platform for students and the instructor to review a deliberation. In such a review, everyone can reflect on what was useful to the deliberation, how to improve deliberative skills, or what missing elements to include in future deliberations. This type of review leads to increased self-awareness and group awareness that may slow the pace of deliberation, which allows students to reflect on and learn from the experience in real time.

5. *Informing external assessment.* The rubric can help instructors meet more formal internal and external assessment requirements by allowing them to assess the strengths and weaknesses of different deliberative pedagogy practices. For teachers involved in interdisciplinary partnerships, the partners can use the DPLO rubric as a common way to evaluate deliberative learning that takes place across courses or curricula. Departments and programs can utilize the rubric in their assessments of student learning outcomes. Also, the rubric allows teachers to make a case to colleagues and administrators about the benefits of deliberative pedagogy in terms of the development of practical and academic skills as well as students' growth in elements specific to deliberation.

Overall, the DPLO rubric can provide a robust tool for instruction, learning, and assessment. Three brief examples demonstrate the potential of using aspects of the DPLO rubric.

One use of the rubric is to have students assess their own learning and the demonstrated learning of their classmates during course activities. Sara A. Mehltretter Drury has used aspects of the DPLO when engaging in interdisciplinary deliberation partnerships at Wabash College. In the spring 2015 semester, Drury's rhetoric course on deliberation partnered with an introductory biochemistry course for a deliberation on genetically modified organisms (GMOs). In this exercise, students from the two classes worked collaboratively with the instructors to develop an issue-framing guide on GMO public policy. The three approaches under deliberation were labeling GMOs in consumer products, allowing GMOs without labeling them as such, and banning GMOs entirely. In the deliberation activity, a group of students from the rhetoric course facilitated a deliberation among the students from the biochemistry course. Since the two instructors could not observe all six groups that were deliberating concurrently, they used a version of the DPLO as a peer-assessment tool. Students in the rhetoric course then used their assessment of the activity to prompt reflection about their own planning and execution of the deliberation, writing journal entries about what they might have done to improve the quality of the deliberation activity around the learning outcomes of deliberative pedagogy.

Drury has also used the DPLO to assess whether students who are exposed to training in public deliberation are able to apply those skills to a new deliberative setting. The public speaking course at Wabash College includes a deliberation assignment. As preparation for the assignment, students learn about public deliberation as a mode of productive discourse, trade-offs and benefits inherent to public decision-making, value hierarchies and tensions, and facilitation strategies to promote participatory deliberation (Abbott, McDorman, Timmerman & Lamberton, 2015; Hogan, Andrews, Andrews & Williams, 2014). For the deliberation assignment, students in small groups give an informative speech on a public problem, along with three or four approaches to addressing that problem. The deliberative speech is in many ways an oral presentation of a deliberative framework. Then the group transitions to facilitating a deliberative conversation among their classmates.

To assess whether students retain their deliberative understanding of public problem-solving, Drury, Andre, Goddard, and Wentzel (2016) created a focus-group study to assess this assignment's learning outcomes. Student participants were grouped according to their previous exposure to deliberation in the public speaking course, resulting in two groups without exposure and two groups with exposure. Each group was given the National Issues Forums guide on national debt (Wharton & McAfee, 2011) to frame deliberations and instructed to have a sixty-minute conversation on the issue using the guide. The research team applied the learning outcome of *understanding of trade-offs and tensions* (see Table 1) to transcripts of all four group deliberations and found that students with previous exposure to deliberative pedagogy through the public speaking course consistently reached higher levels on this learning outcome than the students with no exposure (Drury, Andre, Goddard, and Wentzel, 2016). Although it used only one of the learning outcomes of the DPLO, this application demonstrates the potential for assessing not only student learning but also retention of deliberative pedagogy and, in this case, effectiveness of course goals. Future research should explore additional learning outcomes from the DPLO, as well as the diverse institutional and curricular settings of deliberative pedagogy.

Another example of how to use the learning outcomes of the DPLO comes from a first-year seminar course—Deliberation, Democracy, and Civility—taught by Leila Brammer, professor of communication studies at Gustavus Adolphus College. Brammer worked collaboratively with students throughout the semester, creating situations in which students were asked to deliberate to reach decisions and then act on those decisions. Drawing from a general framework that Brammer provided, students developed their own syllabus, assignments, activities, and timelines. They also identified research resources on campus and in the community and selected an issue for community deliberation for their cumulative assignment, in which they organized and facilitated a campus deliberation. Throughout the course, students reflected on how things were going and made adjustments as needed.

Early in the semester, students demonstrated their *awareness of relationships* with others, recognizing that they knew little about issues of interest to the campus and the local community. The group thus began at the benchmark, or first, level (see Table 1). Because they were seeing themselves in relation to the larger community, they were already beyond the entry level. Students then decided to conduct interviews to learn more about their community and identify issues. Their efforts to decide which issue to choose for their forum resulted in two issues upon which they were divided. Their preoccupation with differences places them at the milestone (second) level at this point. These students appear to have reached the capstone (third) level by early November when they recognized, as one student observed, "The issues were not that different, [they were about] how we live together in community."

In their discussions of the final two issues, students struggled with *understanding of trade-offs and tensions*. Issues that require deliberation are "What should we do?" kinds of questions. They tend to be ethical in nature, demanding that we weigh competing claims made by things that we value, such as freedom, security, and fairness. Tensions arise when the things we value conflict, either internally or as a community (e.g., the need to give up some freedom to attain greater security). As they worked to select an issue, initially students relied on quantitative strategies such as counting how often an issue came up in the interviews or voting (which always ended in deadlock). At times students considered simply going along with what others wanted (compromise) or flipping a coin. As they worked through the choices, they articulated both orally and in writing the trade-offs associated with each issue. They focused on selecting a topic that would be beneficial for the community to address and would help participants understand deliberation and develop deliberative skills. As they worked through the frustration of their impasse, they moved through the milestones of understanding trade-offs together. Because they had developed a clear awareness of the complexity of their relationships with others in the class and the community, as well as the intricacies within issues and positions, their deliberation extended beyond the analysis of information across different positions and frameworks into the *synthesis of ideas and information*. Eventually, they were able to move forward by reframing the issue, focusing their preferred frame on how best to live together as a community, a question that highlights the ethical nature of living together in community.

Reflections and Future Opportunities

Deliberative pedagogy has the potential to meet the challenges of specific course instruction, civic learning, democratic engagement, and the issues facing us in our communities. However, effective teaching and learning of deliberative practices requires clear instruments that define, clarify, and assess deliberation in the classroom. The DPLO rubric and the applications of the rubric described here support the adoption, teaching, and assessment of deliberative pedagogy practices. The rubric also provides a foundation for teachers to develop innovative deliberative pedagogy practices to enhance student learning.

A significant challenge of education and assessment is that students rarely start or stop developing skills in the course of a single semester. While some students may already possess some of the skills on the rubric prior to a course, for others, these may take longer to emerge. This is a challenge for all educational assessment, and the DPLO provides a useful means for instructors and students to collaboratively identify benchmarks in the learning process.

Future research on deliberative pedagogy learning outcomes could report on use of the DPLO rubric and on specific strategies for teaching each of the learning outcomes of deliberative pedagogy.

Scholarship might focus on how particular deliberative learning outcomes can be developed over a curricular experience, such as a major field of study, or over the course of earning a two-year associate's or four-year bachelor's degree. Additional case studies that use this rubric would contribute to knowledge about how deliberative pedagogy is taught across the curriculum.

Other chapters in this volume begin that task, with examples of how to incorporate deliberative pedagogy into communication, political science, philosophy, and STEM fields. Future work could expand understanding of how deliberative pedagogy works across the curriculum by employing the rubric for assessment and for developing evaluation instruments. While case studies tend to focus on a single course experience, they also open space to discuss how instructors employ deliberative pedagogy in a variety of settings. Additional scholarship should encourage the further development of deliberative learning methods across educational settings.

NOTE

1. Within the deliberative context, empathy is not defined as a shared emotional state (i.e., to feel what someone else is feeling), but rather the capacity to understand "*why* someone feels a certain way in a given situation," even if one does not agree with that perspective (Morrell, 2010, p. 40). Empathy as used here is closely associated with a willingness to listen to others even if one does not agree with them.

REFERENCES

Abbott, J. Y., McDorman, T. F., Timmerman, D. M., & Lamberton, L. J. (2015). *Public speaking and democratic participation: Speech, deliberation, and analysis in the civil realm.* New York: Oxford University Press.

Alfaro, C. (2008). Reinventing teacher education: The role of deliberative pedagogy in the K–6 classroom. In J. R. Dedrick, L. Grattan & H. Dienstfrey (Eds.), *Deliberation and the work of higher education: Innovations for the classroom, the campus, and the community* (pp. 143–64). Dayton, OH: Kettering Foundation Press.

Association of American Colleges & Universities. (n.d.) VALUE rubric development project. Https://www.aacu.org/value/rubrics.

Black, L. W., Burkhalter, S., Gastil, J., & Stromer-Galley, J. (2011). Methods for analyzing and measuring group deliberation. In E. P. Bucy & R. L. Holbert (Eds.), *The sourcebook for political communication: Methods, measures, and analytical techniques* (pp. 323–45). New York: Routledge.

Cooper, D. D. (2008). Four seasons of deliberative learning in a department of rhetoric and American studies: From general education to the senior capstone. In J. R. Dedrick, L. Grattan & H. Dienstfrey (Eds.), *Deliberation and the work of higher education: Innovations for the classroom, the campus, and the community* (pp. 113–42). Dayton, OH: Kettering Foundation Press.

Dedrick, J. R., Grattan, L. & Dienstfrey, H. (Eds.). (2008). *Deliberation and the work of higher education: Innovations for the classroom, the campus, and the community.* Dayton, OH: Kettering Foundation Press.

D'Innocenzo, M. (2008). From "youth ghettos" to intergenerational civic engagement: Connecting the campus and the larger community. In J. R. Dedrick, L. Grattan & H. Dienstfrey (Eds.), *Deliberation and the work of higher education: Innovations for the classroom, the campus, and the community* (pp. 17–40). Dayton, OH: Kettering Foundation Press.

Doherty, J. (2008). Individual and community: Deliberative practices in a first-year seminar. In J. R. Dedrick, L. Grattan & H. Dienstfrey (Eds.), *Deliberation and the work of higher education: Innovations for the classroom, the campus, and the community* (pp. 59–88). Dayton, OH: Kettering Foundation Press.

Drury, S. A. M., Andre, D., Goddard, S., & Wentzel, J. (2016). Assessing deliberative pedagogy: Using a learning outcomes rubric to assess tradeoffs and tensions. *Journal of Public Deliberation*, 12(1), Article 5.

Dudley, L. S., & Morse, R. S. (2008). Learning about deliberative democracy in public affairs programs. In J. R. Dedrick, L. Grattan & H. Dienstfrey (Eds.), *Deliberation and the work of higher education: Innovations for the classroom, the campus, and the community* (pp. 165–92). Dayton, OH: Kettering Foundation Press.

Farland, M. (2008). The deliberative writing classroom: Public engagement and Aristotle in the core curriculum at Fordham University. In J. R. Dedrick, L. Grattan & H. Dienstfrey (Eds.), *Deliberation and the work of higher education: Innovations for the classroom, the campus, and the community* (pp. 89–112). Dayton, OH: Kettering Foundation Press.

Finley, A. (2011). Civic learning and democratic engagements: A review of the literature on civic engagement in post-secondary education. Http://www.politicipublice.ro/uploads/LiteratureReview.pdf.

Harriger, K. J., & McMillan, J. J. (2008). Contexts for deliberation: Experimenting with democracy in the classroom, on campus, and in the community. In J. R. Dedrick, L. Grattan & H. Dienstfrey (Eds.), *Deliberation and the work of higher education: Innovations for the classroom, the campus, and the community* (pp. 235–66). Dayton, OH: Kettering Foundation Press.

Hogan, J. M., Andrews, P. H., Andrews, J. R., & Williams, G. (2014). *Public speaking and civic engagement* (3rd ed.). Boston: Allyn & Bacon.

Ingham, L. (2008). Introducing deliberation to first-year students at a historically black college/university. In J. R. Dedrick, L. Grattan & H. Dienstfrey (Eds.), *Deliberation and the work of higher education: Innovations for the classroom, the campus, and the community* (pp. 41–56). Dayton, OH: Kettering Foundation Press.

Jacobs, L. R., Cook, F., & Delli Carpini, M. X. (2009). *Talking together: Public deliberation and political participation in America*. Chicago: University of Chicago Press.

Johnson, J., Rochkind, J., & DuPont, S. (2011). *Don't count us out: How an overreliance on accountability could undermine the public's confidence in schools, business, government, and more*. Dayton, OH: Kettering Foundation and Public Agenda.

Kadlec, A., Sprain, L., & Carcasson, M. (2012). *Framing for democracy: Exploring the impacts of adversarial and deliberative framing, understanding the longer-term benefits of deliberation*. Kettering Foundation Working Paper. Http://www.kettering.org.

Kuh, G., & Ikenberry, S. (2009). *More than you think, less than we need: Learning outcomes assessment in American higher education*. National Institute for Learning Outcomes Assessment. October. Http://learningoutcomesassessment.org.

Longo, N. V. (2013). Deliberative pedagogy in the community: Connecting deliberative dialogue, community engagement, and democratic education. *Journal of Public Deliberation*, 9(2), Article 16.

Mathews, D. (2014). *The ecology of democracy: Finding ways to have a stronger hand in shaping our future*.

Dayton, OH: Kettering Foundation Press.

Morrell, M. E. (2010). *Empathy and democracy: Feeling, thinking, and deliberation.* University Park: Penn State University Press.

Nabatchi, T. (2012). An introduction to deliberative civic engagement. In T. Nabatchi, J. Gastil, M. Leighninger & G. M. Weiksner (Eds.), *Democracy in motion: Evaluating the practice and impact of deliberative civic engagement* (pp. 3–18). New York: Oxford University Press.

National Task Force on Civic Learning and Democratic Engagement. (2012). *A crucible moment: College learning and democracy's future.* Washington, DC: Association of American Colleges and Universities.

Rhodes, T. L. (Ed.). (2010). *Assessing outcomes and improving achievement: Tips and tools for using rubrics.* Washington, DC: Association of American Colleges and Universities.

Stromer-Galley, J. (2007). Measuring deliberation's content: A coding scheme. *Journal of Public Deliberation*, 3(1), Article 12.

Thomas, N. L. (Ed). (2010). *Educating for deliberative democracy.* (New Directions for Higher Education 152). San Francisco: Jossey-Bass.

Walters, D. J. (2008). Deliberation, civic discourse, and democratic dialogue in the context of academic change. In J. R. Dedrick, L. Grattan & H. Dienstfrey (Eds.), *Deliberation and the work of higher education: Innovations for the classroom, the campus, and the community* (pp. 209–31). Dayton, OH: Kettering Foundation Press.

Wharton, T., & McAfee, N. (2011). *A nation in debt: How can we pay the bills?* Dayton, OH: National Issues Forums Institute.

Assessing Language and Power in Deliberative Conversations in Educational Settings

Telma Gimenez and Andressa Molinari

The recognition that education is inherently political has led many academics to argue that educators need to abandon a "neutral" stance and work toward raising awareness about the deep relationship between schooling and political participation. Educational experiences in schools and universities involve social practices in which language plays a vital role as part of semiotic processes that enable social actors to attribute meanings to their actions. Knowledge, attitudes, and values emerge and are sustained or transformed by the constant interactions between teachers and learners (and other school agents) and the meanings associated with their ways of acting and interacting.

Thus, educational institutions are sites for socializing experiences that can be responsible for shaping worldviews and creating dispositions that can be more—or less—amenable to the idea of democracy. However, civic education often focuses on strengthening what Carr calls "thin" democracy—that is, superficial features of the political process like voting and elections—in contrast to what he calls "thick" democracy, which emphasizes critical engagement and social justice. For him,

> progressive, critical democratic education work in classrooms and schools, along with the resultant experience for the students, will be greatly diminished if teachers have a weak or disaffected attachment to democracy themselves. While there are numerous factors involved in the formulation and framing of democracy in schools, clearly educators have an important role to play in cultivating and shaping the educational experience for students in relation to their present and future attitudes, behaviors, ideologies and engagement regarding democracy. (2008, p. 149)

Indeed, this has been the direction encouraged by educational institutions adopting civic engagement as part of their mission. Deliberative pedagogy is an attractive strategy for educators who want to develop skills and attitudes necessary for navigating across differences and finding common ground for action. By going beyond voting, it is a critical tool in education for democratic engagement.

Because deliberative pedagogy focuses on forms of talk and relationships in the classroom, it may conflict with the traditional roles attributed to teachers and students; that is, typical classroom interactional patterns may be incongruent with the patterns suggested by a deliberative conversation. Discourse in which one person holds authority may be interpreted as authoritarian discourse, with little room for consideration of how issues are framed and how this framing constrains or liberates participants to construct an informed judgment. More than that, authoritarian discourse is unidirectional and does not invite argumentation.

In the United States, deliberation in the classroom and in higher education has already established itself in research and practice (Dedrick, Grattan & Dienstfrey, 2008; Shaffer, 2014). In the Brazilian context, however, this concept is relatively new. This chapter focuses on how to assess issues of language and power in this context, based on the experiences of faculty members in a teacher education program at Universidade Estadual de Londrina in Brazil. The intention is to join the conversation with other authors who have considered ways of assessing deliberation in the classroom (Stromer-Galley, 2007; Black, Burkhalter, Gastil & Stromer-Galley, 2011).

The purpose of assessment in this case is not to find out whether deliberation occurred, but rather to use concepts from critical discourse analysis to judge the exercise of power in the use of language in deliberative forums introduced into a language teacher education program. The goal was to minimize an authoritarian classroom ethos by introducing deliberative conversations in which the participants could resist or challenge the framing proposed by a pre-defined "issue book," have more opportunities to express their own views, and engage in argumentative processes. The idea was that these conversations would create different power relations among participants by enabling students to take a more active role in constructing the course of the discussion.

Educating for Democracy: Power and Language

Considering the key role of language in deliberation and, therefore, in deliberative pedagogy, discourse analysis is a useful method for assessing power and language in the classroom. Others interested in assessing deliberation have also adopted discourse analysis as one of their tools (e.g., Black, Burkhalter, Gastil & Stromer-Galley, 2011), although often with the purpose of establishing whether the interactions exhibited a deliberative focus (Stromer-Galley, 2007).

In our efforts, we follow Norman Fairclough, a critical discourse analyst who has developed a theoretical framework that connects the social and the linguistic (Fairclough, 1992, 2003). He does so by adopting a "three-dimensional" view of discourse: "any discursive event is seen simultaneously as a piece of text, an instance of discursive practice, and an instance of social practice" (Fairclough, 1992, p. 4). As a social practice, deliberative forums in higher education may create dispositions that are more accepting of differences and more inclined toward identifying common ground and collective action and thus counter the more teacher-centered, authoritarian forms of talk. Critical discourse analysis studies seek to connect social events to linguistic practices in order to understand this dialectical relationship (i.e., language simultaneously constructs and is constructed by social reality). In this view, deliberative forums are social practices that are enacted through discourse.

Going beyond the sentence level, discourse scholars argue that communication becomes stable through genres, or relatively structured forms of oral or written language that are associated with particular social events or activities (e.g., an interview, a cooking recipe, a letter to the newspaper editor, a lesson). Genres offer relatively stable ways of (inter)acting through discourse because they are associated with a particular social activity that has its own vocabulary and style.

Concerning classroom discourse, Sinclair and Coulthard (1975) developed a descriptive system to study the classroom as a formal space governed by rules of discourse that could be traced through the analysis of transcripts. In their system, they suggested units of discourse in a ranking order: lesson, transaction, exchange, move, and act. A lesson is the largest unit and an act the smallest. An act can be categorized according to its effect; for example, an act labeled as "elicitation" is realized by a question. Its function is to request a linguistic response. A transaction consists of exchanges, and a typical classroom exchange includes three moves: initiation, response, and feedback (IRF). The teacher initiates (usually with a question), students respond, and the teacher gives feedback. The feedback is evidence that the teacher has the power to evaluate, and much of the classroom discourse is about testing students' knowledge. The IRF pattern is predominant in most school settings, and its rigidity suggests a cultural practice in which power (the ability to initiate topics, ask questions, and evaluate the answers) lies with the teacher. This pattern matches what Fairclough (1989) calls "power in discourse" in describing inequality among participants; students remain in a passive role during classroom discourse, rarely initiating topics or asking questions. The importance of experiencing alternative ways of (inter)acting seems evident if we want to contribute to active citizenship—that is, if we want students to appreciate diversity, challenge the status quo, and identify themselves as agents of change.

Prospective language teachers, perhaps even more than other students, may be affected by practices that reinforce or challenge authoritarian ways of interacting in school. For them, these practices may affect not only their experience as students but also their own teaching. Deliberative forums can be introduced as part of an alternative pedagogy that can help create democratic mindsets as learners and teachers engage in processes that encourage the consideration of multiple perspectives, weigh trade-offs and tensions, and move toward action through informed judgment. Deliberative forums have the potential to break the IRF pattern and redistribute power as students engage in dialogue that encourages dissent and the expression of alternative viewpoints. That said, the lack of language proficiency in a language-learning setting may affect participation parity and thus challenge the legitimacy of the deliberations (Fraser, 2014). That means that students who cannot express themselves because of their low proficiency levels will have their participation limited, thus showing power imbalance resulting not only from the persistence of a fixed IRF pattern but also from the insecurity of self-expression. Introducing deliberative pedagogy in foreign language–learning contexts brings the additional challenge of ensuring equal right of participation despite the asymmetry in language competence among the participants.

Language in Deliberative Forums

In the language teacher education course, the instructors included deliberative forums as one genre with the potential to combine the development of oral skills with education for democracy. Table 1 shows the proposed format of such a forum, along with the language associated with its different stages, according to moderators' guides developed by the Kettering Foundation.[1]

As the table shows, most forms of language encountered in this type of forum are associated with points of view expressed with a high level of modality (can, may, should), hypothetical statements, acknowledgement of others' opinions, open questioning, and verbs expressing mental and material states—all linguistic realizations of deliberation. Stromer-Galley (2007) also characterizes deliberation as focusing on language elements that are typical of argumentative processes: reasoned opinions, references to external sources when articulating opinions, expressions of disagreement and hence exposure to diverse perspectives, equal levels of participation during deliberation, coherence with regard to the structure and topic of deliberation, and engagement among participants with each other.

When we bring deliberation into the classroom, however, we cannot ignore the impact of power relations—not only between teachers and students but also among students, particularly those with differing degrees of language proficiency. Classrooms are rarely spaces for equal levels of participation, since power imbalances are inherent in the classroom setting. Deliberative pedagogy may help minimize those differences, but in order to do so, we need to move beyond assessing deliberativeness by considering only the discoursal features of interactions and also reflect on the extent to which such features reveal evidence of power imbalances (Mendonça, 2013).

Our experience has shown that by introducing forums in the classroom as part of the curriculum, teachers may provide opportunities for students to express their views on issues, but they may also constrain participation by taking the role of an instructor and not a neutral moderator. This may lead to the creation of a hybrid genre—that is, a deliberative dialogue with characteristics of classroom talk that ends up reinforcing power relations rather than challenging them. The next section presents an experience that illuminates this issue, including an assessment of language and other features of discourse that both demonstrated and affected power structures in the classroom.

Deliberative Forums in a Language Teacher Education Program

During one semester in 2014, we conducted three deliberative forums in an Oral Comprehension and Production class in the language teacher education program at Universidade Estadual de Londrina. This section describes one of these forums in detail to demonstrate the power and pitfalls of this approach.

Five students ranging in age from twenty to thirty-five took part in the forum. All five students worked as English teachers: three in language institutes and private schools, and two in a state program in which student-teachers work in public schools under a mentor's guidance (in this case, a professor from the university). The forums were conducted in English as part of students' language instruction. One challenge was that no one participating had experienced a forum before, including the university teacher. Language proficiency was also an issue, although all students were able to communicate in English with advanced, upper intermediate, or intermediate skill levels.

In preparing the students to deliberate, the teacher started the class with a warm-up by asking students what the purpose of higher education was in their lives, and what the purpose of education should be. Questioning plays an important role in forums, as shown earlier in table 1, yet questions are indicators of positions of power; the person asking questions puts others in a passive role of responding to the topic as he or she has framed it.

Table 1. The Deliberative Forum Genre

STAGE	MODERATORS' LANGUAGE	PARTICIPANTS' LANGUAGE
Welcome	Greeting, purpose of meeting	Greeting response, introductions
Ground Rules	Questions and statements	Agreement and disagreement
Starter Video/Initial Information	Statements, different points of view, problem posing	—
Personal Stake	Questioning: • How has this issue affected you personally?	Extensive use of personal pronouns, narrative of past experiences, references to other people's experiences
Approaches	Questioning: • What things are most valuable to people who support this option? • What is appealing about this approach? • What makes this choice a good idea—or a bad one? • What would result from doing what this approach proposes? • What could be the consequences of doing what you are suggesting? • Can you give an example of what you think would happen? • Does anyone have a different estimate of costs or consequences?	Interdiscursive references, hypothesis formulation, modal verbs, opinion markers, acknowledgment of points of view, agreement and disagreement, evaluative comments, verbs expressing material processes
Individual Reflections	Questioning: • How has your thinking about the issue changed? • How has your thinking about other people's views changed? • How has your perspective changed as a result of what you heard in this forum?	Personal pronouns (I), verbs expressing mental processes, evaluative comments
Group Reflections	Questioning: • What do you see as the tension between the approaches? • Where are the conflicts that grow out of what we've said about this issue? • Why is this issue so difficult to decide? • What are the gray areas? • What remains unsolved for this group? • What didn't we work through? • Can we identify any shared sense of purpose or direction? • What trade-offs are we, or are we not, willing to make to move in a shared direction?	Personal pronouns (we), verbs expressing mental and material processes, evaluative comments
Next-Step Reflections	Questioning: • What do we still need to talk about? • How can we use what we learned about ourselves in this forum?	Personal pronouns (we), verbs expressing mental processes

Source: The content of this table is based on "Too Many Children Left Behind: How Can We Close the Achievement Gap?" Kettering Foundation, https://www.kettering.org/sites/default/files/product-downloads/too_many_children_mg.pdf.

Power was also revealed by strict adherence to the issue book, in contrast with the students' ways of seeing the issue of higher education. Despite bringing supplementary material with data from the Brazilian context, the teacher/moderator insisted on following the naming and framing provided by the issue book. The students had difficulty in moving away from their own framing of the issues in terms of unequal access to higher education. As the theoretical framework of critical discourse analysis suggests, this resistance was a sign of the power relations in operation; resistance makes visible a power struggle over the meanings that are jointly constructed.

Our experience has shown that social events are connected through a network of practices and cannot be isolated. A forum in a classroom carries not only the history of the relationships constructed so far but also the roles attributed to the participants. In the excerpt that follows, the difficulty experienced by the teacher in performing the role of a moderator while being the source of knowledge is a sign of the tacit rules governing the classroom and forum genres. For instance, when the teacher/moderator was introducing the issue to be discussed, she projected slides with the aim of getting the students to become familiar with the views presented in the issue book. She adopted a typical classroom activity (students reading aloud) in order to present them.

Excerpt 1: Reading the Issue Book[2]

TEACHER [presenting a slide]: All right, before the question: Are you able to read [the slide]?

STUDENTS: No.

TEACHER: OK, so I am going to ask you to read Adam's post and then tell us on what points you agree or disagree with him and why. I'll put it bigger for you. His name is Adam Burk—he is the director and founder of the Tree House Institute in the U.S., and the question he is answering is, "In your opinion, what should be the purpose of education?" This is the question I gave to you [as a homework assignment]. This is OK? Do you prefer to read it together or in silence? [Pause.] What do you think?

ERICA: *Pra mim tanto faz.* [It doesn't matter.]

TEACHER: Girls?

MARA: Let's read it together.

TEACHER: Let's read? OK. Can you start first?

MARA [reading]: "Education is a prominent cultural institution used to perpetuate the prevailing values of a society. Our modern education system has a sordid past largely rooted in indis- indis-" How can I say that?

TEACHER: Industrialism.

In this excerpt we observe how the teacher/moderator makes sure the students can see what they are going to read and suggests a collective task because the homework had not been done (the students were supposed to have read the issue book at home). When she engages them in the decision on whether to read aloud or silently, one student replies that it doesn't matter and another proposes reading aloud, a suggestion the teacher accepts. She points to one student to start and then steps in to provide the pronunciation of a word the student can't read. She exercises her power (generated by her knowledge of the language) by giving the final word on pedagogic decisions and on the linguistic correctness of the student's performance. At this point, the typical classroom genre predominates over the deliberative forum.

On the other hand, there were times during the forum when the teacher juxtaposed her role as a teacher/moderator with that of a forum participant. In the excerpt that follows, of a conversation about dropouts, she again points to a particular student to prompt participation (a typical teacher strategy to get students to talk). In addition to providing prompts and linguistic guidance, however, the teacher contributes with her own experiences and even gives advice on how to deal with older people who had quit school when they were young. The empathy created between the teacher and the students during the personal stake stage of the forum shows that this genre has the potential to break from traditional teacher roles. It also shows how hard it is to balance the roles of moderating and teaching within this kind of environment. During this interaction, power relations were less asymmetrical and participants interacted on a more equal basis.

Excerpt 2: Personal Stake

TEACHER: All right, Beatriz, can you relate to any of the experiences here?

BEATRIZ: I knew a girl in my school who got pregnant, but she didn't drop out because it was a private school so her parents could help her, but she, like, *afastou* . . .

TEACHER: That's when you have a maternity leave, right? For four, five months—she has the right to do that.

BEATRIZ: But she didn't have to drop out to work or to stay with the baby because her parents and grandparents helped her. I know a man who had to drop out in the fourth grade, I think, to work, to have a family. He never went back to school but he managed to get a job, a really good job and to earn a really good amount of money, even though he didn't finish the *fundamental*.

TEACHER: High school.

MARA: Basic.

TEACHER: Yes, basic education.

BEATRIZ: He stopped at the fourth grade, but he managed to get a good salary.

TEACHER: My father stopped in the second year of math because he had to support the family. He is really good with numbers, by the way, something I didn't get from him [laughs], but he never went back as well. And my mother, she finished high school and took *magistério*, but she was able to go to university only in her forties after we were all grown up and she had the time to work and study and take care of family.

ERICA: My mother also finished high school and she tried to, to . . .

TEACHER: Go to university.

ERICA: Go to university, but she didn't manage it, didn't pass the test, so she went to Japan, and then she came back, and now she says she is too old to go back to study.

TEACHER: No, tell her she is not.

ERICA: I try to, but she is kind of stubborn [laughs].

MARA: I'm trying to convince my mother to do the technical course in nursing, because she really likes to take care of people, and everything, but it is hard to convince her.

TEACHER: Yeah, they think they are old [laughs].

MARA: Yeah.

TEACHER: There's no age for such a thing. And you can also talk to your teachers to arrange for alternatives in your internship time. Because I—even though I didn't need to because my parents at least could support me at the time—I worked the four years until graduation. When I came to the internship, in the third year, it was really bad because I worked nine hours a day, plus university, plus internship, so . . . of course I took longer to finish.

As the forum continued, the teacher adopted the role of a moderator more smoothly. In the third excerpt, below, she paraphrases students' comments and invites further elaboration by posing questions to trigger different viewpoints; however, when the interlocutors struggle to find the word in English, the teacher comes in and gives the vocabulary they are looking for. Once again, the teacher's role predominates.

Excerpt 3: Discussing One Approach

TEACHER: So you are saying that we should focus some of the courses, or universities should help to make Brazil stay competitive in the global market, educate more engineers.

ERICA: And it's not just engineers, that's the problem, we stay just focus on, you know in science, we are not thinking about develop a person, the education.

ANDRÉ: Cultural education, for example?

TEACHER: Yes, but then you are talking about economy, right?

ANDRÉ: We should focus on that, we should focus on market, should focus on economy, for example, we are always willing to work in groups, we never explore, for example, rarely salaries, jobs. Fields are discussed in the classes, for example, although lots of students already work as some kind of trainee.

TEACHER: And, if you are saying that higher education should help, should the roles be different from private institutions to public institutions?

ANDRÉ: No, they shouldn't, why should they?

TEACHER: That's my question [laughs]. Should they be different?

ANDRÉ: No, they shouldn't. But, I believe the private sector, for example, takes advantage of this reality we are facing, you know, that requires everyone to take higher education degrees.

TEACHER: To make money.

ANDRÉ: Because actually they don't focus on quality . . . teaching, they focus on graduating people, having numbers. . . . If you agree to that.

LUCIANA: In some universities, yes, and, I think more in the private ones, there are like, forty people in one class and they pay little to the course, to do the course and they pass, but my mom told me that, there's a person who, that must be, é, *retido*?

ANDRÉ: Must be what?

LUCIANA: *Retido*. One. There's a person—

TEACHER: Has to flunk?

LUCIANA: Yes, like the owners of the university show the, the teachers, and they have to do it to reprove?

TEACHER: Flunk.

At this stage of the forum, the students were interacting more freely among themselves, as corroborated by excerpt 4.

Excerpt 4: Considering Alternatives

TEACHER: It says here, instead of giving up, upon students at risk of not graduating college or university, professors and counselors should be required to invest more time in tutoring and mentoring and should offer more effective remaining courses.

ANDRÉ: A perfect world.

ERICA: I don't like that. I think if I am a student you have to, you know, *se virar* [find a way].

ANDRÉ: Yeah.

LUCIANA: But I think that is a good idea, it's an option.

BEATRIZ: Yeah, for many courses is a big deal but I think that people should be like . . . *correndo atrás* [chasing after].

LUCIANA: Yeah!

ANDRÉ: They are not able to, you know, they will flunk and they will give up and be garbage men. Society is as simple as that, why do we have to—

ERICA: Because we say that. All the time of the time tutoring helping and, you know, *como que fala* [how do you say it]? Aid?

ANDRÉ: Aiding?

ERICA: Aiding them, they will never be independent professionals; they will always need someone to help them.

LUCIANA: I don't think so; I think that some students have some difficulties and some help will be very nice. But at the same time it's an option.

TEACHER: So are you saying that the student should ask for tutoring?

LUCIANA: Yes.

ANDRÉ: They should, but as I said—

LUCIANA: And if the professor notices that the student isn't taking it seriously, then . . .

MARA: I mean, you said it? You said that in our course that's not a problem, like, I'm taking someone else spot, because we don't have so much—how can I say that?

LUCIANA: Complaints?

ANDRÉ: Competition?

MARA: Yeah, but for other courses, there are some rich people that could pay for college and they have a good basic education so they get in the university they took someone else spot in here and they don't care they are just in here because their parents told them to be here, that's what I'm trying to say, it's not nice.

ANDRÉ: OK let's think the other way around, if we for example have these financial able people, you know, studying in private institutions just because they can pay, then we will have the same students from public schools using the public university, then I guess the roles will just be inverted, you know? Private institutions will be better than public institutions or universities because we know that elementary and primary schools already suck, then the same will happen to the public universities, then the government will be real happier. What do you think, Luciana?

MARA: I, I agree with you.

LUCIANA: The same as you.

In this interactional sequence, the students dominate the conversation, and calls for vocabulary help are answered by their colleagues, not the teacher, who is sidelined in the discussion. One student actually prompts another to give her opinion, a role performed by the teacher in previous interactions. At this stage of the forum, power was redistributed among the participants, with few interventions by the teacher, although with the dominance of one student (André).

Assessing Power in Deliberative Conversations in the Classroom

As stated in the beginning, our interest in assessing power in a context where deliberative forums were integrated into the curriculum of a language teacher education program led us to look at the ways in which student participants resist or challenge the framing proposed by a predefined issue book, have more opportunities to express their own views, and engage in argumentative processes.

The first observation from this exercise is that when introduced into classrooms, deliberative forums carry the history of relationships among the participants as well as the characteristics of the classroom genre. In a typical class, teachers have the power to determine the topic and the activities to be carried out; communication follows the IRF pattern, with roles clearly specified. The introduction of forums may invite resistance to those roles by giving students the opportunity to question the way the issue under discussion has been framed. This is one measure of power, and therefore an opportunity to assess how the exercise of power affects discourse. If teacher/moderators insist on sticking to the framing provided by issue books, they may not only hinder participation but also affect the outcomes of deliberation.

Another way of assessing power is to observe whether students taking control of the conversational turns can reshape the roles of the teacher and students. In our forum, when the teacher acted as a moderator, paraphrasing and mirroring back the students' comments, students were able to initiate and respond. This suggests that in educational settings, traditional power/knowledge roles have to be suspended by encouraging students to ask questions, prompt answers, and provide clarifications and feedback. In other words, the IRF pattern has to be subverted so students can be responsible for all the moves, and the role of the instructor has to recede into the background—to give way to the moderator role.

In the same vein, consistent referencing of external sources, with the implication that they have more legitimacy than participants' views, may limit the quality of participation. Students' engagement in argumentation requires opportunities to articulate their own opinions on the issue, and for this they need to feel that their voices will be treated as equally valid.

A critical discourse analysis perspective on deliberative forums in the classroom can help us assess power relations through language use by looking at who is controlling and constraining other participants' contributions. Because classes are a particular genre with roles traditionally attributed to teachers and students, deliberative forums have to break with this tradition to allow other roles to be played out.

The forum described here showed signs of a transition from authoritarian to egalitarian contributions. This transition can be explained by situating the event as part of a wider network of social practices constructed through other interactions among participants, thus highlighting the need to consider the context of these practices in analyzing contributions. A critical discourse analysis perspective looks not only at how language is used in context but also how it connects to the social roles performed in specific genres. In this sense, assessing power and language in specific circumstances—such as deliberative forums in classrooms—requires looking at whether the external framing presented is accepted or resisted; whether participants' contributions are distributed evenly, with no dominance by the teacher/moderator; and whether student participants acknowledge each other's views.

What we hope to have demonstrated is that language is constrained by institutional roles and the social genres associated with them. We believe that by experiencing interactions in which students themselves can feel the right to ask questions, to challenge assumptions, and to subvert the roles prescribed by the social genre, they can start imagining other possibilities and create alternative worlds that, balanced against their actual world, will help them move toward more egalitarian and respectful dialogue.

NOTES

1. One example of a moderators' guide can be found at https://www.kettering.org/sites/default/files/product-downloads/too_many_children_mg.pdf.

2. Pseudonyms are used throughout the excerpts to protect students' privacy. The excerpts are from transcripts that have been edited very slightly for clarity and space.

REFERENCES

Black, L. W., Burkhalter, S., Gastil, J., & Stromer-Galley, J. (2011). Methods for analyzing and measuring group deliberation. In E. P. Bucy & R. L. Holbert (Eds.), *The sourcebook for political communication: Methods, measures, and analytical techniques* (pp. 323–45). New York: Routledge.

Carr, P. (2008). Educators and education for democracy: Moving beyond "thin" democracy. *Revista Interamericana de Educación para la Democracia*, 1(2), 147–65.

Dedrick, J. R., Grattan, L., & Dienstfrey, H. (Eds.). (2008). *Deliberation and the work of higher education: Innovations for the classroom, the campus, and the community.* Dayton, OH: Kettering Foundation Press.

Fairclough, N. (1989). *Language and power.* London: Longman.

Fairclough, N. (1992). *Discourse and social change.* Cambridge: Polity Press.

Fairclough, N. (2003). *Analysing discourse: Textual analysis for social research.* London: Routledge.

Fraser, N. (2014). Transnationalizing the public sphere. *Kettering Review*, 32(1), 39–46.

Mendonça, R. F. (2013). Teoria crítica e democracia deliberativa: Diálogos instáveis. *Opinião Pública*, 19(1), 49–64.

Shaffer, T. J. (2014). Deliberation in and through higher education. *Journal of Public Deliberation*, 10(1), Article 10.

Sinclair, J. M., & Coulthard, M. (1975). *Towards an analysis of discourse: The English used by teachers and pupils.* Oxford: Oxford University Press.

Stromer-Galley, J. (2007). Measuring deliberation's content: A coding scheme. *Journal of Public Deliberation*, 3(1), Article 12.

Conclusion

Nancy L. Thomas

This book evolved from a series of conversations among a diverse group of committed college and university faculty members who see a connection between what happens in the college classroom and what happens in the public square. It is a tribute to them that they value teaching as both an art—something far removed from "teaching as telling"—and as relevant to the health and future of emerging and established democracies. The work of these authors is also a credit to the Kettering Foundation and its persistent dedication to "making democracy work as it should." The foundation facilitates this and other unique collaborative endeavors. I hope other academics will accept the authors' invitation—and the foundation's challenge—to examine their teaching practices with a critical eye not only toward improving student learning but also toward increasing student democratic agency and engagement.

In some ways, this book echoes calls for education reform by a long string of educators in noted works ranging from John Dewey's *Democracy and Education* (1916) to Ted Sizer's *Horace's Compromise* (1984), the *Nation at Risk* report (National Commission on Excellence in Education, 1983), Campus Compact's *Presidents' Declaration on the Civic Responsibility of Higher Education* (1999), and, recently, *A Crucible Moment* (National Task Force on Civic Learning and Democratic Engagement, 2012). Research on the positive learning outcomes of democratic education, discussion-based teaching, intergroup dialogue, and other close relatives to deliberative pedagogy is conclusive and compelling (Brookfield & Preskill, 2005). Discussion-based, interactive teaching fosters in students advanced skills in critical thinking, reasoning, intergroup understanding, application, and transference of knowledge (McKeachie, 1994). Yet surprisingly, these effective approaches to student learning continue to face both practical and political barriers in higher education. Deliberation advocates need to renew the case for educating for democracy while simultaneously helping educators overcome these barriers.

The authors in this book offer strategies for tackling the most immediate barrier: unease with the method. Simply stated, deliberative pedagogy feels risky. It requires of the professor a certain relinquishment of control, as well as sophisticated facilitation skills. Chris Christensen, who helped develop case method teaching at Harvard Business School and eventually the entire university, wrote,

> The discussion teacher is a planner, host, moderator, devil's advocate, fellow-student, and judge—a potentially confusing set of roles. Even the most seasoned group leader must be content with uncertainty, because discussion teaching is the art of managing spontaneity. Nonetheless, a good chart can help a mariner navigate safely even in fog. (1991, p. 16)

This book provides that needed chart. Specific recommendations for effective deliberative pedagogy include establishing ground rules, listening, asking the right questions, and responding with respect and curiosity.

Leila Brammer's first-year seminar, discussed in this book, in which deliberation among a classroom community serves as the key organizing principle, points to the risks and challenges that arise when student empowerment and deliberation skills are viewed as learning outcomes. Sara Mehltretter Drury offers an account of deliberative pedagogy in science classes. For disciplines that are more accustomed to following norms and predetermined approaches to technical problems, Drury's approach can broaden students' thinking about complex issues. As Drury puts it, wicked problems "are better addressed when multiple stakeholders are included in the process, but bringing together the experiences of scientists and citizens requires a different sort of process—namely, deliberation." She continues, "as students began to see facts related to public choices about climate change and energy policy, the deliberation activities encouraged moving from the scientific-technical realm to discussion in the public sphere, which takes into account public values as well as knowledge." For students across disciplines, there is a need to push beyond what is comfortable or familiar and to embrace a degree of uncertainty as they wrestle with diverse viewpoints and perspectives about what might otherwise seem like straightforward issues. In fact, as Timothy J. Shaffer reminds us, the use of discussion and deliberation has long been present in higher and continuing education settings—we've just forgotten or overlooked those approaches to teaching and learning.

Cutting across all of these ideas is the fundamental notion that the classroom or learning experience should be viewed as a community. This is, after all, the very purpose of college—a collegial sharing of responsibility for learning. Most students would not know what to do if they were told that they shared responsibility for others' learning and for creating a classroom environment that is conducive to learning for everyone. They rely on professors to control the syllabus, assign readings, cover the materials effectively, manage discussions, and handle disruptions. Deliberative teachers need to reset student expectations at the beginning of a course. They need to build trust over time and demonstrate that diverse perspectives add energy to a discussion. For many students, college is one of the few times they have had experiences with people in different social, religious, economic, and political groups. To be effective collaborators in a diverse democracy, students must learn how to build community among such groups.

Sharing responsibility involves transferring power from the professor to the collective so that students see themselves as colearners and as contributors to each other's learning. I am not suggesting that professors abandon responsibility for the course content, but rather that they give students ample control over the discussion, the process for learning, and even ways to augment the content. I recall reading a story by a faculty member at a New York university who allowed local community members to audit his large lecture course on race in America. One evening, he was lecturing about Malcolm X when one visitor raised his hand and said, "Excuse me, professor, but you have it all wrong. I was Malcolm X's bodyguard. Would you like to hear my perspective?" It was at that moment that the professor began questioning his teaching method and shifting to a more reciprocal, discussion-based approach.

Teaching Deliberation

Students have long been conditioned to view their educational experience as competitive rather than collaborative. Changing that deeply held view will take time and intentionality. When I taught Law and Higher Education at the University of Massachusetts–Boston, I borrowed a teaching trick from one of my favorite professors, Jay Heubert, who is now at Columbia University's Teachers College. I told the students that they could all earn an A and that they should work together on the take-home final exam to ensure that they all succeeded. I reserved conference rooms for the week they had to complete the exam. They were required to write essays answering three out of seven questions. Throughout the week, the students met regularly. Partly as a result of this process, the quality of the essays was higher and learning was broader. One student told me years later, "even though I only wrote three essays, I learned the materials for all seven by discussing them with my classmates."

Treating the class as a community means respecting diversity and navigating inevitable conflict. The classroom often consists of people with different socioeconomic backgrounds and political perspectives. Discussing controversial topics can be particularly interesting, albeit challenging, when students are encouraged to speak from the basis of their lived experiences. It's important to allow differences to surface. And while professors should not appear biased or politically motivated, it may be unrealistic to expect them to hide their personal views. This poses an ethical dilemma, which professors can address by backing arguments with evidence, respecting opposing and diverse views, and encouraging students to evaluate the reasonableness of all views presented, including their own (Hess & McAvoy, 2015). That isn't to say that professors should always be transparent about their political opinions, but doing so can be a powerful pedagogical tool.

Excellent deliberative teachers prepare to manage both the content and the process. I took a class with Chris Christensen of the Harvard Business School (quoted above) and he warned that for every hour of class, he prepared for three hours. Most people know the difference between a good discussion and a bad one. They know the negative effect on a conversation when people monopolize speaking time, insult or intimidate others, refuse to listen or compromise, or disengage. It is not unreasonable to insist on a certain tone of voice and respect. Nor is it unreasonable to require students to come to class prepared. Effective discussion-based teachers establish a contract with students by having the groups set the boundaries to discussions ("stay on subject"), encouraging listening ("ask questions"), discouraging disruption ("share the air"), calling out bad behavior ("if you are offended, say so, and say why"), and identifying language that is sure to derail a conversation ("don't personalize").

Agreements may need to change based on the classroom dynamics, so checking in with students at the beginning of every class (at least until positive dynamics are established) is a good idea. Ask, "How are our agreements working for us?" It may be that the class is too cautious, too polite. Consider suggesting a ground rule on risk-taking. It may be that some students remain shy about contributing to the conversation. Consider offering reflection time or pausing the discussion to ensure that those who prefer to collect their thoughts are not overlooked. Agreements build trust among students in the class.

Deliberative Pedagogy and Equality

In the United States, free expression and academic freedom have long been viewed as essential to the robust exchange of ideas. Such freedom cannot be assumed across cultures; indeed, even in the history of American higher education, politically motivated challenges periodically emerge that deter the kind of teaching discussed in this book. While these pressures are not new, as U.S. society and political decision-making become more polarized and vitriolic, academia becomes a target. To some, the academy supports liberal indoctrination and political correctness. To others, higher education is part of the problem because it preserves—or worse, exacerbates—an unequal status quo. State legislators respond to specific curricular content or student protests by cutting funding. Students challenge some speech as evidence of an unwelcoming and discriminatory campus climate. I have written on this topic before; challenging discriminatory speech is an understandable response to the growing frustration among some groups of students over the slow pace of social justice in public life and on campus (Thomas, 2015). But chilling speech, rather than exposing and discussing it, is an inappropriate response.

It's important to bring deliberative pedagogy to the classroom as a way to tackle inequality and oppression, a challenge facing all established and emerging democracies. The U.S. higher education system is not one of equal opportunity or representation. Currently, low-income students are far more likely than their more affluent peers to attend institutions where the per-student resources and spending are low. Selective four-year institutions spend up to $27,900 per student annually, versus as little as $6,000 per student in open-access two- and four-year institutions, where low-socioeconomic-status (SES) students are overrepresented (Carnevale & Strohl, 2013). With the multiple demands of family and work, low-income students have less time to spend on cocurricular activities, and most do not have a residential college experience; only 1 percent of community college students and 23 percent of students at four-year public institutions live on campus (American Association of Community Colleges, 2015). More resourced institutions (and students) have more opportunities for internships, community service, living-learning communities, and other experiences outside the classroom.

If we want our students to be able to engage in matters of political consequence once they graduate, we need to model and teach ways for them to do so. The classroom offers that promise to students who might not be able to learn such engagement in other forums. The best opportunity to reach low-SES students—the very students we want to reach to increase political equality and proportional representation—is in the classroom.

An Urgent Democratic Learning Agenda

The United States "functions on deliberation, thrives on difference of opinion, and operates on principles of representation" (Schoem et al., 2001, p. 1). Yet academics and others would not be unreasonable to question whether democracy as it is currently practiced in the United States is up to the challenges facing communities, the nation, and the globe. American democracy works only when its people have the capacity, willingness, and opportunity to share the rights and responsibilities of democratic governance. More specifically, Americans need to possess a certain amount of knowledge, or at least the ability to study an issue and gain the requisite knowledge. They need to have access to information and the ability to examine that information critically. They need to be able to reason and act, not only as individuals, but also collectively. They need to care and have a sense of responsibility for their communities and each other, which means a willingness to subordinate their rights and even property, if necessary, for the common good. The rights to life, liberty, and the pursuit of happiness are not unconditional; they require a baseline level of political and social equality. Justice cannot be contrived. People know if they have horizontal standing and power equal to that of others. Low levels of any of these attributes are symptoms of a weakened democracy.

According to the Pew Research Center, the United States ranks thirty-first in voter turnout among the thirty-four most developed democracies (DeSilver, 2014). Approximately 60 percent of Americans vote in a presidential election, and that number drops to 40 percent for midterm elections. Voting is one objective gauge of citizen interest in public affairs. A more significant challenge is who votes. At least 80 percent of wealthy Americans vote, compared with fewer than 50 percent of low-income Americans (Leighley & Nagler, 2014). For years, conventional wisdom held that who votes doesn't matter, that elected officials respected the interests of all Americans. New research dispels that myth. Women and most racial minority groups are severely underrepresented in government at the local, state, and federal levels. In 2016, women held only 24.5 percent of the state legislative seats and under 20 percent of the seats in the 114th U.S. Congress (Center for American Women and Politics, 2016). Whites hold 90 percent of the forty thousand elected positions from the federal to the county levels, numbers extremely disproportionate to U.S. population (Vinik, 2014). As a result, public policies are written overwhelmingly by affluent, white, male Americans. Disengagement by particular demographic groups thus results directly in political inequality, a problem facing all democracies.

While not unique to U.S. politics, polarization is particularly crippling to policymaking and social change in the United States. Through the 1980s, Democrats and Republicans in the U.S. House of Representatives voted on policy matters in similar ways, but starting in the 1990s, the parties started pulling apart. And within the parties, representatives are voting in more of a block. Starting in the 2000s, little overlap exists between the perspectives of Democrats and Republicans in Congress (Andris et al., 2015). While some argue that partisanship energizes the public and increases political engagement (Abramowitz, 2010), it also creates gridlock. Unwilling to compromise, the parties lock horns and policymaking stagnates.

Gridlock and polarization alienate everyday citizens. Only 19 percent of Americans say they trust the federal government to do what is right, the lowest trust in government in more than fifty years (Pew Research Center, 2015). Nearly 60 percent of Americans say that the government needs "very major reform," up from 37 percent in 1997 during the Clinton administration. This distrust extends to the American judiciary, historically viewed as the most trusted of the three branches of government. In November 2015, the National Center for State Courts released the results of its survey of registered voters (a sample that, as noted earlier, is already skewed to include more affluent voters). The researchers conducting the survey stated, "What we found was a disturbingly pervasive belief in an unequal justice system that systemically produces different results based on race, income, and other socio-economic factors . . . not surprisingly . . . there is a massive racial gap, with African Americans much more distrustful of the courts and the broader justice system" (National Center for State Courts, 2015, p. 1). Gallup (2016) reported that in September 2016, 47 percent of Americans polled "disapprove of the way the Supreme Court is handling its job," up from 29 percent in September 2000 when the poll began. The Pew Research Center (2015) reported that just 19 percent of Americans say they can trust the federal government always or most of the time.

Polarization affects everyday Americans, not just politicians. In their personal lives, Americans gravitate to homogeneous communities, social experiences, and work environments where they find others who share their social identity, values, and viewpoints (Bishop, 2008). Americans who are passionate about a political ideology say most of their friends share their political views. Indeed, 30 percent of "consistent conservatives" and 23 percent of "consistent liberals" say they would be unhappy if an immediate family member married a member of the other party (Pew Research Center, 2014). As people gravitate to their silos, they develop perspectives and convictions without having to consider the views of people with different social identities, lived experiences, and political perspectives. Indeed, according to the 2014 Freshman Survey, nearly one in four students grew up in neighborhoods that were either completely white or completely nonwhite. The report notes, "Students who come from such neighborhoods were less likely to 'frequently' socialize with someone of another racial/ethnic group compared to their peers who hail from more racially mixed neighborhoods" (Cooperative Institutional Research Program, 2014, p. 16). As a result, Americans are inexperienced in talking and working together across lines of social, economic, and political diversity.

As a result of these dynamics, Americans have little faith in each other in matters of public affairs. Just 34 percent of Americans say they have confidence in the collective wisdom of the American people when it comes to making political choices, and 63 percent say they have little or no confidence. These opinions are nearly reversed from 2007, when 57 percent had a good deal of confidence in the wisdom of Americans (Pew Research Center, 2015).

These challenges are self-perpetuating: a polarized, ineffective government alienates citizens, which in turn reduces their political power to demand more of their elected officials. Schools and colleges offer the best hope for intervening in this spiraling decline. These dynamics call for a paradigm shift, a rethinking of the way students are taught. Deliberative pedagogy is a powerful tool for helping students develop critical analytic skills, think independently, reason collectively, make evidence-based judgments, and cocreate solutions to problems. By engaging the diversity of perspectives among their fellow students, they learn to engage with others who think differently.

Colleges and universities should view addressing the problems of democracy as both an obligation and an opportunity. If we want our students to acquire the knowledge, skills, and commitments necessary for effective democratic participation, we need to identify the most significant opportunities on campus for doing so, and according to our research, that locus is the classroom. For the past two years, researchers at Tufts University's Institute for Democracy and Higher Education have been conducting qualitative case studies at a broad range of colleges and universities selected partly for their high levels of student political and electoral engagement. Based on our analysis of focus groups and interviews at seven institutions, political discussions in the classroom, across disciplines, emerged as a significant contributor to their campus climate for political engagement.

The authors of this book understand the context and necessity of democratic teaching and learning. The challenges of this form of pedagogy—unease with and politicization of the process of deliberative teaching—have been addressed throughout these chapters. My advice to readers is this: try it. Find like-minded faculty members, either at your institution or elsewhere, and form a study group. Teach as part of a team with more experienced discussion-teachers. Study facilitation and intercultural communication. Experiment. Take risks, but measure the effectiveness of your approaches by surveying your students regularly. ("What is working in our deliberations? What can we do better?") Deliberative pedagogy provides students with the opportunity to be active participants in their learning, which will serve them well as they become active participants in their communities, the nation, and the world.

REFERENCES

Abramowitz, A. (2010). *The disappearing center: Engaged citizens, polarization, and American democracy.* New Haven, CT: Yale University Press.

American Association of Community Colleges. (2015). *Data points: On-campus housing.* Http://www.aacc. nche.edu.

Andris, C., Lee, D., Hamilton, M. J., Martino, M., Gunning, C. E., & Selden, J. A. (2015). The rise of partisanship and super-cooperators in the U.S. House of Representatives, *Plos One,* 10(4). Http:// journals.plos.org/plosone.

Bishop, B. (2008). *The big sort: Why the clustering of like-minded America is tearing us apart.* New York: Houghton Mifflin.

Brookfield, S., & Preskill, S. (2005). *Discussion as a way of teaching: Tools and techniques for democratic classrooms.* San Francisco: Jossey-Bass.

Campus Compact. (1999). *Presidents' declaration on the civic responsibility of higher education.* Providence, RI: Campus Compact.

Carnevale, A., & Strohl, J. (2013). *Separate and unequal: How higher education reinforces the intergenerational reproduction of white racial privilege.* Washington, DC: Georgetown Public Policy Institute, Georgetown University.

Center for American Women and Politics. (2016). Women in elective office 2016. Eagleton Institute of Politics, Rutgers University. Http://www.cawp.rutgers.edu/women-elective-office-2016.

Christensen, C. R. (1991). Premises and practices of discussion teaching. In C. R. Christensen, D. A. Garvin & A. Sweet (Eds.), *Education for judgment: The artistry of discussion leadership* (pp. 15-34). Cambridge, MA: Harvard Business School Press.

Cooperative Institutional Research Program. (2014). *The American freshman: National norms fall 2014.*

Http://www.heri.ucla.edu/monographs/TheAmericanFreshman2014.pdf.

DeSilver, D. (2014). The polarized Congress of today has its roots in the 1970s. *Pew Research Center Fact Tank*, June 12. Http://www.pewresearch.org/fact-tank/2014/06/12/ polarized-politics-in-congress-began-in-the-1970s-and-has-been-getting-worse-ever-since/.

Dewey, J. (1916). *Democracy and education: An introduction to the philosophy of education*. New York: Macmillan.

Gallup. (2016). *Supreme Court*. Washington, DC: Gallup. http://www.gallup.com/poll/4732/supreme-court. aspx.

Hess, D. E., & McAvoy, P. (2015). *The political classroom: Evidence and ethics in democratic education*. New York: Routledge.

Leighley, J. E., & Nagler, J. (2014). *Who votes now? Demographics, issues, inequality, and turnout in the United States*. Princeton, NJ: Princeton University Press.

McKeachie, W. J. (1994). *Teaching tips: Strategies, research, and theory for college and university teachers* (9th ed.). Lexington, MA: D. C. Heath.

National Center for State Courts. (2015). *National survey of registered voters*. Washington, DC: GBA Strategies.

National Commission on Excellence in Education. (1983). *A nation at risk: The imperative for educational reform—A report to the nation and the Secretary of Education, United States Department of Education*. Washington, DC: U.S. Government Printing Office.

National Task Force on Civic Learning and Democratic Engagement. (2012). *A crucible moment: College learning and democracy's future*. Washington, DC: Association of American Colleges & Universities.

Pew Research Center. (2014). *Political polarization and the American public: How increasing ideological uniformity and partisan antipathy affect politics, compromise and everyday life*. Washington, DC: Pew Research Center for the People and the Press.

Pew Research Center. (2015). *Beyond distrust: How Americans view their government*. Washington, DC: Pew Research Center.

Schoem, D., Hurtado, S., Sevig, T., Chesler, M., & Sumida, S. (2001). Intergroup dialogue: Democracy at work in theory and practice. In D. Schoem and S. Hurtado (Eds.), *Intergroup dialogue: Deliberative democracy in school, college, community, and workplace* (pp. 1–21). Ann Arbor: University of Michigan Press.

Sizer, T. R. (1984). *Horace's compromise: The dilemma of the American high school*. Boston: Houghton Mifflin.

Thomas, N. L. (2015). The politics of learning for democracy. *Diversity & Democracy*, 18(4). Https://www. aacu.org/diversitydemocracy/2015/fall/thomas.

Vinik, D. (2014) Report: Every level of government is suffering from a serious woman problem. *New Republic*, October 8, 2014.

About the Contributors

Ibtesam Al-Atiyat is an associate professor of sociology, women's, gender, and Middle East studies at St. Olaf College in Northfield, Minnesota. Al-Atiyat is a native of Jordan. She received her BA and MA degrees in Sociology from the University of Jordan and received her PhD from Freie Universität Berlin, Germany.

Leila R. Brammer is a professor of Communication Studies at Gustavus Adolphus College. She received her PhD from the University of Minnesota. Her research interests include social movements, rhetoric and argument, and deliberation and civility. She is the author of *Excluded from Suffrage History: Matilda Joslyn Gage, Nineteenth-Century American Feminist*. She developed Public Discourse, a nationally recognized model for teaching deliberative discourse and citizenship. She has been honored for her teaching with numerous awards, including the Edgar M. Carlson Award for Distinguished Teaching and the Swenson-Bunn Memorial Teaching Award.

Christy M. Buchanan is a professor of psychology and the senior associate dean for academic advising at Wake Forest University. She received her PhD from the University of Michigan in 1988. Her research and teaching addresses adolescent and young adult development, especially the impact of beliefs and expectations about adolescence, family, and culture. Her administrative responsibilities include the orientation of new students and academic support for undergraduates.

Martín Carcasson, PhD, is a professor in the communication studies department of Colorado State University and the founder and director of the CSU Center for Public Deliberation (CPD). He also serves as a Senior Public Engagement Fellow with Public Agenda, works with Colorado State University Extension, serves on the faculty of the Kettering Foundation's Centers for Public Life program, and is on the board of directors of the National Coalition for Dialogue and Deliberation. His research focuses on contemporary public affairs and the interdisciplinary theory and practice of deliberative democracy and collaborative governance. The CPD serves as an impartial resource for the Northern Colorado community dedicated to enhancing local democracy through improved public communication, community problem solving, and collaborative decision-making. His research has been published in *Rhetoric & Public Affairs*, the *Journal of Public Deliberation*, *Higher Education Exchange*, the *International Journal of Conflict Resolution*, *New Directions in Higher Education*, *Public Sector Digest*, *Communication Theory*, *Journal of Applied Communication Research*, and the *Quarterly Journal of Speech*.

Joni Doherty is a program officer at the Kettering Foundation. She directs research on the deliberative framing of historical issues, and she leads exchanges with libraries and humanities groups. Doherty has a longstanding interest in discourse ethics and the ways in which the arts and humanities can foster democratic practices. She is also involved with projects that investigate the ways in which deliberation and democracy intersect with teaching and learning in higher education. Before coming to Kettering, Doherty was the director of the New England Center for Civic Life at Franklin Pierce University and taught in the American studies and philosophy programs. She has more than twenty years of experience with National Issues Forums and is an alumna institute member. Doherty earned a BFA in painting at the University of New Hampshire in Durham, a MA in cultural studies at Simmons College, Boston, and a PhD in philosophy and art theory from the Institute for Doctoral Studies in the Visual Arts in Portland, Maine.

Sara A. Mehltretter Drury is an assistant professor of rhetoric at Wabash College and the director of the Wabash Democracy and Public Discourse Initiative. Drury teaches and researches the quality and character of U.S. public discourse, with particular interest in deliberation. She has received grants to work on deliberation and civic communication from Indiana Humanities and the National Science Foundation (in collaboration with principal investigator Laura Wysocki) and has served as a deliberation process consultant on the Brookings Supports Breastfeeding project, which was supported by the Bush Foundation. Prior to her position at Wabash, Drury worked as a research assistant at the Kettering Foundation; she now is a research deputy for that organization. She received her BA in communication studies and political science from Boston College, and her MA and PhD in communication arts and sciences from Pennsylvania State University.

Cynthia M. Gibson, PhD, is an independent consultant specializing in evaluation, public policy research and analysis, program development, strategic planning, evaluation, and communications. Previously she was a program officer at Carnegie Corporation of New York in the area of Strengthening U.S. Democracy, overseeing grants and programs in the nonprofit and philanthropic sector. She has held leadership roles in several other national foundations and nonprofits. She is also a widely published author and blogger on issues ranging from civic engagement and philanthropy/nonprofits to health care and education.

Telma Gimenez is associate professor at the State University of Londrina, Brazil, and is currently serving as the international relations advisor to the president of the university. She holds a PhD from

Lancaster University (England). In 1997 she was an International Fellow at the Kettering Foundation and has since maintained relations with the foundation, participating as a member of the Faculty for Deliberative Democracy Workshop (DDW) and Deliberative Democracy Exchange (DDEX) for several years. She is interested in developing understanding about democracy and the role of higher education institutions in creating an active citizenry. One of her recent publications in this area is the chapter entitled "Institutionalizing Social Participation in Brazil: Dialogue Mechanisms in the 'National Policy on Social Participation,'" in *Initiatives in Active Citizenship* (2015), edited by Ileana Marin and Esther Velis.

Stephanie Gusler completed her bachelor's degree in psychology at Radford University and obtained her master's in psychology at Wake Forest University in 2015. While at Wake Forest, she worked as a graduate research assistant on the Democracy Fellows longitudinal study under the supervision of Christy M. Buchanan, Katy J. Harriger, and Jill J. McMillan. Stephanie is a doctoral student in the University of Kansas's Clinical Child Psychology Program.

Ferenc Hammer is associate professor and chair of the media and communications department at Eötvös Loránd University in Budapest. He teaches and conducts research on public service media, media representations of inequalities and conflict, and cultural history focusing on everyday life in Communism, mortgage debtors, content use modalities in the digital environment, and the history of television in the Cold War period. He has held research fellow positions in the United Kingdom and the United States. Apart from English and Hungarian, his works have also been published in Spanish, Portuguese, and Korean. His most recent work concentrates on building connections between humanities at the university and creative industries.

Katy J. Harriger is a professor and chair of the Department of Politics and International Affairs at Wake Forest University. Her research and teaching interests include American constitutional law, American politics, and civic engagement. She is coauthor with Jill J. McMillan of *Speaking of Politics: Preparing College Students for Democratic Citizenship through Deliberative Dialogue* (2007).

Scott London is an independent scholar who has written extensively about social innovation and civic renewal. His work has appeared in many books, newspapers, magazines, and scholarly journals. He is the author of several influential white papers and reports, including *Doing Democracy* and *Higher Education for the Public Good*. He lives in Santa Barbara, California.

Nicholas V. Longo is chair of Public and Community Service Studies and professor of Global Studies at Providence College. His publications include *Why Community Matters: Connecting Education with Civic Life* and several coedited volumes, such as *From Command to Community: A New Approach to Leadership Education in Colleges and Universities* and *Publicly Engaged Scholars: Next Generation Engagement and the Future of Higher Education*. Nicholas lives in Providence, Rhode Island, with his wife, Aleida. Together, they have a great passion for educating the next generation of democratic citizens, starting with their children, Maya and Noah.

Ekaterina Lukianova taught in the Department of English Language and Culture at Saint Petersburg State University in Russia from 2005 to 2016. She is a program officer at the Kettering Foundation in Dayton, Ohio.

Idit Manosevitch, PhD, is the founding director of the Center for Teaching and Learning and a faculty member in the School of Communication at Netanya Academic College in Israel. She holds a PhD from the Department of Communication at the University of Washington in Seattle and has served as a research associate at the Charles F. Kettering Foundation in Ohio (2006-8). Idit's research investigates how varying forms of communication and media may help create conditions for enhancing democratic ideals of informed, inclusive, and respectful public debate. Since 2013, Idit has been working with Kettering Foundation on applied research projects in the field of deliberative pedagogy, which focuses on ways of integrating deliberative processes of working through issues with teaching, learning, and engagement in higher education settings. Specifically, she seeks to understand the particular challenges involved when implementing deliberative practices in a deeply divided society such as Israel and build on these insights to develop an applicable theory for facilitating deliberative processes in such contexts.

David Mathews is president of the Kettering Foundation, a nonprofit research foundation rooted in the American tradition of invention. Prior to his work with the foundation, Mathews served as Secretary of Health, Education, and Welfare in the Ford administration. From 1965 to 1980, he taught history at the University of Alabama, where he also served as president from 1969 to 1980. Mathews earned an AB degree in history and classical Greek. After graduating Phi Beta Kappa from the University of Alabama, he received his PhD in history from Columbia University. Mathews has served on the boards of a variety of organizations, including the Gerald R. Ford Foundation, National Issues Forums Institute, the Southern Institute on Children and Families, and Public Agenda. He has received numerous awards, and in 2007, the Alabama Center for Civic Life was renamed in his honor. He is also the recipient of seventeen honorary degrees. Mathews has written extensively on Southern history, public policy, education, and international problem solving. His books include *Politics for People: Finding a Responsible Public Voice*, *Reclaiming Public Education by Reclaiming Our Democracy*, and *The Ecology of Democracy: Finding Ways to Have a Stronger Hand in Shaping Our Future.* Mathews is married to Mary Chapman Mathews, and they have two daughters and six grandchildren.

Janice McMillan is senior lecturer and director of the University of Cape Town's (UCT) Global Citizenship (GCP) program, which she cofounded in 2010. Janice has a PhD in sociology from UCT with a focus on analyzing service learning as a form of boundary work in higher education. From 1999–2001, she was UCT representative on a national service-learning project funded by the Ford Foundation. From 2010-14 Janice was also service-learning Coordinator of Stanford University's program in Cape Town. Janice's teaching and research interests include community engaged learning, active citizenship, critical pedagogy, and reflective practice. She is passionate about teaching and engaging students and colleagues as active citizens addressing challenges facing South Africa and higher education. Janice sits on several university committees linked to community engagement.

Jill J. McMillan is professor emerita of communication and a research professor at Wake Forest University. Her work has focused on communication and rhetoric in organizations and institutions: corporate identity, the strategies and impact of an organization's public messages, communicative dysfunction in organizations, organizational democracy and decision-making, and pedagogy in higher education. Recently she has worked on teaching deliberation in academic and community settings as a means of improving civil discourse and civic engagement.

Andressa Molinari has a master's degree in applied language studies from Londrina State University, Brazil. She has also specialized in teacher education-English, graduated from Letras-Inglês, and has a degree in pedagogy. She is a professor at Londrina State University and also works in public schools in Paraná with high school students.

Jack Musselman is an associate professor of philosophy and the director of the Center for Ethics and Leadership at St. Edward's University in Austin, Texas. He teaches ethics, legal ethics, environmental ethics, and philosophy of law and is working on a book about ethics in arts administration.

Marshalita Sims Peterson is a consultant and researcher committed to public scholarship, deliberative pedagogy and transformative action within the work of democratic practice. As founder of M.S. Peterson Consulting & Research, LLC, she is also dedicated to processes involving strategic planning, communication constructs, effective leadership indicators, and facilitation of national issues forums. Peterson's research and work spans the field of education and focuses on practices and experiences of engagement in support of quality and equitable educational experiences for students (K-16), school improvement/achievement, curriculum design/ implementation, academic programming, and teacher education preparation. In addition to her work in the field of education for the past thirty-six years, she has worked with colleges/universities and public and private sectors in a variety of industries regarding effective processes from initial phases of goal-setting to implementation continuum, models of support, accountability, and innovative processes of engagement to enhance organizational productivity. Peterson is former chair and associate professor of teacher education at Spelman College (Atlanta, Georgia) and researcher with the Kettering Foundation.

David Procter is a professor of communication studies and the director of Kansas State University's Center for Engagement and Community Development and the Institute for Civic Discourse and Democracy. He received his PhD from the University of Nebraska. From 1993–2006, he was head of Kansas State University's Department of Communication Studies, Theatre and Dance. In 2004, he helped establish the Institute for Civic Discourse and Democracy at K-State to help provide citizens with a stronger voice in local, state, and national politics and help communities build the capacity for informed, engaged, and civil deliberation on salient civic issues. Procter has served as a coeditor of the online *Journal of Public Deliberation* and has provided community facilitation training in Canada, New Mexico, Wisconsin, Ohio, Georgia, and communities across Kansas. He has also been part of many facilitation teams moderating community forums on a host of wicked civic issues including issues of food access, water, mental health, and climate change.

Angela Romano is associate professor at the Queensland University of Technology in Brisbane, Australia. She teaches journalism and coordinates the honors program for the Creative Industries Faculty. She conducts research on different elements of the media in Australia, the United Kingdom, United States, Indonesia, and East Timor. Her work is focused on a wide range of elements related to the quality and regulation of journalism, journalism's political function, and innovative philosophies, such as public journalism.

Timothy J. Shaffer is assistant professor in the Department of Communication Studies and assistant director of the Institute for Civic Discourse and Democracy at Kansas State University. He is also principal research specialist with the National Institute for Civil Discourse at the University of Arizona. Additionally, he is an associate editor of the *Journal of Public Deliberation*. As a scholar, Shaffer centers his research on the advancement of democratic practices through deliberative politics and civic engagement in higher education and other institutional and community settings. He has published in the *National Civic Review*, *The Good Society*, and the *Journal of Public Deliberation*, among others. He received his PhD from Cornell University.

Timothy Steffensmeier is the department head and associate professor of communication studies at Kansas State University, where he serves as a research associate for the Institute for Civic Discourse and Democracy. He has published a book, chapters, and essays focused on deliberative democracy, argumentation, and community development. He teaches courses in public deliberation and rhetorical theory. He is currently researching Public Square Communities' community development process. He also serves as faculty for the Kansas Leadership Center. Steffensmeier received his PhD in communication studies from the University of Texas at Austin.

J. Cherie Strachan received her doctorate in political science from the State University of New York at Albany in 2000. She is the director of Student and Civic Engagement for the College of Humanities, Social and Behavioral Sciences and professor of political science at Central Michigan University. She is the author of *High-Tech Grassroots: The Professionalization of Local Elections*, as well as numerous articles and book chapters. Her publications focus on the role of civility in a democratic society, as well as on college-level civic education interventions intended to enhance students' civic skills and identities. Her applied research, which focuses on facilitating student-led deliberative discussions sessions and on enhancing campus civil society, has resulted in on-going work with the Kettering Foundation. She is also the cofounder of the Consortium for Inter-Campus SoTL Research, which facilitates cross-campus data collection for campus-wide civic engagement initiatives and political science pedagogy research.

Maxine S. Thomas is secretary and general counsel at the Charles F. Kettering Foundation. As a program officer, Thomas directs a number of projects in community leadership and leads Kettering work with the American Bar Association and the Ohio Supreme Court. Before coming to Kettering, Thomas was associate dean of the University of Georgia School of Law. She previously served as assistant attorney general for the state of Washington serving in the office of General Counsel of the University of Washington. Thomas received her BA degree in English from the University of Washington and her JD degree from the University of Washington School of Law.

Nancy L. Thomas directs the Institute for Democracy and Higher Education at Tufts University's Jonathan M. Tisch College of Civic Life, conducting research and providing assistance to colleges and universities to advance student political learning and participation in democracy. The Institute's signature initiative, the National Study of Learning, Voting, and Engagement (NSLVE), is a large dataset for research and provides each of the more than nine hundred participating colleges and universities with their students' aggregate voting rates. Her work and scholarship center on higher education's democratic mission, college student political learning and engagement, free speech and academic freedom, and deliberative democracy on campuses and in communities. She is the author of multiple book chapters, articles, and the monograph *Educating for Deliberative Democracy*. She is an associate editor of the *Journal of Public Deliberation* and a senior associate with Everyday Democracy.

Rebecca M. Townsend, PhD, studies deliberation, public engagement, and local communication. She is currently the professor in residence at the civil and environmental engineering department at the University of Connecticut, on leave from her role as professor of communication (and former department chair) at Manchester Community College. The White House awarded her the "Champions of Change for Transportation Innovation" for her scholarship on public engagement in transportation planning. Her work has also been honored by the International Association of Public Participation, Commonwealth of Massachusetts, State of Connecticut, National Communication Association, Urban Communication Research Foundation, and the CT Board of Regents' first Scholarly Excellence Award. She received her PhD and BA in communication from the University of Massachusetts Amherst and her MA in speech communication from Indiana University. She is also the first woman elected as her town's Moderator.

Index

A

Abu-Lughod, Leila, 108, 109
Addams, Jane, xxii, 39
adult education, 22–31
Alfaro, Cristina, 191
Anderson, Jenn, 75
argumentation courses, 74–75
Aristotle, x, 71
Arnone, Ed, 155
Auer, J. Jeffrey, 27

B

Barnett, Ronald, 162–63
Barr, Robert, xxv
Belcher, Ellen, 155
Benhabib, Seyla, 110
Birtalan, Gergő Gy., 119
Bittle, Scott, 80–81
Black, Laura W., 193
Black Lives Matter, xxiii
Bloch-Schulman, Stephen, xxi
Blumler, Jay G., 117
Boggs, Carl, Jr., 117
Boyte, Harry C., xxii, 40–41, 135, 143
Brammer, Leila, 197
Briand, Michael, 8

Brown, Shelby, 171
Bultitude, Karen, 80
Burk, Adam, 208
Burkhalter, Stephanie, 193
Butin, Dan W., 170

C

Carcasson, Martín, 44, 45, 171, 193
Carli, Linda L., 94–95
Carr, Paul, 203
Cartwright, Morse A., 22
centers for civic life, 127–32
Challenger, Douglas, 129
Chautauqua Institution and movement, 22–24
Christensen, Chris, 215–16, 217
Citizens' Initiative Review, 75
civic agency, 135–36, 139, 143, 147–48
civic engagement, 38, 81, 127, 130, 143–48, 170, 180
civil rights movements, xx, xxii
Coate, Kelly, 162–63
Colorado State University, 42, 45, 75, 76
communication studies, xx, 26, 71–76; at Kansas State University, 135, 138–40
community colleges, scholarly neglect of, 169–70
convergent thinking, 3, 10–12, 16
Cook, Fay Lomax, 51, 192

Cooperative Extension Service, 28, 29, 30

Corvinus University, 116

Cossart, Paula, 30

Coulthard, Malcolm, 205

Crucible Moment, A (report), 51–52, 84, 191, 192, 215

D

Dahlgren, Peter, 135

Dedrick, John R., 45

deliberation, 9, 169, 191; etymology of, x; mind-set for, 4–5, 16

Deliberation and the Work of Higher Education (Kettering Foundation), xv, 52, 192

deliberative democracy, x–xi, xx–xxi, xxiv–xxv; limitations of, 40, 46

deliberative pedagogy: assessments of, 179–88, 191–99, 204, 212; campus priorities and, 14–16; challenges of, 215–16, 221; community applications of, 37–47, 54, 112; course examples of, 51–59, 62–69, 137–40, 144–48, 170–75; criticism of, 40, 46; definitions of, xi–xii, xiv–xv, xix, xxi, xxv–xxvi, 3, 18, 38, 61, 90, 159–60, 191–92; in engineering courses, 160–66; faculty roles in, xxiv, xxv, 18, 44, 56–58, 75–76, 118, 170–71, 216–17; feminist potential of, 89–97, 113; global online example of, 99–106; historical roots of, 21–31; in journalism courses, 153–58; in science courses, 79–84; teaching approaches to, 217–18, 221; in women's and gender studies, 107–13

Deliberative Pedagogy Learning Outcomes (DPLO), 194–99

deliberative politics, xxi, 38; women's early exclusion from, 91–92, 96

Delli Carpini, Michael X., 51, 192

democracy, xi, 90; current state of, 219–21; Dewey and, 12; interaction and, 8; "thin" vs. "thick," 203

Democracy Consortium, xxii

Dewey, John, xxv, xxvi, xxxii, 12, 26, 27–28, 31, 215

Dialogue, Deliberation, and Public Engagement (DDPE) certificate, 139–40

Difficult Dialogue Initiative, xxiii

divergent thinking, 6–7, 13–14, 16

Doherty, Joni, 107, 129

Doyle, Michael, 7

Drury, Sara A. Mehltretter, 75, 196–97

Dubanoski, Richard, 131

Dudley, Larkin, 129, 131

E

education, banking model of, xxv, 13–14, 21

Elon University, xxi

empathy, xiv, 5, 13, 194–96, 199n1

Eötvös Loránd University, 115, 116

Everyday Democracy, xxvi

Ewbank, Henry L., 27

F

Fairclough, Norman, 204

farmer discussion groups, 28–30

Farr, James, 143

Farrell, Thomas B., 72

Federal Forum Centers, 25

feminism. *See* deliberative pedagogy: feminist potential of

Fielding Graduate University, 139

Fishkin, James S., 9

Flanagan, Maureen A., 24

Follett, Mary Parker, 26, 28, 31

forums, 114n2; language in, 205–11; merits and limitations of, 115; public forum movement, 22–25, 28, 30; student forums, 117–22, 144–48

Franklin, Benjamin, 22

Franklin Pierce University, 128

Freire, Paulo, xxv, 13, 21

Friedman, Will, 8

G

Garland, J. V., 26–27

Gastil, John, xxiv, 23, 74, 171, 193

Gaventa, John, 46–47

Gazillo, Stephen, 171

Gilbert, Jess, 28

Gitlin, Todd, 117

Goodlad, John, 39

Graff, Gerald, 15
Gustavus Adolphus College, 52–58, 197–98

H

Harkavy, Ira, 46
Harriger, Katy J., 180, 184, 185
Harwood, Richard C., xiv, 156–57
Hauser, Gerald, 14, 72
Held, David, xxiv
Hess, Diana, 47
Heubert, Jay, 217
Highlander Folk School, xxii
historically black colleges and universities
    (HBCUs), 143–44, 148
Hofstra University, 42
Holmes, Janet, 93
hooks, bell, xxv
Horton, Myles, xxv
Hungary politics, 115–17, 122n2

I

Institute for Civic Discourse and Democracy
    (ICDD), 136–41
International Institute for Sustained Dialogue, 139
Isocrates, x, 72
Israel, politics in, 61–63

J

Jacobs, Lawrence R., 51, 192
Jane Addams School for Democracy, 41–42, 45
Johnson, Allan G., 90
Johnson, Barry, 18
Johnson, Jean, 80–81
Johnson, Matthew, xxv
Journal of Public Deliberation, xxii

K

Kadlec, Alison, 193
Kaner, Sam, 3, 5–9, 11–14, 17, 19, 81. *See also*
    participatory decision-making (Kaner model)
Kansas City University, xx
Kansas State University, 130, 135–41

Kassam, Karim-Aly, 159
Katriel, Tamar, 62
Katz, Zivah P., 170
Kavanagh, Dennis, 117
Keith, William, 22, 23, 26, 30, 72, 74, 171
Kettering Foundation, Charles F., x–xi, xiii–xv, xxii,
    xxiii, 9, 83, 114n1, 139; ICDD and, 136–37; mission
    statement of, 141n2, 215
Kingston, Robert J., 155
Knighton, Betty, 155
Knowles, Malcolm S., xxv
Kuehl, Rebecca A, 75
Kuh, George, xxvi

L

labor movements, xx, xxii
Lacy, Charles, 132
Lakoff, Robin, 92
Lanham, Richard A., 15, 71–72
Lazarus, Amy, 44
Levine, Peter, 46, 180
Lindblom, Charles, 13
London, Scott, 41
Longo, Nicholas V., 159–60, 161, 191–92
Loss, Christopher, 25
lyceum forums, 22–24
Lyman, Rollo, 24

M

Manchester Community College, 169–75
Maricopa Community Colleges, 130
Mathews, David, xxxi, 5, 22, 38, 135, 141n1, 148
McCrehan, Jeff, 156–57
McKenzie, Robert, 155
McMillan, Janice, 41
McMillan, Jill J., 180, 184, 185
Meyers, Arthur S., 24
Miller, George, 155
Morse, Ricardo, 129
Morton, Keith, 43
Murillo-Castaño, Gabriel, 130

N

National Coalition for Dialogue and Deliberation, xxii, 171

National Issues Forums Institute (NIF), xxiii, 42, 52, 75, 83, 93, 114n2, 143-48

National Task Force on Civic Learning and Democratic Engagement, 180

Netanya Academic College, 62, 63-68

O

Occupy movements, 115-16, 119-20

P

Participatory Budgeting Project, 75

participatory decision-making (Kaner model), 5-12, 17-18; individual adaptation of, 12-13

Partnership for Inclusive, Cost-Effective Public Participation (PICEP2), 169, 170, 174

Pearce, Barnett, 139

Pennsylvania State University, 74

Pericles, x

Phillips, Charles F., 26-27

Pillay, Suren, 160-61

political mobilization, 117, 121-22

Poulakos, Takis, 72

pracademics, 75

Program on Intergroup Relations, xxiii

Program Study and Discussion (PSD), 29-30

Providence College, xix-xx, 43

Public Agenda, 80-81, 83

Public Conversations Project, xxiii

Public Dialogue Consortium, 139

public speaking, 15, 25, 26, 72, 73-74, 172, 197

Q

Queensland University of Technology, 154

R

race and racism, xxiii, 160

rhetoric, 26, 71-72

Rhodes University, 155, 156, 157

Robinson, Karl F., 27

Roosevelt, Theodore, 23

Ross, Tara, 155

Ryfe, David M., 143

S

Saint Petersburg State University, 99-100

Salmi, Jamil, 181

Saltmarsh, John, xxiv, 44, 45, 46

Sanders, Lynn M., 94

Sanderson, Dwight, 26

Schools of Philosophy for Extension Workers, 29-30

service-learning, 15, 38, 40-45, 129-30, 147, 170

Sheffield, A. D., 26

Silva, Joana, 80

Sinclair, John McHardy, 205

Sizer, Ted, 215

Skelton, Nan, 45

Spelman College, 144-48

Spencer Foundation, 180

Sprain, Leah, 193

St. Edward's University, 99-100

St. Olaf College, 107-8

Stromer-Galley, Jennifer, 193, 206

Studebaker, John W., 24-25, 26, 28

Study Circles, xxiii

Sustained Dialogue Institute, xxiii

T

Taeusch, Carl F., 28

Tagg, John, xxv

Temple University, 154-55, 157

Thomas, Maxine, 155

Thomas, Nancy L., 192

Tocqueville, Alexis de, 127

town meetings, 22, 30, 128

Traver, Amy E., 170

Tufts University, 221

U

United States Department of Agriculture (USDA), 28-31

Universidad de los Andes, 130

Universidade Estadual de Londrina, 204, 206

University of Canterbury, 154

University of Cape Town, xix, 41, 159–66

University of Massachusetts, 217

University of Michigan, 129

University of Western Sydney, 139

University of Wisconsin, xxiii

Utterback, William E., 27

V

Vincent, John J., 22

Virginia Tech, 129

W

Wabash College, 74, 76, 79, 196–97

Waghid, Yusuf, 159

Wake Forest University, 42, 182–87

Wallace, Henry A., 28

Wheatley, Margaret J., xix

White, Gordon, 119

wicked problems, 3–6, 9–12, 14, 16–18, 75, 79, 80–81, 137

Wilson, M. L (Milburn Wilson), 28–29

women's movements, xx, 91

Y

Yankelovich, Daniel, 5, 8, 9